Understanding American Power

Understanding American Power

The Changing World of US Foreign Policy

Bryan Mabee

© Bryan Mabee 2013

First published 2013 by
PALGRAVE MACMILLAN

Palgrave Macmillan in the UK is an imprint of Macmillan Publishers Limited,
registered in England, company number 785998, of Houndmills, Basingstoke,
Hampshire RG21 6XS.

Palgrave Macmillan in the US is a division of St Martin's Press LLC,
175 Fifth Avenue, New York, NY 10010.

Palgrave Macmillan is the global academic imprint of the above companies
and has companies and representatives throughout the world.

Palgrave® and Macmillan® are registered trademarks in the United States,
the United Kingdom, Europe and other countries

ISBN 978–0–230–21772–0   hardback
ISBN 978–0–230–21773–7   paperback

This book is printed on paper suitable for recycling and made from fully
managed and sustained forest sources. Logging, pulping and manufacturing
processes are expected to conform to the environmental regulations of the
country of origin.

A catalogue record for this book is available from the British Library.

A catalog record for this book is available from the Library of Congress.

Contents

List of Tables and Figures

Tables

Figures

Preface and Acknowledgements

The book that follows is the product of attempts over many years to not only better understand US foreign policy, but also to broaden out the ways in which we might examine it. I focus on the much broader concept of 'American power' as a way of moving away from the 'foreign policy process' as the main explanation of how the American state engages with the external world (note: I use 'United States' and 'American/America' interchangeably in the text that follows; where I mean the Americas more generally the usage will be clear). It is not because such views are unimportant (indeed I take them very seriously in Chapter 3), but they tell us less than we might want to know about the wider dynamics of American society, the international system, and the state as a mediator – both as an active actor and as a structure – between these realms. Power is also a core way that the US is commonly examined and argued about in wider conversation, and looking at the US in terms of the scope of its power – past and present – will enable a better understanding of the future of US power. In this light, the book is also intended as an intervention into recent debates about American 'decline', providing a clearer analysis of power as a means to better contemplate current tendencies in American power, and also relate them to American historical development.

The book therefore is both an attempt at justifying a particular approach to thinking about American foreign policy through power dynamics as well as an analytic overview of the past, present and future of American power in the world (and therefore American foreign policy as well). It is intended to be a contribution to a political and historical sociology of international relations, with the intention of analysing American power in the context of international and domestic-societal dynamics. This presents a more complicated (and perhaps messier) picture of US power in the world than may be presently available, but it is one that in my opinion better situates the US in the world, and provides us with a richer understanding of the US as an actor in international relations.

With the general scholarly background out of the way, it remains to acknowledge the people and institutions that aided the completion of the book. First, I must thank Steven Kennedy, my publisher at Palgrave (and the rest of his team), who asked me to write the book in the first place, and has continually pushed and encouraged me over the years. Second, I have to give special thanks to colleagues who have read drafts, discussed ideas, and given me feedback that has had a major impact on my thinking about the book: Tarak Barkawi, Alex Colas, Mick Cox, Toby Dodge, Jean-François Drolet, James Dunkerley, Adam Fagan, Sophie Harman, Ray Kiely, Patricia Owens, Chris Phillips, Rick Saull, Srdjan Vucetic and Jeff Webber. Ray and James have been particularly supportive of this research project (and beyond), and I really owe them a great deal. Third, I'd like to thank my colleagues at the School of Politics and International Relations at Queen Mary, University of London, who have provided a collegial and supportive environment for producing scholarship. I also must thank the students of POL358 US Foreign Policy, where I have tested a number of the ideas and arguments of the book over the past few years, and the discussions and feedback I've had in those classes have been important in thinking and rethinking the content of the book. Fourth, I'd also like to thank the Center for Advanced Security Theory at the University of Copenhagen – and especially Lars Bo Kaspersen and Ben Rosamond for facilitating my visit – which generously put me up in the summer of 2012, and gave me a fantastic intellectual space to finalize a first draft of the manuscript. Fifth, the Teder family gave me a great deal of support while visiting Sweden, and I've appreciated their hospitality and patience while ostensibly on holiday. Finally, Maja Cederberg has not only been incredibly supportive of a project that has taken up an inordinate amount of time, but also read and commented on the manuscript, and gave me a much needed outside perspective. The book is undoubtedly clearer because of her: *tack Maja!*

BRYAN MABEE

Introduction: American Power in the World

Since the end of the Cold War, the future of American power has been much debated. The collapse of the Soviet Union ended an era where the US role in the world was well understood, and the new era saw the US as a sole superpower, and much contention in terms of what that might mean for America's future role. Would the US become predominant or preponderant in the international system? Would the US squander its newfound power through an increasing insularity? Would challengers rise to circumvent American power? In the wake of the terrorist attacks of 11 September 2001, such questions became even more heated. Were there new transnational threats that could undermine US power in different ways? Would the US reaction to such challenges jeopardize American legitimacy in the world? More recently, the economic crisis of 2007/08 has again brought the debates to the forefront, and with the Western capitalist system seemingly mired in continual problems, new economic challengers to American power are seen as on the rise (or as already arisen). Are we headed for a 'post-American world', where states such as China, India and Russia are peer competitors to the US? Is the unipolarity of the US in the international system to be replaced by a multipolar system?

What are we to make of such debates? How are we to evaluate them? This book is an attempt to better understand American power, but one that endeavours to go beyond the limits of the current debates, by paying more attention to the ways in which we define and analyse power, and how we examine it in terms of the historical development of the US state. Finding a way of navigating the question of the future of American power is important not just as an academic exercise, but also as an issue that goes to the core of the future of international relations. While the book is not about forecasting the future, it does attempt to develop an improved understanding of the development of American institutions over time in order to provide a better critical understanding of the progress and prospects of American power.

Though now a decade old, the 2003 invasion of Iraq highlights a number of concerns with US power. In 2003, the United States, with an assortment of allies (a 'coalition of the willing'), attacked the state of Iraq, in an effort not only to prevent what its leaders and policy-makers perceived as an increasing international security threat, but also as part of a wider bid for regional order-making. The Iraq War became a highly controversial focal point for all manner of discussion of American power: the overall strength of US power (in terms of the ability to achieve the stated goals of the invasion), the potential for credible opposition (in terms of other key states which opposed the invasion), the perceived recklessness of the wielding of US power (by not having more broad-based international support), the goals and shape of US power (the clarity of the goals articulated), and the future of US power (would the invasion enhance or decrease American power?). That all of these issues were up for debate shows not only the problems associated with highly contentious foreign policy actions, but also a concern with the contours of power in international relations. While the Iraq War certainly brings moral and political concerns about the use and abuse of power in international relations to the fore, it also allows us to probe more deeply into the sources of American power. For example, it raised numerous questions about the role of power in US foreign policy-making, from the power of the executive branch over Congress in terms of the 'war power', through social forces in the US state in influencing the policy agenda, to the articulation of US power (and US 'imperialism') in international relations.

The 'Arab Spring' of early 2011 raised similar questions about American power in a new context: in the aftermath of years of war in both Iraq and Afghanistan, but also under a new American president, Barack Obama. Questions were raised concerning both the ability and the vision of the US in supporting the democratic movements in a variety of Arab states: Tunisia, Egypt, Syria, Libya, Bahrain and Yemen. The Obama Administration took a pragmatic approach: while earlier speeches (such as that in Cairo in 2009) had provided a moral vision of the US supporting democracy, there was also an increased sense of restraint. The new foreign policy vision can be seen in two ways: as a repudiation of the previous Bush Administration's emphasis on imposing regime change; and as emphasizing the decreasing ability of the US to provide direct leadership everywhere in the world. The use of American power in this context was pragmatic and cautious: support was given for democrats in Egypt (after initial support for President Mubarak), while no support was given to protesters in Bahrain. While intervention was never contemplated in the ongoing civil war in Syria, the US pushed for direct military intervention (though limited to air support for rebel forces) in Libya. The questions here surrounded the ability or desire of the US to wield power in the region: did it have the ability to influence actors in other regions? was there a coherent vision of US leadership? Furthermore, in the case of Libya, the power of the president was also questioned, in terms of overreaching his authority to bring the country into war: Congress was never properly consulted about the use of force, and questions were raised as to whether or not this was appropriate (or legal).

As will be elaborated upon later, part of the core argument of the book is that we need to go beyond looking at the US from only the perspective of international politics to actively incorporate the domestic institutions of American power into our analysis. In academic International Relations (IR), US foreign policy-making is often examined in the context of its international relations, looking at grand strategy and approaches to the world of international relations (such as realism and idealism). Alternatively, a narrower focus on the policy process could be seen as fundamental to understanding foreign policy outcomes. Here, analysis of policy-making starts with an emphasis on the formal powers of government, looking at the powers of the executive branch versus those of Congress and how the two bodies interact to form policy. Further extension of the examination of policy process would look at the role of bureaucracies, the impact of interest groups, and of course, the external environment. These approaches, while important, neglect broader societal influences on US foreign policy-making, and have a tendency towards presentism: that is, they do not see the dynamics of American power as embedded in institutions that have developed over time. A core argument of the book is that there is a need for a broader approach to US foreign policy and power that goes beyond both traditional approaches in IR and those that focus narrowly on the foreign policy process.

The book has two core analytic claims. First, it claims that in order to grasp the dynamics of US power, we need to understand more about the US itself: the way in which the American state draws upon domestic power resources to project internationally; how such power has developed historically and institutionally; and how the international environment impinges on (and provides opportunities for) the expression of US power. To accomplish this, we need more than an analysis of the policy process (though we do need to understand this as well), as power is diffused throughout the state in different ways, and not everything can be accounted for through the mechanisms of formal politics. Second, the book claims that the analysis of American power requires a more nuanced understanding of power in order to get a better grip on what its future might be. Power needs to be understood not just as 'power over' – the power of the US to get what it wants in relation to other actors – but also as the power to structure outcomes (and interests) in the international system more generally. The book will argue that the 'institutional' and 'structural' power of the US is core to thinking about the past and future of American power, and crucial for putting current arguments about American decline into perspective. In essence, the book will argue that while US power (especially in the economic sphere) is in *relative* decline, its institutional and structural power is still rather robust. In fact, the case will be made that the main issue with US power in the future concerns the internal dynamics of the US state – politically and economically – rather than problems of relative power internationally.

The book further examines the debates about the sources of US power and their global projection, beyond the mechanics of foreign policy, analysing the broad array of social forces – ideological, economic, military, political – that contribute to America's global position. The book will also put American power in a historical context, arguing that increases in American power were largely historically contingent and shaped by a variety of domestic and international factors. Therefore, the book puts the American state at the nexus of the international and domestic, arguing that both facets of politics are crucial for understanding American power now and in the future. The Introduction continues by first setting the future of American power in the context of debates about American decline, in order to get a better sense of the debates about power (and the possible deficiencies), before moving on to provide an overview of the argument and structure of the book that follows.

Debates about the future of American power

The future of American power has been debated repeatedly in recent years, especially in the context of the aftermath of the wars in Iraq and Afghanistan, the impact of the global (but American-centered) financial crisis in 2007/08, and the purported rise of a number of developing states challenging the centrality of the US in the global economic system. However, concerns about relative decline have been prevalent since the late 1960s, and throughout the period of the 1970s and 1980s they were a prominent part of political, popular and academic discourse about the US. As Michael Cox (2001: 320) describes the earlier debates:

> Divided at home, confronted by new competitors abroad, faced with new uncertainties in an increasingly crisis-prone world where both enemies and allies alike were eroding its previous position of strength, there seemed to be little room for complacency. At best the United States was becoming what Richard Rosecrance termed an 'ordinary country' with its wings 'entangled' like the metaphorical 'eagle'; at worst an indebted, has-been superpower, with a declining capacity to shape the world around it.

A core example of these tendencies (or one that became more popular because of them) can be found in the 1988 publication of Paul Kennedy's (1989) work, *The Rise and Fall of the Great Powers*, which provoked a substantial debate when it first appeared. This large work, covering some 500 years of history, with detailed footnotes, was in essence an erudite historical survey, though one with a purpose: to demonstrate that great powers had a tendency towards 'overstretch' in their ambitions abroad. Kennedy argued that the expansive use of military (and imperial) power needed to maintain dominance (or primacy) inevitably strained the domestic economy until power was lost (Kennedy, 1989; cf. Gilpin, 1981). There were large costs to maintaining leadership or dominance in the international system that inevitably could no longer be met when a state's resources were stretched to the point of collapse.

Kennedy's book became prominent due to his analysis of the US, claiming that the US was a great power like any other, and subject to the same pressures of over-extension. For Kennedy, the internal tensions from over-extension were already there to be seen: the Reagan Administration's massive defense expenditures were putting the US in great amounts of debt, from which it would never fully recover. Challengers of the Kennedy thesis saw the US as still the leading state in the international system – they contended that Kennedy had wilfully misinterpreted the facts, or missed out on crucial pieces of evidence – they also believed that America *must* not decline (Cox, 2007: 646–7); not in the sense that it was impossible, but that it was supporting world order, and needed to retain its over-all primacy in order for the world order itself not to collapse. However, the debate was side-lined with the end of the Cold War and the emergence of the US as the sole superpower. The consider-able growth in the economy in the 1990s also helped to shift the focus away from decline, and it seemed that Kennedy's critics were proven right.

It is important how Kennedy's book played into a trend that had been around since the early 1970s. The Reagan Administration may have attempted to reverse what had seemed inevitable – 'morning in America' to oppose President Carter's 'malaise' (the nickname given to his national Address of July 1979) – but many of the structural problems were still there. The early 1970s had seen American power challenged in every area. It pulled out of the increasingly intractable war in Vietnam in 1973. In 1971, the Nixon Administration started the beginning of the end of the Bretton Woods international economic system, by stopping the dollar's direct convertibility to gold, which ultimately led to the development of an open exchange in currencies. Relative American productivity had also been in decline since the 1960s, with the states of Western Europe returning to pre-war levels of productivity, and states such as Germany and Japan having significantly improved economic growth. The American share of global productivity became about a fifth of world output by the early 1970s, down from half in the immediate post-war period (Kennedy, 1989: 558–9). There had also been a growing recognition of the growing complexity of the international system in terms of providing effective security, as well as an increasingly inter-dependent global economy (only highlighted by the ease with which the 1973 OPEC oil embargo effectively crippled the American econ-omy, now very reliant on foreign sources of oil). Soviet gains in the 'Third World' also demonstrated the limits of American power, as did the tacit acceptance of Soviet power that was seen in the 1972 agreement of the Strategic Arms Limitation Talks (SALT I) and the 1975 Helsinki Accords. Finally, the American economy had entered a period of structural economic problems that had been unheard of previously – stagflation, where inflation remained high and overall growth low. The election of Ronald Reagan was meant to deal with all of these problems, at least partially seen in terms of a moral decline within the US, and variously blamed on the previous administrations' approaches to foreign policy (especially those of Presidents Nixon and Carter). However, the Reagan years saw several other perceived challenges to American power, mainly in the rise of the East – and especially the threat of Japan – and it is in this context that Kennedy's thesis became the source of popular contention.

The decline debates of the 1970s and 1980s are of much relevance to current debates about American decline, especially in the context of what appear on the surface to be very similar conditions to those of the 1970s: the aftermath of two problematic wars, economic crisis, and the rise of rival economic powers. First, the wars in Iraq and Afghanistan showed that American power was not all-encompassing: that despite having by far the most powerful (and expensive) military in the world, the US could not impose itself on either state in terms of the vague goals of national reconstruction and regional order building. Second, the wars and the campaign against terrorism that accompanied them showed an America that was often unwilling to play by the rules of the international system that it itself had set up, with a potential corresponding loss of legitimacy. Third, the economic crisis of 2007/08 initiated a recession that was as large as that of the Great Depression of the 1930s, with an accompanying crisis in American-led capitalism. Fourth, the economic crisis once again highlighted the problems with American public debt and trade deficits, and put in question the future of the dollar as the international reserve currency. Finally, a number of economic competitors emerged that are seen as real challengers to US economic power, most predominantly in the industrial powers of China and Germany, traditional challengers in the EU and Russia, but also in developing economies, such as India and Brazil (for different perspectives see, e.g., Beckley, 2011/12; Brooks and Wohlforth, 2008; Ikenberry, 2008; Kaplan, 2011; Kupchan, 2012; Layne, 2009; Luce, 2012; Moran, 2012; Nye, 2011; Rachman, 2010; Zakaria, 2009).

These factors have all been put forward to question the durability of American unipolarity or hegemony in the international system both today and in the near future. Of course, not everyone agrees on the present condition of American power, nor the future prospects. But three things are important about the current debates for the purpose of the book that follows. First, the decline debates need to be put in context, as the debates themselves ebb and flow with international events that challenge American perceptions of its role in the world. The debates of the 1970s and 1980s were soon forgotten with the end of the Cold War and the booming economy of the 1990s. The current decline debate continues to draw on the past articulations of decline, which is one reason why we need to be critical of the current discourse. Why were the 'declinists' wrong then? What changed to bring America out of relative decline (or was it really in decline at all)? Second, we should also draw attention to the importance of perceptions of decline because, if American policymakers themselves believe in the reality of relative decline they will act upon it; and there is real evidence that the Obama Administration has conceded this point (see discussions in Indyck et al., 2012; J. Mann, 2012; Singh, 2012), as have important policy reviews (US National Intelligence Council, 2008; 2012).

Finally, at the core of the present debates about American decline and power in the international system is the question of how we examine power itself. For the 'declinists' American decline is seen in terms of relative power that affects the ability of the American state (for better or worse) to achieve its interests in relation to other key actors in the international system. Many of those who have been critical of the discourse of decline have homed in on a problematic conceptualization of power as being at the heart of misunderstanding American power today (e.g. Beckley, 2011/12; Brooks and Wohlforth, 2008; Nye, 2011: ch. 6). The discussion of decline therefore requires a critical discussion of what power itself is international relations, as the debates on decline too often rely on a view of power mainly conceived of as a direct 'power over', avoiding other important aspects of power relevant to American power, and also avoids a sense of 'power to', a core articulation that is important for thinking about what kinds of powers the US has had and will continue to have.

The argument and organization of the book

Too often debates about the future of American power have been pitched at the level of clear clashes of interest, and ignore other contours of power. In particular, the book argues that 'institutional' power and 'structural' power are crucially important in examining the future of American power. Institutional power derives from the power the US has embedded in international institutions; structural power from the broader ways in which the US makes its own interests those of the rest of the international system. These forms of power are fundamental for two reasons. First, the institutional dimension is essential for seeing the degree to which the US has managed to secure its interests through the creation and reproduction of international institutions, which have given other states a stake in the system. To the extent to which these institutions remain buoyant there is little incentive for challengers to overthrow them in favor of something else. While this does not necessarily mean that there will not be American decline, it emphasizes that institutions provide a framework in which relative decline can be managed. Second, the overlooking of more structural elements of power is likely the most problematic aspect of the decline debates. While the US as an economic actor is clearly in *relative* decline, the structural power that has allowed for American success has not disappeared. The real sources of international decline here can be seen in three core areas of challenge: in attempts to undermine the legitimacy of American leadership in the international system; in the potential undermining of the dollar as an international reserve currency, which would challenge the centrality of the US to the global economy, and also undermine its extravagant deficit spending; and in direct attempts to challenge the US geopolitically.

We have an added problem when thinking about power in international relations. While it is useful to think of states (and potentially other entities) as 'actors' with power capacities, it does not entirely get to the heart of where power resides. States are essentially collective actors *and* structures, which mobilize groups of people to achieve their own specific ends, but also structure the possibilities of those groups within the scope of state power. Therefore there is a clear need to understand American power through an analysis of the American state in its international role, but also in terms of its domestic institutions and sources of power. We need to move beyond the 'domestic/international' divide to better understand how American power is organized, and how the domestic sources of power relate to its international position and power projection (and vice versa). The power that states wield can be seen as a form of 'social power', defined as organized collective action. This is not to say that social power is 'good' or 'soft' as some might want to see it, but just that the power that states wield is through institutions that utilize the collective power of individuals working together.

The book develops these two further positions in relation to American power by utilizing Michael Mann's valuable four-stranded model of social power, which focuses on ideological, economic, military and political power (the IEMP model) (Mann,

1986: 22–8; Mann, 1993: 6–10, chs 2 and 3; cf. M. Mann, 2012). Ideological power derives from the organization and control of meaning, which can include both sources of 'ultimate meaning' such as religion, or norms of social interaction. Economic power 'comprises the circuits of production, distribution, exchange, and consumption' (Mann, 1986: 25). Military power concerns the organization of violence for whatever ends (e.g. for the usefulness of aggression or defense and protection of life, i.e. security). Finally, political power 'derives from the usefulness of centralized, institutionalized, territorialized regulations of many aspects of social relations' (Mann, 1986: 26). Political power is therefore organized in the state, but the function of the state varies in terms of its overall purpose and the relationship with other networks of power. The book uses Mann's four sources of power as a way of analytically separating different strands of US power, as a means to better understand the role each plays and how they interact. While a separate chapter will be devoted to military, economic, and ideological power, the American state forms the core of American political power, and discussion of its role will be woven in and out of all of the chapters that follow.

Chapter 1, 'The Rise of American Power', situates the US state in the context of power, charting the overall rise and expansion of US state power from the beginning of the Republic up until the present day, in order to get a better sense of where the core institutions of American power have come from, how they have changed over time, and how they influence the present. The chapter hinges upon a longer reflection on the key moment for contemporary American power: the post-World War II expansion of state power and the rise of the 'national security state'. The purpose of the chapter is to demonstrate how important the expansion of state power – both territorially and institutionally – has been for the American experience, and to argue that we cannot properly understand the potential for international power projection without examining domestic developments.

Chapter 2, 'American Power and International Relations', complements the discussion in the first chapter by using the introductory history as a means to examine the international role of the United States. It first provides a bridge to the previous chapter by analysing a number of core concepts that emerged in Chapter 1 – such as isolationism and internationalism – and relating them more clearly to the debates on power. The chapter continues by providing an extended discussion of how to conceive of power in international relations, in order to get a clearer sense of the scope of the debates around the concept of power, and why they are important for understanding American power. Drawing on the work of Barnett and Duvall (2005), the chapter utilizes a four-fold distinction of how power operates, in order to clarify the core arguments about power made in the book. The chapter then provides a discussion of different theories about the role of American power in the world, examining the ways in which approaches to international relations relate to the power debates. Tying the argument together is the contested concept of legitimacy, which has become core to thinking about the problems and possibilities of the future of American power. Finally, the chapter examines the ways in which we can conceive of power using the four sources employed by Mann.

Chapter 3, 'State Power and the Foreign Policy Process', surveys the domestic dynamics of state power, and starts off the analysis of different sources of power by focusing on the political. The chapter first examines the structures of the American state, and puts forward an outline of a theory of the American state, in order to provide a context for understanding American power. It then moves on to a deeper examination of the diffusion of political power within the American state, examining the contest for control over American power through foreign policy. The chapter details the restraints on the presidency by examining the politics of foreign policy in a number of areas: congressional oversight (both formal and informal), the role of interest and pressure groups, the role of the media, and cultural and institutional legacies. The key insight of the chapter is that the foreign policy-making process is highly circumscribed by societal factors, and especially the historical legacy of foreign policy-making within the federal government, and conceptions of the role of the US in the world.

Chapter 4, 'The Evolution of Military Power: An American Way of War?', examines the role of military power in the American state. Having the largest military spending of any country in the world, as well as the most technologically advanced armed forces, has been important for America's role in the world, and its global reach. The evolution of military power from the founding of the Republic to the present is used in the chapter as a way of framing past and present concerns about militarism in American political life. The use of force internationally is also analysed, especially in terms of direct interventions that have been important for considering US power projection, but also in terms of the institutional and structural power of the military globally. These insights are further utilized to explore the idea of a distinct 'American way of war', which examines both American military policy, and civil–military relations and the role of the military in society. The chapter concludes with a discussion of the efficacy of military power in the contemporary world, considering the problems the US has had in recent years in using military power as a solution to international problems. The core argument of the chapter is that since the beginning of the Cold War the US has had a difficult relation with military power, seeing military power as fundamental to expressions of power in international relations, but also being subject to an increasing militarization of its international power projection and domestic life.

Chapter 5, 'The Rise (and Fall?) of American Economic Power', examines the role of the US economy in power projection. The main aim of the chapter is to clarify the role of economic power within the broader contours of American power: the US remains a highly dynamic capitalist state, and the relationship of civil society and the state and economy is an essential part of understanding the future of American power. Here, the examination of the different types of power is crucial, in that much of the debate about American economic decline is premised on just looking at forms of 'power over', and often overlooking the continued institutional and structural power the US holds in the international political economy. The chapter looks at the historical background of economic power; the relationship between national political economy and the national interest, noting real divides within the economy and their effects on how the state acts in terms of economic interest; the importance of American leadership in the world economy, and how it has managed to maintain structural power over such a long period; and finally the major problems of the American economy, from the 2007/08 crisis to the future of the dollar as the international reserve currency. The chapter argues that economic power has been fundamental to US primacy and hegemony, and that the key challenge is less to do with peer 'competitors' and contingencies that emanate from the openness and interdependence of US-led capitalism, and more with the current fragility of the US domestic economy, which is becoming increasingly affected by public debt and the inability of the political system to deal with structural problems.

All of the previous chapters emphasize in different ways the role of values in framing the exercise of power, from the means by which the

US was shaped by both anti-militarism and anti-statism, to the role of liberal individualism and the US as a 'market' society. These ideas are expanded upon in Chapter 6, 'The Power of American Values: Ideology and Identity in American Foreign Policy', which starts by demonstrating the importance of values (expressed as a form of ideology) in US foreign policy formation. The chapter then examines the scope and content of 'American exceptionalism', and how exceptionalism provides a framework for thinking about US foreign policy and its relation to American identity. The final section examines how the US has actively used exceptionalist values to shape international relations more generally, noting two important ideas. The first is that exceptionalism does not lead to uniform policies, as it has both shifted over time (along with the role and power of the state), and only provides a blueprint for action and understanding, rather than a specific set of policies. Second, the extent to which American ideology is a core part of the international system, providing legitimacy for the expression of American power, also demonstrates ways in which such power might be undermined: either through states that are opposed to the American ideology, or through the US acting in ways that undermine that legitimacy.

Chapter 7, 'Responses to American Power', considers global responses to American power by looking back at the debates on power discussed in Chapter 2 (and utilized throughout the book), as a means of discussing the possibility and potentials (and desirability) of resisting power, which has been a prominent theme in contemporary debates on the future of international relations. The chapter argues that we can see these challenges more clearly by embedding them in the power debates and by referring back to the four sources of power.

The conclusion brings all of the strands together in order to demonstrate the analytic purchase of the discussion of American power, and revisits the debates about American decline.

Chapter 1

The Rise of American Power

In 1783, after the Treaty of Paris concluded the Revolutionary War against Britain, the 'US state' consisted of about a third of the territory of the current continental United States. This included the original thirteen states with the addition of territory to the west that was conceded by Great Britain at the end of the American Revolution. Until the ratification of the Constitution in 1788, the United States were held together in a loose confederation, and were still very much a collection of quasi-independent states. In 1803 a vast swathe of the center of the continent was purchased from France. Westward expansion continued throughout the first half of the nineteenth century until 1848, when, with the Mexican Cessation, the United States had filled territorially what we now think of as the continental United States (if not yet formally being composed of all the states existing today). While historians have long been interested in this westward expansion, what role does it play in thinking about US power and foreign policy?

A core contention of this book is that the domestic politics and power resources of states (and the US in particular) are crucial for understanding both foreign policy and the dynamics of power in international relations more generally. The power of the US and its role in international relations changed dramatically over the course of two centuries, from the creation of the republic on the eastern seaboard of the North American continent, through westward expansion and moves towards empire in the nineteenth century, to the rise of the US as a 'superpower' in the twentieth. Core to the development of the power of the modern state is its expression geographically: Max Weber (2009a) famously defined the state in terms of its territorial manifestation and it is important we see the development of the American state in this light as well. The western expansion of the United States is central for understanding not only the growing power and territorial reach of the American state, but also the intersection of foreign policy and state power. The chapter therefore details the rise of US power from the founding to the present in terms of both the expansion of state power and key expressions of international power, thereby examining the influence of both the international and domestic realms in this expansion, as well as the development of key institutions through history (Chapter 2 will follow this by bringing the historical discussion forward to a conceptual and analytic overview of how we can understand US power theoretically). Overall, I will argue that the rise of American state power is a crucial facet of US power in general, and integral to its international role both past and present.

In terms of the founding ideology of the US, the rising power of the American state was a paradox. The US was established on the basis of a very limited form of federal government, necessary in bringing together the thirteen states against foreign encroachment. In fact, some of the most fascinating rationales for the creation of the national government by the authors of *The Federalist* clearly surround the issue of national defense (e.g. Madison et al., 1987: n 23). This was also related to the problems created by the limited government formed through the Articles of Federation in 1781, which, as Herring describes, 'proved at best an imperfect instrument for waging war and negotiating peace' (Herring, 2009: 25). The debates within the early Republic were framed in terms of the expansion of state power, the scope of federal or national power, but also as to whether or not to expand the geographical size of the state (e.g. Madison et al., 1987: n 51; cf. Stephanson, 1995: 17). But the United States was always different from other states in terms of where power lay: while relying on military power for its expansion, it was influenced by the dynamism and independence of its civil society, and from its origins in a revolution against aristocratic modes of government, and as such its democratic form was very important to its foreign policy (Mead, 2002: ch. 2).

The chapter provides a narrative of the rise of American power through the nineteenth and twentieth centuries, drawing on these themes but also focusing attention on a pivotal moment for US state-building: post-World War II and the early Cold War. Since we can see state power very broadly in terms of its administrative capacity, its geographical extension, and in terms of its overall reach into civil society, it is important to contemplate the rise of US power in the paradoxical context of the overall anti-statism within the US (an ideological tendency that still survives to the present day), and the post-war moment is an essential shift in US power and our understanding of that power. The chapter contends that over time the US state built up a very particular capacity for the institutionalization of power, which drew on its distinctive traditions, which is important for understanding both US foreign policy and power projection.

The state, power and foreign policy: 1776–1945

Many accounts of American power and US foreign policy start with World War II and after, logically seeing this period as the beginning of American hegemony and a pronounced internationalism, and they tend to draw the main lessons about both the expression and logic of American power from this time frame. Following a number of recent authors (e.g. Kagan, 2006; Mead, 2002), I will stress the importance of embedding our understanding of American power in a much longer continuity. While the discussion of some 200 years of history of the US will be necessarily brief, schematic and thematic, an understanding of US power today is heightened by getting a better sense of the past. This becomes very clear looking at the development of state power, and the traditions from which US power has derived. The present section will look at this history focusing on two broad eras: the nineteenth-century expansion of US state power, and the early twentieth century rise of the US as a great power.

The making of a great power

The US state went through a number of phases in the nineteenth century, starting from a very limited government focused on internal improvement, to an expansionist power, ever moving westwards, through the Civil War period, which unified the states in a much firmer fashion, and finally, by the end of the century engaging in out-and-out imperialist adventures, especially seen in its war with Spain. These shifts in American foreign policy tend to revolve around a number of core issues: the limits of the power of the state; debates about the ideal size of the US; and the virtues of expansion and engagement with the world. From the start, the US saw itself as a virtuous republic that would be a beacon of freedom, detached from the problems of Europe. What this meant in practice became more difficult to define, as various presidents stressed different roles for the US, and, as the state grew geographically, different explanations were given for expansion. While there is not space to deal comprehensively with all of these debates, a number of key administrations are chosen to highlight the dilemmas of foreign policy and power in the nineteenth century.

The foreign policy of the early republic was based on ideas that came from the revolutionary experience, well articulated by the first president (and Commander-in-Chief of the Continental Army in the War of Independence), George Washington. The character of Washington's foreign policy (and that of the early republic) is well accounted for in his Farewell Address of 1796 (a published letter to the American people, in part written by Alexander Hamilton, explaining Washington's reasons for declining to take up a further presidential term of office) (Gilbert, 1970). In the Farewell Address, Washington discussed numerous issues pertinent to the future of the union (especially his view that Americans need to avoid the factions and partisanship that come with political parties), and it is particularly famous for its discussion of foreign policy. He stated that 'The great rule of conduct for us, in regard to foreign nations, is, in extending our commercial relations, to have with them as little political connexion as possible', and 'it is our true policy to steer clear of permanent alliances with any portion of the foreign world, so far, I mean, as we are now at liberty to do it' (Viotti, 2005: 151). However, while this can sometimes be taken as a bold isolationism, it is one that is also connected to America as a peculiarly moral nation. As he states earlier in the Address:

> Observe good faith and justice towards all nations; cultivate peace and harmony with all. Religion and morality enjoin this conduct; and can it be, that good policy does not equally enjoin it – It will be worthy of a free, enlightened, and at no distant period, a great nation, to give to mankind the magnanimous and too novel example of a people always guided by an exalted justice and benevolence. (Viotti, 2005: 150)

This view of foreign policy became the basis for the foreign policy of the Federalist Party (followed by Washington's presidential successor John Adams and staunch federalist Alexander Hamilton), which charted a mid-point between a more revolutionary foreign policy and a more peaceful one.

While the Farewell Address is often seen as the beginnings of an American tendency to isolationism, this reading is misleading. First, the Farewell Address needs to be seen in its historical context. After managing all the problems that came with the 1778 alliance with

France (necessitated by the need for support in the war against the British), including much interference in American domestic affairs, there was a recognition by Washington from his experiences that such alliances were not viable if the US was to become truly independent. France was furthermore attempting to interfere in the 1796 election, insinuating that the signing of the Jay Treaty (with Great Britain) and the re-election of Washington for a third term would be the path to war with France. The French thought it much better for Americans to support the Democratic-Republican candidate Thomas Jefferson, whose party was far more amenable to France and French interests. On one level, the Farewell Address was an intervention into the election itself. Having decided not to run for another term, Washington wanted to promote the Federalist Party, but also note that parties had become a means of foreign influence on American interests domestically through Congress (Bemis, 1937; Herring, 2009; Perkins, 1993).

The Farewell Address was also situated in a time where the power of the US was much attenuated, and the only suitable course was a pragmatic one, as McDougall notes, more akin to 'unilateralism'. As he states, 'neutrality was the only moral *and* pragmatic course for the new nation. Entangling alliances would only invite corruption at home and danger abroad, while neutrality could not but serve Liberty and national growth' (McDougall, 1997: 42). The lack of isolationist sentiments in the Address has been noted by numerous scholars, but is worth stressing (e.g. Bemis, 1937; Herring, 2009; Mead, 2002; McDougall, 1997; Perkins, 1993). Not only is there no mention of 'isolationism' (a concept that only became popular in the late nineteenth and twentieth centuries), but the pragmatism of the policy is also made clear in Washington's reference to the need for 'temporary alliances'. Additionally, as Herring notes, Washington also 'vigorously advocated commercial expansion' (Herring, 2009: 83), which highlights how much emphasis is on *political* independence, rather than shutting America off from the world. Regardless of the misinterpretations, there is an important sense that the Farewell Address did become a blueprint for American foreign policy (and American power). As argued many years ago by Bemis, 'for over a hundred years no responsible American statesman ever gainsaid it. It became so firmly established as American policy as still to stand, even in our days in a vastly altered world' (Bemis, 1937: 110).

In this light the 'Model Treaty' or 'Plan of 1776' is also of great interest. With the Declaration of Independence in 1776, the

Continental Congress sought to have a set of general principles for setting up relations with other states (and was also meant to be the starting basis for a treaty with France). The Model Treaty (designed by a committee, but mainly written by John Adams) was set up as an ideal, a treaty of 'amity and commerce' that would have two core sets of principles: the first the firm principle of shunning political connections with trading partners, thus avoiding entangling alliances; the second a set of rather daring liberal commercial principles. The key ideas of commerce mainly revolved around shipping, which was of course crucial for commercial trading (and dominated in the Americas by Britain and its naval power); and especially important were the principles of 'free ships, free goods', as well as a set of essentially anti-mercantilist principles against tariffs and for the promotion of neutral trading during wartime. All were principles aimed at the undermining of British commercial power. As Herring notes, the Model Treaty was 'breath-taking in some of its assumptions and principles' (Herring, 2009: 17), as the common practice in the global economy was towards mercantilism, and 'the Americans thus entered European diplomacy as heralds of a new age' (Herring, 2009: 17). As Perkins summarizes, 'in commerce, in short, there would be no nationality; all the civilized world, at least all those who accepted the American scheme, would trade as equals' (Perkins, 1993: 24).

Although the principles could not hold entirely in the need for a relationship with France, as the French demanded (and received) some limited political guarantees in its recognition of American independence, France also did concede in a limited way to some of the principles of 'amity and commerce' set out in the Model Treaty, especially conceding trading on a 'most favored nation' status and limited maritime neutrality. The origins of American power in the world were therefore pragmatic, but also linked from the outset to firm principles of commerce and politics, which did have an important legacy for American diplomacy and power projection more generally. As Bemis has pointed out, the Model Treaty 'has exerted a profound influence on the history of American diplomacy because it crystallized the policy which the United States has generally pursued throughout its history in regards to certain fundamental concepts of maritime law and neutral rights' (Bemis, 1937: 25).

With the election of Thomas Jefferson as president in 1800, there was a shift in emphasis in foreign policy matters. Whereas the Hamiltonian Federalist Party (followed by both Washington and his successor, John Adams) had stressed trade, industrial development and a more 'realist' foreign policy (and were much more sympathetic with Britain), Jefferson and the Democratic-Republican Party (usually seen as the forerunner of the modern Democratic Party) were much more focused on the (re)development of 'republican virtue' at home, mainly found in the promotion of yeoman farmers, and building a space for the 'empire of liberty' to flourish (Stephanson, 1995: 22). These considerations played an important role in both the Louisiana Purchase of 1803 (which doubled the geographic size of the US), and the War of 1812 against the British (though Jefferson was no longer president, his party's successor, James Madison, carried on these traditions). However, the role of the federal state at this point was still quite small, and overly focused on the maintenance of states' rights.

The first real shift in US foreign policy in terms of expansion began to occur under the presidency of James Monroe (1817–25), along with his Secretary of State, John Quincy Adams. Although a member of Jefferson's party, Monroe moved towards more expansionist practices of US foreign policy. Adams especially has been seen as not only one of the most successful Secretaries of State, but one who managed to secure America's interests without giving up core principles, thus setting a framework for American foreign policy for the long term (see e.g. Bemis, 1949; Gaddis, 2004). Whatever the long-term judgement, it is clear that Adams vigorously believed in and pushed for American continental expansion. The United States, he had written, was destined to be 'coextensive with the North American continent, destined by God and nature to be the most populous and powerful people ever combined under one social contract' (cited in: Perkins, 1993: 4). Part of this was to be achieved through territorial expansion, also backed up by commercial expansion abroad. As Herring notes, 'sensitive to the needs of the shipping and mercantile interests of his native New England, he viewed free trade as the basis for a new global economic order' (Herring: 2009: 139). Monroe and Adams attempted (with limited success) to do this by expanding US diplomatic missions abroad, but also by enacting reciprocal trading agreements, in an attempt to abolish mercantilist principles.

In practice, two areas of expansion and assertion were hugely important. First, the annexation of Florida in 1819 by a treaty with Spain both secured the territory of the US across the Eastern continent and established US territorial claims all the way to the Pacific (although north of the present border with Texas). The treaty was accomplished through adept diplomacy, but also through coercion, primarily the belligerency of General Andrew Jackson, who extended orders to 'pacify' the indigenous Seminole population of Western Florida, using this as an excuse to invade Florida. While the move invoked much controversy at home and abroad, it was also used skilfully by Monroe and Adams as a means of incorporating the Floridas into the US (Herring, 2009: 148).

The expression of the 'Monroe Doctrine' of 1823 further demonstrated US desire to expand its influence in the Americas, or to keep the influence of the Europeans out. In the context of the recognition of newly independent states of Central and South America (formerly Spanish and Portuguese colonies), Monroe gave his 1823 Annual Address to Congress dealing with the problems of colonial interference in the hemisphere. What came to be known as the 'Monroe Doctrine' mainly concerned European (and other) powers not interfering with the newly independent colonies (while refraining to comment on those that were already established). The key message was that 'the American continents, by the free and independent condition which they have assumed and maintained, are henceforth not to be considered as subjects for future colonization by any European powers' (Viotti, 2005: 154). Additionally, the message carried on the principles of non-intervention and 'isolation', or at least the sense that the US would also remain aloof from conflicts in Europe (and in this context, the contemporaneous Greek struggle with the Ottoman Empire was mainly in the thoughts of many Americans). It was in essence a theory of 'two spheres': one the new world of republican governance, the other the old world of Europe, and the two should no longer meet (Herring, 2009: 155–6).

Many European leaders reacted with disdain, and saw in it the roots of an American radicalism (especially noted in the reaction of Austrian Chancellor, Prince Metternich) (Perkins, 1993: 166). However, the immediate legacy in the US was much less muted than the weight often placed on this doctrine would seem, and it was not until the end of the nineteenth century that it would be resurrected as a core guiding principle for the US (Perkins, 1993: 167–8). But as Herring notes, despite its immediately limited influence, it was 'by no means a hollow statement': 'it publically reaffirmed the continental vision Adams had already privately shared with the British and Russians: "Keep what is yours but leave the rest of the continent to us"' (Herring, 2009: 157). Indeed, Bemis (1937: 209) sees the Monroe Doctrine rather as a 'capstone' to what had successfully come before it. As such, it is best to see it in terms of its essential continuity with what was already present, but also that the US could assert itself more readily in many ways due to its growing power and independence, the increasing retreat of the European colonial powers in the Americas, and their own exhaustion from the Napoleonic Wars in Europe.

The presidency of Andrew Jackson (1829–37) added a militarist drive to American expansionism, and also left a real legacy for foreign policy making. The Jackson presidency saw a real re-dedication to an anti-statism against overarching state power, and the promotion of individual freedom. While the presidency of Jackson's predecessor, John Quincy Adams, had been seen as a relative failure in terms of its attempts at national improvement, Jackson re-invigorated American 'exceptionalism'. As Stephanson described the Jacksonian ideology: 'opportunity and expansion for everyone amid minimal or no government regulation, a rhetoric of republican equality that actually masked a profoundly unequal society' (1995: 30). Such ideas were taken even further by Jackson's follower James Polk (1845–9), who inaugurated a series of wars and foreign policy moves that completed the westward expansion of the United States. First came the annexation of Texas in 1845, followed by war with Mexico (1846–8), and agreement with Britain over the Oregon territory (1848). All were done with the sense of the US's right to these lands – 'Manifest Destiny' – and aggressive expansion from both settlers and the military when seen as necessary, and also entailing the destruction of native populations. What was pronounced in this era was the vastly differing ideas about the role of the state in national development and expansion, divisions over slavery (and debates about the expansion of slavery into newly annexed regions) and the limited role of federal government.

The Civil War (1861–5), in many ways a culmination of the tensions that came with expansion (both in economic and moral terms over the practice of slavery – whether it should be expanded to the new regions of the US) shifted the overall scope and capacity of the state in a number of ways. First, like numerous wars in US history, the impact of war was to further the reach of the state in its administrative capacity (Bensel, 1990; Skocpol, 1992; Skowronek, 1982). Second, the North's victory over the South also meant a tightening of federalism, bringing a stronger and more imposing national state (especially through the policies of reconstruction) (Foner, 1988). Third, the Civil War (with the ratification of the Thirteenth Amendment of the Constitution in 1865) also brought an end to the practice of slavery that had been dividing the republic for some fifty years: while this by no means ended issues with race relations, especially in the South, it did mean that there was the outlawing and transformation of the plantation economy as well as a greater uniformity to the American state (see Foner, 1988; Kolchin, 1995; McPherson, 1990). However, despite the increases in state capacity seen after the Civil War, the US state still remained different to its European forebears in terms of the overarching dominance of the state. The domination of national politics by Congress, the continued weakness of the institution of the presidency, and the problems of Civil War debt continued to mean that the US state was not strong in the way we see it now (Zakaria, 1998: 11–12). It would take the combination of industrial dominance and a stronger presidency to shift the American state towards what it is today.

The US in the world

The first half of the twentieth century in many ways provided the consolidation of American power. The US had been on the rise for most of the nineteenth century, a fact recognized by the European powers. The expansion of the American state across the continent, the dramatic rise in the population of the US, its relative geographic safety (both in terms of the protection of two oceans, and the actual continental scale), and, finally, the rise in American industrial productivity, left the US in a very strong position relative to the other great powers of the world. The development of the US as an industrial power at the end of the nineteenth century was particularly impressive, and worrying for European competitors (P. Kennedy, 1989: ch. 4). As Zakaria notes, 'the 1880s and 1890s mark the beginnings of the modern American state, which emerged primarily to cope with the domestic pressures generated by industrialization' (Zakaria, 1998: 11). However, despite much involvement in foreign relations, the US was still primarily domestically focused. The pivotal turning point for the US in many ways was its involvement in a series of wars starting in 1898.

The war with Spain in 1898 (often referred to now as the 'War of 1898' to indicate the broader context of the conflict, in both Cuba and the Philippines) was a significant change for the US. It marked the point where Americans started to look more expansively abroad in terms of their foreign policy, here becoming directly involved with a European power over the issue of Cuba. At this time, Cuba was in a state of revolution over Spanish rule, and increasingly dominated by the US in terms of its economy; the US wanted Cuba to be independent, but was wary of a revolution that impinged on its interests (LaFeber, 1995: ch. 7). The war also marked a transformation in American rhetoric in terms of how they would deal with international relations: from an insecure state that entered into foreign relations pragmatically in order to foster the future of the American 'experiment', to one that acted much more in line with the imperial prerogatives of the other European states. The victory over Spain also left the US with some of its first overseas possessions (Puerto Rico, Guam, and the Philippines), and an eventual colonial conflict in the Philippines (1899–1913). The war also started a debate about American imperialism – the US was meant to be an anti-imperialist state, different from those in Europe, but the war with Spain saw it playing a similar role. As George Kennan put it, 'in 1898, for the first time, territories were acquired which were not expected to gain statehood at all at any time but rather to remain indefinitely in a status of colonial subordination' (Kennan, 1951: 15; cf. Hofstadter, 1996). What was the US to become? Would it be a formally colonialist imperial power like the European countries? Or would it remain something exceptional?

At the same time, the US continued aggressively to pursue its particular commercial interests abroad (LaFeber, 1995). In this light, much retrospective attention has focused on the 'open door' Notes of 1899 and 1900. These diplomatic notes, written by Secretary of State John Hay, were basically appeals to the great powers to maintain open access to China, rather than establishing a system of imperial preference (Herring, 2009: 331; cf. Hunt, 2007: 47–8). Much has been made of these notes: with William Appleman Williams' famous interpretation that they set the stage for US foreign economic policy for decades; and George Kennan arguing that they were indicative of the American tradition of 'idealism' (W. Williams, 1962; Kennan, 1951; cf. Hunt, 2007: 48). However, while the Notes should be seen as important in terms of a fairly consistent statement of principles – that is, appeals for openness that would also benefit American economic interests – they had little impact at the time (Herring, 2009: 333–4). As such, it is probably best to see the Notes both as setting a context for a US vision for its own economic role in the world, and as the means by which it would pursue its interests in other developing regions, one that was based on openness in the pursuit of American interests.

In many ways these two instances of the expression of American power internationally did set some precedents for the future, even if we should not see them as entirely deterministic. The 'indirect' approach to imperial possessions was one that would be an American trend for years to come, along with the economic approach emphasizing openness in a way that was certain to be beneficial to American interests. But perhaps what is of most interest was the way in which the US began to be formally inducted into the more bellicose traditions of European diplomacy. While Americans had never been disinclined to use force to expand, much of this had been haphazard and had also always encouraged buying property rather than fighting for it (even in the forced Mexican Secession of California, the US government insisted on payment) – the other important part was that, as noted above, this expansion had always been to grow the territorial reach of the US state. The new imperialism at the end of the nineteenth century was very much predicated on the importance of action in the world (and less about settler colonialism), and overly bellicose figures like Theodore Roosevelt (president from 1901 to 1909) drew on the idea of war and violence as something good for the nation itself. In fact, as McDougall (1997: ch. 2) argues, this is one of the first eras where the language of 'isolationism' begins to be invoked, as a pejorative term used against those who felt that the US shouldn't be an imperialist or expansionist internationally. Critics such as naval strategist Alfred Thayer Mahan and Senator Henry Cabot Lodge insisted that the US follow geopolitical and moral imperatives to be an imperial power.

The consequence was an increasing interventionism in the Americas, and especially in the former Spanish territories in the Caribbean and Pacific. The Platt Amendment of 1901 formalized the US quasi-control of Cuba. In 1903, the US intervened in Panama's dispute with Colombia in order to pursue its goal of building a canal in the Central American isthmus. A further dispute with Argentina led to President Theodore Roosevelt's 1904 modification of the 1823 Monroe Doctrine, often referred to as the 'Roosevelt Corollary' – here, not only were the European powers to be denied access to the Americas, but the US would have the right to intervene in states that were lacking stability. As he stated in his fourth Annual Address to Congress:

Chronic wrongdoing, or an impotence which results in a general loosening of the ties of civilized society, may in America, as elsewhere, ultimately require intervention by some civilized nation, and in the Western Hemisphere the adherence of the United States to the Monroe Doctrine may force the United States, however reluctantly, in flagrant cases of such wrongdoing or impotence, to the exercise of an international police power. (Roosevelt, 1904)

The Corollary was used as justification for a series of interventions in the region, many predicated on maintaining order where American economic interests needed to be preserved. There were numerous examples from the period, with the US intervening in the Dominican Republic in 1904; Nicaragua in 1910; Mexico in 1914; and Haiti in 1915.

On the domestic front, the power of the state had also increased substantially since the Civil War. The Office of the President was becoming even more important and powerful, beyond what the founders had intended (Gould, 2003: ch. 1). Roosevelt's bellicose foreign policy was shaped internally by something seemingly different (cf. Leuchtenburg, 1952), an overall recognition of both 'populism' and 'progressivism' that had arisen as dual reactions to the massive changes wrought by industrialization in the late nineteenth century, which shifted the context of American democracy from a primarily rural, agrarian society to an increasingly industrial and urbanized one (Hofstadter, 1955; cf. Jenkins, 2012: ch. 4). Additionally, the pressures of industrialism had also led to demographic shifts, with increasing international migration. Starting in the 1890s, there were growing demands for more equity, less corruption, and less domination of the population by big business. National level reforms, such as those found in a series of constitutional amendments (for example creating a national income tax, legislating the direct election of senators, and introducing women's suffrage), all emphasized the need for political reform. There was also a newfound move towards expanding the state's role in the economy, especially after economic crises in 1893 and 1907. Probably one of the most important economic examples from the era was the 1913 establishment of the Federal Reserve Bank, which not only imposed an important set of regulations on the banking industry (a response to a growing number of financial crises in the US), but also set the foundations of the present US monetary and banking system (for more discussion, see Chapter 5).

World War I provided the next great challenge to American foreign policy. While the US had not been shy in intervening abroad when its interests were seemingly at stake, the start of World War I in 1914 led to a muted response in the US, showing to some extent the lack of interest in a broader, more global approach to foreign policy (or potentially just a continuation of previous pragmatism). However, when the US did get involved, it also invoked a new set of principles that helped to shape the future of American exceptionalism. In 1917 President Woodrow Wilson declared a famous list of 'Fourteen Points' that outlined the motives for US intervention in the war. The points, which later became the main conditions for peace that were agreed as part of the Treaty of Versailles in 1919, mainly outlined the moral reasons for US intervention, stressing the importance of national self-determination, the immorality of secret diplomacy, the problems of the European alliance system and the need for an alternative system of collective security (Herring, 2009: 412; Hunt, 2007: 57–61). While Wilson's post-war plan didn't entirely work out (the collective security system, found in the League of Nations, was never very effective, in part due to the lack of US participation in it), the development of a 'liberal internationalism' found in Wilson's fourteen points was very influential in shaping future foreign policy. In fact, it is likely one of the most influential statements in articulating a liberal vision of how US values could be spread universally. How this played out in practice varied in a number of ways, as we shall see below (in Chapter 6).

The rejection of Wilson's plan is often seen as a decisive blow to internationalism, one that would not be revived until America's entry into World War II, and the post-war internationalism that was maintained (though not exclusively in a liberal form) to the present day. Indeed, the interwar period is usually the one that is most readily placed in terms of 'isolationism'. Here we have a period where the US, despite pretentions to great power status, specifically declined to take up leadership in the international system. However, as has been pointed out by a number of critics, this isolationism was limited. First, while the US certainly declined a leading role in international affairs, it definitely did not entirely retreat from internationalism in its economic position. The post-World War I period saw the real beginnings of the US as a global financial power, with the dollar beginning to overtake sterling as an international reserve currency. Second, as revisionist critics of 'isolationism' such as Williams (1962) have noted, there may have been a retreat from the great power system of Europe, but the US continued to be proactive internationally in pursuing its economic policies. Finally, many diplomatic efforts also were made by the US in the era, including the important Washington Naval Conference (1921–2), and the 1928 Kellogg-Briand Pact (co-named after US Secretary of State Frank B. Kellogg), an attempt to outlaw aggressive war.

But the area where isolationism was clearest was in domestic debates about the economy. McDougall points out that interwar 'isolationists' actually referred to themselves as 'nationalists', and for the segment of the economy where this was most relevant (mainly manufacturing and agriculture), a protectionist spirit certainly played out in the period (McDougall, 1997: 39–40). As Frieden has noted, 'the contradictory role of the United States in the interwar period can be traced to the extremely uneven distribution of international economic interests within American society' (Frieden, 1988: 61). The preference for economic isolationism mainly came from the broad sector of the American economy that was not interested in internationalism, while the internationalists were in the financial sector.

The internationalists did eventually win the argument about the American economy, but the Great Depression of the 1930s, spurred on by the Wall Street stock market crash of 1929, also set a new course for both the American state and American economic development. The crash first of all led to the triumph for the nationalists with the imposition of the 1930 Smoot-Hawley Tariff, a highly restrictive set of tariffs on imports meant to protect American industry (but something that is now seen as prolonging and worsening the depression). However, continuing economic depression led to increasing insecurities for Americans, and a desire to find some way out of the economic crisis. The election of Democratic President Franklin Delano Roosevelt in 1932 promised to do just that. Roosevelt's overall idea was to stimulate demand in the economy through a 'New Deal', focused on massive infrastructural programs that would help end the depression. As Roosevelt announced in his Inaugural Address of 1933, 'I shall ask the Congress for the one remaining instrument to meet the crisis-broad Executive power to wage a war against the emergency, as great as the power that would be given to me if we were in fact invaded by a foreign foe' (Roosevelt, 1938: 15). What was striking about this period was not only the new capacity of the state generated by the interventions of the New Deal, but also how it shifted the debate about the role of the state in the American economy, a debate that continues along similar lines today, between 'liberals' who support state intervention, and 'conservatives', who wanted a smaller state that allowed the market to take its course. The reference to 'war' in Roosevelt's Inaugural Address should also be seen as important in this light, as war was the one area of public policy where a strong state (at least during national emergencies) was to be tolerated, and the notion of war was being expanded to domestic policy, as a rationale for expanding the state to deal with domestic crises (Leuchtenburg, 1964).

Roosevelt also changed the idea of how the US should act in the world. The moves to a more aggressive imperialism and interventionism of the early twentieth century were replaced by a much more internationalist worldview, though one that was not necessarily shared by the Congress. For example, the Monroe Doctrine and Theodore Roosevelt's Corollary were replaced by the 'Good Neighbor policy', which was meant to set a different standard for dealings with Latin America. Again, Roosevelt addressed this new approach in his Inaugural Address: 'In the field of world policy I would dedicate this Nation to the policy of the good neighbor – the neighbor who resolutely respects himself and, because he does so, respects the rights of others – the neighbor who respects his obligations and respects the sanctity of his agreements in and with a world of neighbors' (Roosevelt, 1938: 14).

The start of World War II in Europe began to solidify the shift to a more comprehensive internationalism in US foreign policy (and the perspective of power) as well as a dramatic shift in the scope and capacity of the state. By temperament, Roosevelt was keen to get involved in the war on the side of the allies, fearing the consequences of a Nazi takeover of Europe (Dallek, 1979). However, Congress was still inclined to pursue neutrality. Roosevelt found ways of helping the forces against Nazi Germany (particularly through the Lend-Lease Act of 1941), but it was the attack on Pearl Harbor by Imperial Japan on 7 December 1941 that ended any pretence of isolationism. The success of the US involvement in the war – essentially helping to turn the tide of the war in the Allies' favor, first with material support, and later with increasing combat effectiveness as well – was an essential demonstration of American power (Overy, 2006; Parker, 1989). No longer just a domestic-oriented power with potential, the war proved that the United States was indeed a great power. The devastation of the traditional European powers after the war meant that the US was the only 'Western' state left to lead the international system. Unlike after World War I, this time the US took up the mantle of responsibility for leadership, helping to create the key international institutions of the post-1945 world, both in the international economy (the Bretton Woods institutions: the International Monetary Fund and World Bank – see Chapter 5 for further discussion) and in international politics and security (the United Nations). For the American idea of itself, it saw the essential end of republican isolationism, though it lingered on in the early post-war period, as not everyone was convinced of the need for internationalism (Senator Robert Taft was probably the most vocal exponent of a more traditional republican foreign policy).

To sum up, we see a real expansion of the state over the 150 years or so that led up to World War II. While there are many continuities, it is also clear that the American state and its environment have been much changed over that period. The reach and capacity of the state increased over time, a shift that went along with many of the changes in the state that followed the Civil War, and the increased economic capacity of the American state itself. The forms of state intervention most readily associated with the 'New Deal' (but certainly present in early phases of reform in the early twentieth century) illustrate this shift, and lead us to a war that necessitated leadership and involvement by the state. However, we have seen a continuity in terms of the US role in international affairs that (though tempered and influenced by its relative power position in international politics) mainly emphasized three core features: a dedication to economic openness (inasmuch as it favored the US) that had been present since the founding of the US; a pragmatism in foreign policy that shifted after World War II to a much more internationalist position; and finally an anti-imperialism that also contradictorily allowed for a paternalistic and interventionist approach to the affairs of other states. However, the war and the geopolitical aftermath also brought one of the core dilemmas for the American state in the post-war period: the potential militarization of the American state.

The 'national security state'

The beginnings of the Cold War are important for the discussion of American historical development in a number of ways. First and foremost, it is the place in history where the US state took on the characteristics that we are now so familiar with: its scope, size and capacity were all fundamentally shaped by the experience of World War II and in the post-war focus on the newly minted concept of 'national security' (Dalby, 1997: 21; Hogan, 1998; E. Rosenberg, 1993b; Yergin, 1977: 194–5). Second, the period from 1945 to 1950 also clearly shows the analytic purchase of looking at state power as an interaction between the domestic and international. While international events and actions were of great importance to the development of American power during this time, a series of internal events, actions and crises had a great deal to do with the development of state power.

The legacy of World War II in terms of the US role in the world has already been discussed above, but we need to investigate a number of other elements that were important. First, while the war had been fought successfully, it had been recognized that there were a great deal of organizational problems within the government surrounding the coordination of the military services and overall policy of national defense. President Roosevelt had stamped his own imprint on war organization that was largely due to his own idiosyncratic style, taking a great deal of interest in day-to-day strategic affairs. But beyond that, there was also the innovation of creating a Joint Chiefs of Staff for the military services, which could better coordinate the war effort. Inter-service relationships had been highly problematic at the beginning of the war with communication issues seemingly to blame for the intelligence failures that left the US unprepared for the attack on Pearl Harbor. These various issues of coordination left the US in a situation where there was a greater desire politically to have a stronger peacetime military establishment, which President Truman saw as being best accomplished through the unification of the military services, and the creation of a Department of Defense (see eg Hammond, 1977; Stuart, 2008). The desire for unification was fused with an increased sense of insecurity in the post-war period, mainly to do with technological changes in warfare, especially through the potential for long-range bombers to reach the United States. America would be permanently vulnerable, because, as General Henry H. Arnold reported, nuclear weapons could, 'without warning, pass over all formerly visualized barriers or "lines of defense" and . . . deliver devastating blows at our population centers and our industrial, economic or governmental heart' (cited in Gaddis, 1987a: 24; cf. Stuart 2008: ch. 1). World War II demonstrated to American policy-makers that the US could no longer be complacent in its geographical security, and needed to formulate military policy that put these new realities and dangers at the forefront. As John Lewis Gaddis notes, 'this [new] sense of vulnerability is basic to an understanding of how Americans perceived their interests – and potential threats to them – in the post-war world' (Gaddis, 1987a: 21–2).

The new sense of insecurity was an important part of what necessitated both increased coordination of the military and also a move towards permanent preparedness (and a peacetime military force). In a 1945 speech to Congress that was explicitly about the unification of the armed forces, President Truman stated:

> but all nations . . . know that desire for peace is futile unless there is also enough strength ready and willing to enforce that desire in any emergency. Among the things that have encouraged aggression and the spread of war in the past have been the unwillingness of the United States realistically to face this fact, and her refusal to fortify her aims of peace before the forces of aggression could gather in strength. (Truman, 1961: 548–9)

Unification would achieve this goal, and also provide a more robust peacetime military.

Second, one of the crucial factors in the Allied victory in World War II was the harnessing of economic production, and the character of wartime political economy was also important for the resolution of the problem of defense unification. During the war, the US was to become, in the words of President Roosevelt, the 'Arsenal of Democracy'. But due to the lack of direct threat to the American mainland, the absence of overall disruption to normal economic activity, and American traditions of entrepreneurship, the US was not about to have a top-down approach to directing the economy towards military production (unlike that of the Soviet Union). The switch to military production, while coordinated by wartime government boards (e.g. the Manpower Commission, the War Production Board), was in the main driven by alliances between business and labor, and relied heavily on the innovation of the private sector (Koistinen, 2004; Overy, 2006). The major government boards that were coordinating the production efforts were mainly there to focus on any real deficiencies in the market, and importantly did not defer to the government: that they were in the main led by individuals from the business world says a lot about the US approach to production. For example, the War Production Board, which set priorities for military production and helped to distribute scarce resources, was headed from 1942 to 1944 by

Donald M. Nelson, the Executive Vice-President of Sears Roebuck; additionally, the board contained other prominent members of the business community, such as Vice-Chair Charles E. Wilson, the head of General Electric. The successes of military production will be discussed further in Chapter 4, but what is of greater import for the discussion here is the impact this organization left on the state.

The 1947 National Security Act provided the institutional basis for the new American state. The Act created a National Military Establishment, with a civilian Secretary of Defense at its head (though initially with the heads of the military services – the Navy, Army and newly created Air Force – as cabinet-level secretaries); the National Security Council (NSC), designed to coordinate a common national security policy between the military and foreign policy establishment; and the Central Intelligence Agency (CIA), intended to unify disparate intelligence agencies (as a successor to the wartime Office of Strategic Services). All of these organizations are still active today – in somewhat modified forms – and in essence are the heart of American political and military power and indicative of a shift in the purpose of the state towards national security and a potential 'militarization' that went along with that.

Although this administrative and institutional change was of great importance in general, the particular form it took was also of interest, especially in terms of how it was drawn out of longer traditions of US political culture. While there had been a consensus that the reorganization of the military was a necessity, there was a large debate about what it should look like and its overall scope. The political battle over defense reorganization was key in seeing the growth of state power and capacity, and the reorganization heralded by the National Security Act can be seen as part of a greater debate about what the American state would become (Friedberg, 2000; Hogan, 1998). Would it transform into the dreaded 'garrison state', led by military leaders and infused with a militarist spirit, or could the need for permanent preparedness be tempered with a more 'American' approach to state power? The National Security Act demonstrated that the latter was not only possible, but also necessary, the Act itself drawing a middle ground between the old system and a more thoroughly centralized one. The outcome was a kind of compromise between the two views, one that paid attention to US traditions but also sought to reshape the US state to the new international environment (Friedberg, 2000; Hogan, 1998: ch. 2; Stuart, 2008; cf. Mills, 1956).

The debate could also be seen in other areas that challenged the scope of state power. As part of the program for permanent preparedness, President Truman wanted to initiate a more general program of conscription, referred to as 'Universal Military Training' (UMT). The debate here became whether or not the state would have the power to 'force' individuals to be in the military, combined with the reality of a larger standing army. The President decisively lost this debate: Congress would not accept state intervention or power at this level. Similar debates occurred in the area of defense budgets: while the military wanted huge increases to accompany the need for permanent preparedness, there was little sense that Congress, the business community, or the public at large would accept such increases (Pollard, 1989). The Truman Administration itself was rather divided about increasing defense budgets: the president did not want defense spending to impact on important areas of social spending, and others (especially in the Budget Bureau) shared with Republicans the desire to maintain balanced budgets (Hogan, 1998: ch. 5). It wasn't until the massive rearmament program started with the Korean War in 1950 that defense budgets began to soar. Although defense budgets eventually did rise (and also assumed a rather sacrosanct position in American politics – they became essentially untouchable), there always was a desire that the defense budget needed to allow for both guns *and* butter, and it is very telling that the defense budget expanded along with the American economy (that is to say that after an initial surge in the 1950s, the expenditure on defense never rose much beyond 10 per cent of GDP, and went down after 1970; see Chapter 4 for more details).

As noted above, the role of business in America was shaped by the exceptionalist ideology of US liberalism and capitalism, one that played a further role in setting the tone of the early Cold War period. While state power grew in ways to support the growing militarization of the state, there were also the beginnings of a broader internal monitoring of political difference. While anti-statism may have continued to influence how Americans felt about the federal government, the government was increasingly involved in monitoring the beliefs of its citizens. Direct intervention through anti-communist crusades from Congress (especially the highly influential investigations of Senator Joseph McCarthy), 'loyalty oaths' for civil servants, and FBI investigations into communist activities were only the tip of the iceberg. The 'red scare' became a profoundly normative movement that saw internal subversion become a key focus of life in the

US (Harbutt, 2002; Heale, 1990; Morgan, 2004; Sherry, 2003; Whitfield, 1996). Overall, the 'national security state' that developed began to change profoundly the American approach to both its domestic and international affairs. As George Kennan put it, 'a country which in 1900 had no thought that its prosperity and way of life could be in any way threatened by the outside world had arrived by 1950 at a point where it seemed to be able to think of little else but this danger' (Kennan, 1951: xi).

The Cold War and American power

The early post-war years were therefore ones of great transformations for the US state and American power. These, of course, also took place in a changed international context that developed quickly into a Cold War between the Soviet Union and the US, which also shaped the internal debates. While the origins of the Cold War have been the subject of much contentious debate (eg Gaddis, 1997; Leffler, 1994; 1999), whatever the precise reason, by the end of the 1940s, there was a tense relationship between the US and the Soviet Union. While some of this was clearly to do with the lingering issues of World War II and especially the Soviet Union's insistence in maintaining power and control in eastern Europe, it was also due to the attempts of the US to set up a new international order, based on its own principles, especially founded on a multilateral internationalism. For American policy-makers, the threat of the Soviet Union could not be kept at bay through isolation: the US would need to engage with the world. As President Truman stated in his famous Address to Congress outlining the 'Truman Doctrine': 'the free peoples of the world look to us for support in maintaining their freedoms. If we falter in our leadership, we may endanger the peace of the world – and we shall surely endanger the welfare of this Nation. Great responsibilities have been placed upon us by the swift movement of events' (Truman, 1963: 180). The creation of the United Nations (1945), the Bretton Woods economic institutions (1944), and the eventual commitment of US aid to Western Europe (through the Marshall Plan, 1948–51) all helped in creating a new international order based on liberal market principles (though a 'Western'-based international order, in opposition to the Soviet Union and its allies and satellites). There really was a developing sense of two social systems clashing that came to dominate the early Cold War (Halliday, 1993).

The Cold War context of the 1940s was also heightened by a number of crises. For example, the communist coup in Czechoslovakia in 1948 demonstrated to US policy-makers at least the potential for war in Europe (though often seen in retrospect as exaggerated). But two events transformed the international scene in 1949: the Soviet explosion of the atomic bomb in August, ending the American monopoly on nuclear weapons; and the success of Chinese communists in the Chinese Civil War in October (Harbutt, 2002: ch. 2; Leffler, 1992: chs 7 and 8). Both of these not only confirmed the initial suspicions of national security policy-makers about communism – that it was aggressive, expansionist and spreading – but also that of a more dangerous and tense international environment. The events of 1949 also led to a further tightening of the Atlantic Alliance through the creation of NATO, and eventually the creation of the Federal Republic of Germany (aka West Germany), out of the various Allied occupation zones. Revisionist historians have argued that the danger was likely overstated, and have also noted the importance of international economic problems at the time: the US-led international economy was facing a looming problem with the balance of payments. With the international monetary system reliant on the dollar as reserve currency, and on the US as the key producer, dollar shortages were leading to potentially disastrous consequences for the US economy, not to mention those of its allies (Cardwell, 2011; cf. Leffler, 1992: 314–17).

The problems of 1949 led directly to the signing off of one of the most important documents in the history of American foreign policy: NSC-68 (short for National Security Council Document 68). NSC-68 was the product of President Truman's desire to synthesize various readings of the international context, the dangers for the US, and provide a detailed response. The document – mainly conceived by Director of Policy Planning Paul Nitze and Secretary of State Dean Acheson – saw the Soviet Union as a hostile power, ideologically opposed to the US, and determined to defeat the US and its core principles by whatever means possible. As the document put it: 'there is a basic conflict between the idea of freedom under a government of laws, and the idea of slavery under the grim oligarchy of the Kremlin', and furthermore 'the implacable purpose of the slave state to eliminate the challenge of freedom has placed the two great powers at opposite poles' (United States National Security Council, 1950: 27). For the writers, 'it is only by developing the moral and material strength of the free world that the Soviet regime will become convinced of the falsity of its assumptions and that the preconditions for workable agreements can be created' (United States National Security Council, 1950: 30). The US would be required to vastly increase its spending on defense and to balance out its own traditions of freedom with the needs of national security. As Emily Rosenberg argues, 'simply put, the central dilemma of NSC 68 is how to advocate "freedom" by greatly enlarging the state's capacity for action' (1993a: 161). While it would be wrong to think that NSC-68 was applied without any criticism, it became for many the guiding blueprint of the Cold War, setting its ideological parameters.

The 1950 Korean War – the invasion of South Korea by the communist North – played into a number of these concerns, and needs to be seen in the broader international context: a tightening of bonds in the western alliance, and grand fears over the fragility of both the multilateral trading system and the international security environment. For national security policy-makers, it confirmed the 'expansionist' nature of communism as outlined in NSC-68, fixed the importance of the NATO alliance and West Germany in shoring up US power in Western Europe, and also provided the final push towards the implementation of NSC-68 and the rearmament of the US (Harbutt, 2002: 80–88; Leffler, 1992: ch. 9; cf. Cumings, 1990, 2011). The creation of a national security state came into its own with the start of the Korean War. Military spending went from a modest $13.7 billion in fiscal year 1950 to $23.5 billion in the next fiscal year. By the end of the war in 1953, defense spending was up to $52.8 billion, representing 14 per cent of GDP (White House, 2012a). While this number eventually went down, it never went down to the more modest early post-war years.

The increase in defense spending had a number of important consequences, and also represented some broader qualitative shifts in the government. First, it solidified the nascent 'national security state' by giving it a real depth of resources. Second, it effectively began the militarization of the Cold War, which up to that point, though punctuated by crises and various 'war scares', was still relatively peaceful. Third, and though the causation here is rather disputed, the massive increase in spending was characteristic of a kind of 'military Keynesianism' (where problems of demand in the economy are mitigated by public spending on the military), which helped to bring the American economy out of the economic recession started in 1949 (Block, 1980; cf. Cardwell, 2011). Finally, it brought the US back into war, only five years after the end of World

War II. This final point is important for the centrality it brought to the military, and to the kinds of crises and contention it created internally. The war years were characterized by a continued congressional unease at the newly expansionist state. Congress was particularly aggrieved that President Truman had brought the US to war without approval from Congress or a declaration of war, seen as an overreaching executive power, a complaint that would resonate through the rest of the Cold War period, and one with some force today (Sherry, 1995: 177–87).

President Eisenhower won the 1952 election inheriting these problems. The war was quickly drawn to a close, and there was some re-evaluation of the national security state. While his initial national security policy (as articulated by Secretary of State John Foster Dulles) was premised on the 'rollback' of the Soviet Union, Eisenhower eventually developed a 'new look' foreign policy, which was based on decreasing military spending and an increased reliance on nuclear weapons and strategic airpower rather than perpetuating a large standing army (Herring, 2009: 659–60). As such, the Eisenhower years were very much a step back to a more republican foreign policy, though one that was resolutely internationalist in outlook. Eisenhower's views on military power came out very clearly in his 1961 Farewell Address, where he warned against the prevailing influence of the 'military-industrial complex' (Eisenhower, 1961; cf. Ledbetter, 2011). A series of changes and potential crises also were an important part of US power projection in these years. The death of Stalin in 1953 led to some hope of a more conciliatory leadership, but the 1950s became the years of the Cold War at its most dangerous. The Soviet Union was seemingly intractable, paired with a further sense of insecurity in the growing power of nuclear weapons, and a lack of real diplomacy between the two states (Gaddis, 1997: ch. 8). The crushing of the Hungarian Uprising in 1956, and another crisis over Berlin in 1958 only heightened these matters.

The election of John F. Kennedy in 1960 was meant to inaugurate a fresh approach to relations with the Soviet Union, but in practice was better characterized as a shift of emphasis. The dominating military strategy for the Cold War became 'flexible response', an escalating use of force that was geared towards the actual requirements necessitated rather than a singular focus on 'massive retaliation' with nuclear weapons (Harbutt, 2002: ch. 4; Herring, 2009: 702–5). The defining crisis of the Kennedy Administration was the 1962

Cuban Missile Crisis, which can be seen as a real turning point in the first phase of the Cold War. The showdown between the Soviet Union and the US over nuclear missiles in Cuba was resolved peacefully in the end, but also led to an increased stability of the Cold War, the recognition of better communication, and a real commitment to dealing more sensibly with nuclear weapons. A hotline between the Kremlin and the White House was installed, and the first of a series of international agreements over nuclear weapons began to be created, starting with the 1963 Partial Test Ban Treaty and culminating in the 1968 Non-Proliferation Treaty, which still sets the international framework for nuclear weapons today (Gaddis, 1997: ch. 9).

However, the defining event of the 1960s for American power has to be the Vietnam War. President Kennedy had stepped up US military assistance to South Vietnam, and his successor (after Kennedy's assassination in 1963), Lyndon Johnson, brought the US into a full-fledged intervention in 1965. The war was to last (at least the American involvement in it) until 1973, encompassing the deaths of 58,000 American soldiers (many of whom were conscripted), and against the backdrop of substantial domestic unrest (not only over the war, but in a variety of progressive and radical social movements that had also become quite influential) (Herring, 2009: ch. 16; Sherry, 1995: ch. 6). While the war went on, Johnson also expanded the role of the state in two key ways. In 1964, he signed into law the Civil Rights Act, a set of provisions protecting the rights of African-Americans (and other groups as well), legally abolishing discrimination that had been prevalent through policies of segregation. Additionally, 1965 saw the inauguration of major programs as part of the 'Great Society' including the addition of Medicare and Medicaid to the programs of Social Security (Harbutt, 2002: 160–75). These are important in our context as they indicate another side of the growth of the state: it was no longer just military expenditures that would become prominent.

As the Vietnam War carried on indecisively, causing more and more friction domestically, all was not well internationally in terms of American power. First, the 1960s had seen the rise in prominence of other centers of manufacturing, particularly in Europe (and especially West Germany), and the US was no longer the preponderant power in the international economy (P. Kennedy, 1989: 533–64). This was as expected in many ways, as part of the policy of reconstruction was meant to have a more open and multilateral system, with the hope that trade and production would become more equalized. However, this also had an impact on both American productivity and the position of the US in the international monetary system. The Vietnam War only added to the burdens of the American economy. As we shall see in more detail in Chapter 5, one of the major consequences was the end of the Bretton Woods system, but this also became the key focal point in discussion about American decline. Additionally, the rise of Europe had increasingly led to challenges to American leadership. The example of France is most telling in this context, in both economic and military-security terms. The French government challenged American leadership in the global economy by increasingly threatening the dollar's position as a reserve currency by exchanging dollars for gold. Additionally, France had challenged the American domination of NATO by pulling its own nuclear and conventional forces out of the NATO unified command structure in 1966.

Overall, the 1970s began with the US in relative decline, only further exacerbated by the gradual development of Soviet strategic parity (Crockatt, 1996: ch. 9). Parity was recognized through the 1972 SALT I agreement, as well as the anti-ballistic missile (ABM) treaty: both agreements were ways of recognizing and institutionalizing the nuclear status quo. The recognition of parity was part of a plan by the Nixon Administration (guided by the president and his prominent National Security Advisor, Henry Kissinger) to bring the US into 'détente' with the Soviet Union, a period of perceived cooling off of the Cold War. Détente was a means of normalizing relations – in the sense that the Soviet Union was to be treated like any other great power, rather than as a moral problem for the US. However, it also provided the potential for improving relations with China. Nixon and Kissinger had both recognized that the Sino-Soviet 'split' of the early 1960s (ideological and practical disagreements between the two states had been increasing during the 1950s, but reached an apex in the early 1960s) showed that communism was not monolithic, and better relations with China could be a way of balancing against the Soviet Union. Nixon visited China as part of this plan, in 1972 (Herring, 2009: 791–3).

The Nixon and Johnson Administrations continued to increase the power of the American state, and the president in particular. President Johnson's push over the Vietnam War, as well as the new domestic spending programs, increased the size and power of the American state, in many ways an extension of the policies and ideas of President Roosevelt. The Nixon Administration especially was seen as placing far too much emphasis on presidential power, with the criticism of the development of an 'imperial presidency' (e.g Schlesinger, 2004). The secrecy surrounding the military campaign in Vietnam (such as the bombing of Cambodia) was part of such concerns, and eventually Congress tried to reassert authority through the War Powers Resolution of 1973. While more will be said about this in Chapter 3, the Resolution was meant to provide a way for Congress to have more control over the presidential use of force.

US decline was also seen in the context of broader global politics. First, the 1970s saw a series of revolutions in the Third World, and external intervention by communist states (not only the Soviet Union, but also Cuba), began to demonstrate to American policy-makers that the Soviet Union was contesting the Cold War balance, and attempting to impose itself in other areas of the world (Halliday, 1986; Westad, 2005). There was at the same time a domestic political action against the détente policies of the Nixon Administration. Hawkish Democrats and Republicans resented the lack of a moral dimension to the Cold War, and saw détente as an immoral realism that needed to be rearticulated as a battle between ideologies. Organizations such as the Committee for the Present Danger – the starting point of the neo-conservative movement in terms of foreign policy – advocated a more robust and moralized countering of Soviet power (Halliday, 1986: ch. 5). The Soviet invasion of Afghanistan in 1979 only seemed to confirm their point of view. After the years of détente under Nixon and Kissinger, and the shift to Carter's foreign policy in the later-1970s (seen by many as a disaster – too focused on human rights, and not attentive enough to the Cold War, and beset by a number of major crises, such as the Iranian embassy hostage-taking in 1980), the election of Ronald Reagan to the presidency saw the elevation of a politician whose rhetoric lived up to the Cold War of old (Halliday, 1986: ch. 8).

While Reagan is a controversial figure – reviled by the left for the resumption of and ratcheting up of the Cold War (and for implementing a neo-liberal ideology domestically), loved by the right for those same things – his two terms were important for shifts in US power (Patterson, 2005: ch. 5). First, his fiscal regime was seen as bringing an end to the economic doldrums of the 1970s, by tightening monetary policy, and basically pushing the US into recession to try and get rid of rampant inflation. Second, although the defense budget had been substantially increased at the end of the Carter Administration, Reagan kept pushing it upwards in an attempt to outdo the Soviet Union. He did this through the development of new military technologies (the B2 bomber, cruise missiles, the MX missile) and the funding of a 600 ship navy. As Patterson notes, military expenditures went up 34 per cent in his first term, and over his two terms of office, military expenditures totalled nearly $2 trillion (Patterson, 2005: 200). Third, these spending initiatives also went along with a new heated rhetoric that hadn't been heard since the early phases of the Cold War. The characterization of Soviet Union as an 'evil empire' brought a renewed tension in US–Soviet relations. Fourth, the US attempted to increase pressure in Cold War arenas in the 'Third World', especially seen in the support for a variety of anti-communist movements in Latin America, probably best exemplified by the funding of the 'Contras' in Nicaragua (Westad, 2005: ch. 9) .

Despite all of the rhetoric and ratcheting up of tensions, Reagan was also rather pragmatic, and did have a moral position against deterrence which should not be forgotten. Both of these traits combined prominently in initiatives surrounding nuclear relations with the Soviet Union. While often ridiculed for the pursuit of the so-called 'Star Wars' anti-ballistic missile system (the Strategic Defense Initiative), it was in part a direct attempt to abolish the system of deterrence, part of Reagan's (contradictory) anti-nuclear beliefs (Herring 2009: 895). Reagan managed to follow through with some of these shifts – importantly supported by the newly appointed reform-minded Soviet leader, Mikhail Gorbachev – initiating a series of arms control agreements which went far beyond those of the 1970s. First was an extraordinary meeting between the two leaders at Reykjavik, Iceland – where a summit on arms control was held in the summer of 1986 – that led to proposals to abolish nuclear weapons altogether. Though nothing was resolved, it led to directly to the 1987 Intermediate-range Nuclear Forces Treaty (INF), which abolished a whole class of nuclear weapons (thereby disposing of a major dispute in Europe surrounding the deployment of intermediate-range nuclear missiles). The 1991 Strategic Arms Reduction Treaty (START), though signed by President Bush, was also the result of Reagan's initiatives.

The end of the Cold War, for most analysts and practitioners, came as a real surprise: while there were some who recognized that internal economic problems would eventually undermine the viability of the Soviet Union, that it fell apart so quickly and relatively peacefully was a bit of a shock. While this is not the place to rehearse the debates about the reasons for the end of the Cold War (see, e.g.,

Hogan, 1992), the combination of economic collapse, US international pressure, new thinking within the Soviet Union, Reagan's willingness to compromise (often over the objections of advisors), and the influence of Western ideas within the Soviet Union and communist eastern Europe, led to first the letting go of the east in 1989, and in 1991 the dissolution of the Soviet Union itself.

International order in the post-Cold War world

There was considerable debate concerning what the end of the Soviet Union would mean for international politics and the future of the international order. A growing dispute took place in academic journals and foreign policy circles about what the international order would comprise (for example how many great powers there would be, whether the international system would be characterized by conflict or cooperation), but additionally in terms of what this specifically meant for US foreign policy. Right from the outset of the post-Cold War period there was contestation about the consequences of the new American preponderance (Cox, 2004). Those who leaned towards optimism, such as Francis Fukuyama (1992) and other liberal commentators, saw the end of the Cold War as a victory for American-led democracy and liberal capitalism, which would lead to a new stability in the international system. Such a view was celebrated in a September 1990 Congressional Address given by President George H. W. Bush, in which he described the creation of a 'new world order' where the traditional arrangements of international order – balance of power, polarity of the system, collective security arrangements – could be augmented with commitments to global security, justice, human rights and economic equality. As Bush stated, it would be

> A new era – freer from the threat of terror, stronger in the pursuit of justice and more secure in the quest for peace, an era in which nations of the world . . . can prosper – a world where the rule of law supplants the rule of the jungle, a world in which nations recognize the shared responsibility for freedom and justice, a world where the strong respect the rights of the weak. (Bush, 1991)

Overall, a combination of US power, collective action and the UN would lead to peace.

However, there was also a much gloomier picture painted by sceptics of the potential peacefulness of the new system. Many scholars of international relations had seen the Cold War as an essentially stable system, where the precarious balance between two superpowers with nuclear weapons kept ambitions in check (Gaddis, 1987b). However, the collapse of Soviet power meant that a vacuum was created in its former zone of domination in Eastern Europe, and furthermore, that the US could easily disengage from the world. As such, the liberal visions of peace, security and integration were opposed with visions of chaos, disorder and conflict (e.g. Huntington, 1993; Mearsheimer, 1990). The immediate post-Cold War context saw a supposed vindication of the 'lessons' of the Cold War: the consequences of Soviet collapse were the further failure of states in Eastern Europe and sub-Saharan Africa.

Despite the importance of these different visions of international order, what became paramount to US policy-makers was to determine how to act within this new international context. The immediate post-Cold War years saw President Bush pursue a (mainly) cautious and pragmatic foreign policy that was more geared towards the multilateralism of the 'new world order'. In many ways, the first Gulf War (1991) was a fulfilment of this approach: a UN-supported military operation against an unambiguous aggressor that was easily won through a demonstration of US military power with clear global support. Such liberal internationalist views were continued into the Clinton Administration, despite President Clinton paying much less attention to foreign policy, and much more to the problems of the domestic economy. Critics of Clinton's foreign policy thought that it was lacking in an overall coherence, and that it was too focused on pursuing marginal interests rather than upholding great power relations. For example, critics such as Michael Mandelbaum (1996) accused Clinton of conducting foreign policy as 'social work', condemning the humanitarian uses of force that characterized much of Clinton's foreign policy, as well as a lack of attention to the national interest.

If the Bush (I) and Clinton Administrations were initially couched in terms of a 'moralism' in foreign policy, their approaches were criticized in relation to yet another set of US foreign policy dichotomies: the issue of whether unilateral or multilateral action was the preferred way to act. Those who stressed the necessity of unilateral action referred to the need for the avoidance of alliances or any form of external restraint on US action; those who stressed the importance of multilateralism focused on the need to use international institutions and partners to enhance US action. Charles Krauthammer (1990/91) famously argued the former view in his article 'The Unipolar Moment', where he derided claims that the world was multipolar and internationalist and potentially more peaceful, and argued for a more robust defense of US power, against both realism and isolationism. Much of the criticism of Clinton's foreign policy reinforced this view: that Clinton's multilateral approach was undermining the potential of American power, ignoring real interests, and lacking an overarching vision.

By the end of the 1990s, there was a move (associated with neoconservatism) to recapture the legacy of President Reagan's assertive and moralistic foreign policy. In an influential 1996 article, William Kristol and Robert Kagan outlined the basic idea of a 'neo-Reaganite' foreign policy. Opposed to Clinton's 'Wilsonian multilateralism', the neo-isolationism of conservative Republicans like Pat Buchanan, as well as the amoral pragmatic realism of Henry Kissinger, Kristol and Kagan, advocated a more muscular US foreign policy that exemplified all of the qualities noted by Krauthammer, wrapped up in the exceptionalism of the US. Their overall critique of the squandering of US power came down to a broader criticism of the attitude of (seemingly) isolationist-Republicans like President John Quincy Adams. Whereas Adams famously pronounced that America should not go 'abroad in search of monsters to destroy' but rather is 'the well-wisher to the freedom and independence of all', Kristol and Kagan asked 'why not?': 'the alternative is to leave the monsters on the loose, ravaging and pillaging to their hearts' content, as Americans stand by and watch' (Kristol and Kagan, 1996: 31).

However, there were also defenders of multilateralism (or perhaps better described in terms of pragmatic caution) in the new post-Cold War environment. A number of Clinton's supporters argued that the new international environment made it very difficult to form an overarching strategy, and therefore 'ad hocary' and domestic attention was actually necessary. President Clinton was also heavily constrained by the election of a Republican Congress in 1994, which was exceedingly hostile to the Clinton Administration. As Stephen Walt (2000) argued, the US was still the preponderant power, with tremendous freedom of action, but this created a corresponding problem of trying to find focus, both internationally and domestically (the latter in terms of the public's lack of interest in foreign policy), as well as dealing with the rising difficulties of interest group pressures in the foreign policy arena. Additionally, Clinton did find new areas of concern, all of which became a real of legacy of the 1990s: democratic enlargement, the protection of the world economy, and the threat from potential 'rogue states' (Dumbrell, 2002). Finally, it also needs to be mentioned that the Clinton Administration's foreign policy was not exclusively multilateral, as the intervention in Kosovo (1999) and the pursuit of National Missile Defense (the program's goal of providing a defense against missiles likely was in breach of the ABM treaty) highlight.

The George W. Bush Administration was seen to inaugurate, at least post-9/11, a move towards a much more assertive approach to foreign policy, which was very much influenced by the neo-conservative critique of the Clinton years. Though initially a rather restrained foreign policy that seemed guided by a traditional realism (eg Rice, 2000), the devastating 9/11 attacks provided it with an opportunity to implement an agenda led by a preoccupation with both American power and moralism: a reassertion of American power bound in a sense of exceptionalism about the US (Daalder and Lindsay, 2005). The doctrine of pre-emption, articulated in the 2002 National Security Strategy (White House, 2002), seemed to codify the change from the 1990s: the document not only reconfirmed a commitment to US pre-eminence, but also a vigorous and aggressive unilateral approach to assessing and dealing with threats. The US claimed the right to intervene militarily to curtail *potential* threats to the US, and also put pre-emption in a broader ideological language of US exceptionalism (especially seen in the context of the 'Global War on Terror'). The 2003 Iraq War was seen as a firm articulation of the neo-conservative approach to foreign policy: a pre-emptive use of force designed not only to meet a limited security goal, but also explicitly intended to reshape the regional order in the Middle East on grounds favorable not only to US interests, but also in line with the moral duties of US exceptionalism.

It is unsurprising that the Iraq War was so controversial, as it led both to a long drawn-out war and military occupation in Iraq, and a sense that the US had squandered the international legitimacy it had gained during the 1990s. The moralism expressed internationally was problematic, as it seemed both paternalistic and a means of masking national interests with a rhetoric of humanitarianism. However, the move away from an emphasis on multilateralism, expressed mainly through a strong commitment to international institutions, also led to some real questioning about a need to counter-balance US power. Debates about American 'empire' became prominent (Bacevich, 2002; Callinicos, 2003; Harvey, 2003; Mann, 2005), with some ideas about the potential 'balancing' of US power by the EU, China and Russia (Todd, 2006). Though much of this discussion was rather polemical, it led to many important questions being asked about the international expression of US power, both how it was being articulated (and how that related to past foreign policies or 'grand strategies') and for what reason. The future of US power was never far from consideration either as, despite an overwhelming preponderance of military power, the US was unable to achieve a desired victory in Iraq, begging the question of how useful military 'power' actually is. The financial crisis that began in the US in 2007/08 also added to the debate, now not only challenging the efficacy of US military superiority, but also asking questions about the future of US economic power.

The first Obama Administration

President Barack Obama came to power with a number of different problems to contend with. The most important, initially, was dealing with the aftermath of the 2007/08 financial crisis. The financial crisis itself became the major issue of the 2008 election, showing major differences in policy. While major legislation to buffer the impact of the crisis had been signed by President Bush – particularly the Troubled Asset Relief Program (TARP) to bail out the remaining banks affected by the crisis – President Obama attempted to do a number of things to alleviate the problem, but the main attempt was through a huge economic stimulus plan, signed early in February 2009. The plan distributed $787 billion in an attempt to overcome the recession caused by the economic crisis. While hugely controversial, and possibly very misunderstood (see Grunwald, 2012), the ambitious plan (along with other initiatives) demonstrated a re-dedication to state intervention in the economy.

The major foreign policy concern for the new Obama Administration concerned the future of the wars in Iraq and Afghanistan, and the so-called 'War on Terror'. The success of Obama in the 2008 Presidential Election was at least partially due to the failures in foreign policy associated with the Iraq War (also seen earlier in the 2006 midterm elections, where the Democrats retook majority control of the House and Senate). Here Obama saw an opportunity to recover the prestige that the US had lost during the earlier part of the decade (Obama, 2007). He attempted to do this through a number of means. A set of early Executive Orders attempted to reverse controversial policies of the Bush Administration that had long contributed to the decline of America's reputation in the world (and at home): a push for the release of prisoners at Guantanamo Bay within one year (a promise broken, which was more down to the difficulty of dealing with Congress over the matter); and an end to any 'torture'-like practices by the military or intelligence services (here a promise kept, much to the consternation of the CIA).

The attempt to change specific polices was accompanied by a broader shift in the tone of foreign policy, well articulated in his speech in Cairo in June, 2009 (Obama, 2009d). In the speech, Obama sought to articulate the core beliefs of Americans and America in the world, rather than just what the US is against. In this light, he found ways to show that the US is not at odds with the rest of the world (and particularly the Muslim world), but seeks to help spread these core values elsewhere (but without the imposition of particular regimes – very much stressed as a way of distancing himself and the new foreign policy from that of the previous Administration). While there were similarities with the Clinton Administration, the differences in circumstances (the financial crisis, the perceived 'catching up' of states such as China and India, and the international perceptions of the US after seven years of war) also meant a greater focus on how to regain American prestige and maintain American influence.

However, while the public rhetoric was important in trying to restore the world's confidence in the US, the early approach to foreign policy was very much formed by a realism shared with his inner circle of advisors (such as Denis McDonough and Ben Rhodes) as well as Secretary of Defense Robert Gates (a hold-over from the Bush Administration) (J. Mann, 2012). It was also clear that Obama and his key advisors, shaped by the experiences of Clinton-era staff that joined his Administration, were not resistant to the use of force. The speech given as acceptance of the Nobel Peace Prize attested to these two worldviews (Obama, 2009a). While Obama praised past recipients of the prize – such as Gandhi and Martin Luther King Jr – he also noted that as the leader of a state, he needed to balance the desire for peace with that of security, making a case for the 'just war'. In many ways this was quite remarkable, using the Nobel Peace Prize acceptance to make the case for war, but it was also occurring at the very time when a decision was made to increase troop levels in Afghanistan. Obama's speech at West Point in December 2009 announcing an increase of troop levels by 30,000 in early 2010 was important regarding a number of these themes, as it stressed the need to rethink the level of commitment to global leadership by the US (Obama, 2009c).

The Obama team also saw a real difference of the position of the US in the international system (J. Mann, 2012; Singh, 2012). While still strong, this was not the US of the mid-1990s. China had joined the 'club' of great powers, both in its economic strength and military power and, to some extent, its greater desire to exert itself and fight for its interests internationally. India and Brazil had also taken an increasingly prominent place in the global economy. The financial crisis had also hit the US hard, and meant that states such as Germany, that had previously been seen as part of an old Europe that was no longer competitive, were actually overtaking the US as an industrial exporter, and had managed to endure the crisis with much more stability. As Obama stated, in recognition of these perceived changes:

> if it's just Roosevelt and Churchill sitting in a room with a brandy, you know, that's an easier negotiation. But that's not the world we live in. And you know, that's not a loss for America. It's an appreciation that Europe is now rebuilt and a power house; Japan is rebuilt, is a powerhouse. China, India, these are all countries on the move. And that's good. That means there are billions of people who are working their way out of poverty. And over time, that potentially makes this a much more peaceful world. (Cited in J. Mann, 2012: 173)

There was a real sense that dealing with the power transition globally would be key to US foreign policy.

In this light, the Obama polices really took two divergent streams, but all drawing on past ideas about foreign policy (though less encumbered by the legacy of the Vietnam War). On the one hand was the continuation of Bush-era counter-terrorism policies (especially those of his second term, where there was a real shift of emphasis). While the US withdrew from Iraq, and attempted limited counter-insurgency techniques in Afghanistan, it also focused on counter-terrorism using both its influence in Pakistan to focus that government's efforts on Al-Qaeda in the border regions of

Afghanistan and Pakistan, and the use of unmanned drones to target the Al-Qaeda and Taliban leadership. The use of drones grew dramatically from the Bush Administration, and the CIA program became an important and controversial facet of American foreign policy – one that could project military power without the dedication of personnel in the field. The counter-terrorism program resulted in one stunning result: the killing of Osama bin Laden in 2011. The killing of bin Laden was the result of continued intelligence, but also an audacious decision by the president to send a special forces team into Pakistan to target bin Laden directly (J. Mann, 2012). Despite the perceived success and domestic celebration, the raid did raise numerous issues about the counter-terrorism approach, and especially the future of relations with Pakistan (Singh, 2012: ch. 4). Additionally, the Obama Administration carried on a concern with nuclear proliferation, especially in Iran and North Korea, though one also tempered by Obama's own views on the need for gradual nuclear disarmament by all states (Obama, 2009b; United States Department of Defense, 2010).

On the other hand, there was an eventual acceptance of more liberal international components that were part of the early foreign policy rhetoric, but often undercut by actual actions. For example, the reaction to the Green Movement in Iran in 2009 was very different from that of the Arab Spring two years later. In the former, Obama officials did not want to support civil society movements in Iran directly for fear of alienating the government, with which it wanted to cultivate better relations to try and secure a deal on nuclear proliferation and its weapons program. However, partially due to the influence of liberal internationalists in the Administration (such as Susan Rice, Samantha Power, Anne-Marie Slaughter and Michael McFaul), the reaction to the Arab Spring was much more sympathetic to the protesters, and US support was important for the resolution of the crisis in Egypt, as well as that of Libya (J. Mann, 2012; cf. Obama, 2011). However, the Obama team was also seen by a number of critics as slow to react, and too lacking in a broad strategy for dealing with the region (Singh, 2012).

What may be of most importance was the reaction and debate over how to deal with the future of American global leadership. Obama's core advisors all agreed that the US could no longer afford to keep up the kind of role it had followed previously – partially due to the financial costs, but also because of the changing balance of power (eg Obama, 2009c). The decision was made therefore to try and encourage other states to step up. This was made abundantly clear in terms of the US role in the intervention in Libya in 2011: the US would provide military support, but would draw back after the initial phases and let European allies (manly France and the UK) take over the effort. This strategy was aptly described as 'leading from behind' (Lizza, 2011); though this approach also came with some severe criticism for its implicit recognition of a lessened role for the US in the world (see Singh, 2012: ch. 3).

What accompanied the issue of leadership was the acceptance, rightly or wrongly, of a perceived relative decline of the US in the international system (Singh, 2012). It was no longer a case of talking about China's 'rise' (or that of India or Brazil): as Ben Rhodes stated: 'they have already risen' (quoted in J. Mann, 2012: 190). While the Obama Administration did not want to give up America's leading role, there was an acceptance that the US could no longer be preponderant, and much of the crafting of foreign policy was to be set in this new 'post-American' international system (Singh, 2012). The issue was therefore how to engage with these states. By far the most difficult relationship was with China. After an initial attempt to 'engage' with China in a more conciliatory manner was met with real intransigence (likely seen by Chinese officials as a tacit recognition of China's relative strength and US weakness), a firmer approach was taken (Clinton, 2011). In January 2012, a new strategy for defense was released, demonstrating a shift in emphasis, away from the Middle East and the battlegrounds of the 'War on Terror', and towards East Asia (United States Department of Defense, 2012b). The so-called 'Asian pivot' was meant to be a rearticulation of where American interests and concerns lie, in addition to setting out a new defense plan for a US with fewer resources.

Conclusion

We have seen the rise of the US from a small and fragmented collection of states on the east coast of North America, through its westward expansion, to industrial power, and eventually to pre-eminence after World War II. The narrative since World War II has mainly stressed the increasing strength of the US, and the drastic increase in influence of military power and militarization of the state. The post-Cold War period gave a series of dilemmas for US policy-makers, mainly to do with how to deal with the power of the US in the international system.

The story of the rise of the power of the US state mainly concerns the spatial expansion of the state, and also internally derives from a combination of important factors. First has been the economic power of the US, which has come hand in hand with westward and international expansion. While the power of the US in its original form was rather limited, its spread westward allowed for expansion in agricultural production, combined with the search for raw materials that enabled the US to become an industrial powerhouse. When this commercial growth is also fused with the ideology of economic liberalism, it gives a powerful sense of the enlargement of the role of the US state over time. By the early twentieth century, the US was clearly a leading industrial power, which gradually took on an increasing role in international finance as well. Much of the development of state power in the early part of the twentieth century relied on the interactions with economic power.

Second, although the US in its first century was a limited military power, it used the coercive power of the military continually, as part of westward expansion, in the main, but also increasingly as an international actor. By the end of the nineteenth century, the US was clearly a great power geopolitically, and sought to emulate the other great powers of Europe by using military force as a means of protecting and expanding its interests. The twentieth century saw even further the geopolitical ambitions of the US , as the more unilateral and insular policies of the US gave way to much more internationalism, tentatively in World War I, and more expansively in World War II. The taking on of the mantle of geopolitical leadership in the post-World War II period was at least partially premised on the relative potential of US military power.

Finally, these two factors went together with the expansion of the formal institutions of the US state itself. While by 1950 federalism was still important, the expansion of the US across the continent, and its increasing responsibility for the conduct of wars and their aftermath, greatly expanded the power and the reach of the state. By 1950, the state was a substantial presence in American life. But despite all of this, ideologically the state in the US is seen as playing *less* of a role in people's lives, instead creating a kind of framework for opportunity, the core tenets of US anti-statism. The state may well be large, but it is in practice less interventionist than in much of the industrialized world, and it has also become part of a debate about how much state there should be. Many of the debates in recent presidential elections have been about the role of the state, and especially about how there seems to be a general (though perhaps contradictory) desire to have a more limited state.

While the chapter tried to draw in both an international and domestic role of the state, in order to show ways in which these realms are important to thinking about the development and maintenance of state power, the future of American power is very often discussed in more international terms, in the relationship between its grand strategy of foreign policy and how this plays out in international relations. If we see the state as mediating foreign policy, we get a much richer sense of what American power looks like, but also how foreign policy derives from the internal dynamics and constitution of power, and is attenuated through the international dynamics of war and peace, of global economic development and broader international processes. As such we need to spend some more time discussing the 'purely' international dynamics of American power, which will be the subject of the next chapter.

Chapter 2

American Power and International Relations

The previous chapter accounted for the historical rise of American power, stressing key moments where there were important shifts in the practices or ideas shaping American power that are significant for understanding American power today. These historical perspectives on power and the historical narrative provide the background to the conceptual discussion in the present chapter, which will survey various views on understanding US power in international relations. The debates about power can also be better situated in historical conceptualizations of America's role in the world, and the chapter first visits these concepts – isolationism, internationalism, realism, idealism, unilateralism, multilateralism – both as a means to bridge the previous chapter with the present, and to introduce the varied ways in which these concepts have been used to articulate differing visions of the expression of American power internationally. In the Introduction, it was argued that there are different ways of understanding both American power and power in international relations, alternative perspectives that yield distinctive analytic conclusions. The debates in the social sciences on the character of power are therefore an important starting place for a better understanding of American power. The second section of the chapter analyses these debates in more detail, presenting a four-fold typology of power that will be utilized in the rest of the book. The analysis of four types of power – compulsory, institutional, structural and productive – is necessary for a better understanding of the power resources of the US, and the chapter argues that institutional and structural power need to play a central role in any analysis of American power, past, present or future.

The power debates also need to be linked more closely to debates about American power (and power more generally) in International Relations (IR), in order to provide a more substantive understanding of American power in the world. The chapter therefore engages with a number of analytical understandings of how the US expresses and exercises power internationally, drawing mainly on realist, institutionalist (liberal), Marxist and constructivist approaches to international relations. While these map roughly onto the distinctions made in the general discussion of power, they also go beyond it by demonstrating further mechanisms and behaviors that challenge and reproduce power internationally. Each of these ways of looking at US power have been part of a variety of debates concerning how we should see the current role of the US internationally, and what the future of US power might be. The chapter substantively situates the argument about power outlined in the Introduction: that we need to pay greater attention to institutional and structural forms of power to better understand US power in the world. The chapter concludes by revisiting the analytic distinctions raised by Michael Mann's 'sources' of social power, looking substantively at how these four sources – political, military, economic and ideological – relate to the conceptual discussion of power, and how they will be utilized in the chapters that follow.

Wielding American power

Before we move on to examining the power debates and linking them more clearly to the international relations of American power, we can situate the power debates within the broader claims Americans have made for wielding power in the world. Analysts and policy-makers rely on a number of 'traditional' concepts to frame debates about the present and history of US foreign policy-making and power projection: internationalism and isolationism; realism and moralism; unilateralism and multilateralism. Though the effectiveness of these concepts – mainly in terms of historical accuracy – is often disputed, they are useful in two core ways. First, they can help us get to grips with some core changes and continuities in US foreign policy and power projection over time. Second, they are important to the extent to which those making foreign policy use them as a shorthand for particular policy and political positions, which means that they form a good starting point for considering how policy-makers and pundits understand US power in the world.

Isolationism and internationalism have been core descriptions of the evolution of US foreign policy, especially over the course of the twentieth century, and they have increasingly been used as oppositional concepts. Isolationism usually refers to not a complete disengagement from the international system, but rather a refusal to involve the US in 'entangling alliances'; as well as a focus on US domestic matters, which is sometimes extended to a belief that the US should not be intervening abroad. As noted in the previous chapter, isolationism was not used as a concept until the late nineteenth century, and mainly became a term of abuse for those opposed to an expansionist and internationalist foreign policy. The early 'isolationism' of the US was mainly a pragmatic matter (and is probably better defined as 'unilateralism', described below). Internationalism is usually seen as the opposite: a belief in the necessity of US engagement with the world in order to pursue US interests, through American leadership in the international system (and often in 'liberal' terms). A commonplace historical narrative of US foreign policy is that the US retreated from the world after World War I, only to re-emerge after the Great Depression of the 1930s to re-engage in World War II, and then become a truly international power in the immediate post-war years. World War I saw the US emerge as a great power, but a number of actions during the interwar period were seen in retrospect as the US not taking up a potential position of leadership in the international system. Core examples can be seen in the Congress' refusal to ratify the 1919 Versailles Treaty, which would have committed the US to the League of Nations, and an economic 'inwardness', starting with the onset of the Great Depression in 1930, and seen in policies such as the 1930 Smoot-Hawley Tariffs (see p. 28).

Critical scholars such as William Appleman Williams (e.g. Williams, 1962) have challenged this narrative, effectively demonstrating that the US was highly internationalized and economically expansionist during the course of the nineteenth century, and that it continued such policies in the twentieth century (cf. LaFeber, 1995). This internationalism was seen in US policies such as that of the 1823 Monroe Doctrine as well as President Theodore Roosevelt's 1904 'Corollary', which claimed the right of the US to intervene in the Americas if governments did not preserve domestic order. The expansion and direct imperialism of the US, starting with the war against Spain in 1898, led to a series of interventions, most notably in Cuba and the Philippines. However, in his critique of isolationism, Williams went further, arguing that the expansionism of the US post-World War I was an *economic* expansionism, entailing not the direct possession of territory, but the expansion of liberal capitalism.

The debates over isolationism and internationalism concern the proper approach to power. It is not a coincidence that accusations of isolationism only began in the late nineteenth century, as a term of abuse by more internationally focused (and empire building) critics. The 'isolationists' of the interwar period also preferred the term 'nationalists', signifying an approach to economic (and political) life that was focused on enhancing domestic power, rather than engaging in expansionism. Correspondingly, internationalism has varied over time in terms of the overall levels and kinds of American power. There is a difference between the pragmatic internationalism of the early republic (which was heavily reliant on international trade), the westward expansion of the US in the nineteenth century (which does need to be seen as a form of 'internationalism'), and post-World War II internationalism, which concerned a preponderant America shoring up hegemony in the international system. All of these variants point to differing concerns over how the US can achieve and maintain power in the world. The debates about isolationism and internationalism have also taken on a new twist, with the development of conservative internationalists, demonstrated most readily by the neo-conservative movement (and also seen in libertarian conservatives who promote 'neo-isolationism'). We can see how these traditional dichotomies have both changed with time, and been used by pundits and policy-makers as ways of legitimating (and denigrating) different approaches to American power and foreign policy.

The division between realism and moralism (sometimes called 'idealism') is also a long-standing tradition in debates about the character of American foreign policy (Kennan, 1951). Here, we have a distinction between a US that is pragmatic and calculating in its foreign policy, versus one that is moral and crusading. The 'crusading' tradition in US foreign policy is often seen to be associated with the liberal internationalism of Woodrow Wilson, and his attempt to spread US values internationally. Wilsonianism is thus often contrasted with the more pragmatic strategy of the founding fathers, particularly Alexander Hamilton's commercial realism, and Thomas Jefferson's focus on setting an example for the world, rather than trying to impose American values (Mead, 2002). Since the Cold War, these distinctions have become increasingly important for understanding US foreign policy and power.

The pragmatic-realist view has been expressed by a number of post-war authors, including the diplomat George Kennan, international relations scholar Hans Morgenthau, and scholar-practitioner Henry Kissinger. Kennan was highly influential through his rather unsentimental account of the Soviet Union as an emerging threat, which was published anonymously in 1947 (Kennan, 1947). Kennan contended that the Soviet Union would challenge its borders whenever the opportunity arose. While resolutely anti-communist, Kennan tended to view relations with the Soviet Union in terms of power rather than just ideology. Morgenthau was critical of US engagement in Vietnam in the 1960s, as his realist view was that the war was clearly not in the national interest, and therefore to be avoided (Morgenthau, 1965). Finally, Kissinger's time as National Security Advisor (and later Secretary of State) brought out a shift in relations with China, predicated on the idea that 'balancing' Soviet power was more important than worrying about the ideological threat of communism (Kissinger, 1979).

The 'idealist' side of the debate has also been frequently invoked, from initial expressions of American anti-communism, through new articulations of liberal internationalism, to the neo-conservative movement. While Kennan (1951) saw this as a form of 'moralism' in international relations that should be avoided, many US policymakers have seen a commitment to liberal principles as an important motivation for action in the world. This implies the US upholding its own values and either attempting to set an example for the world or actively trying to impose such values. The long tradition of 'liberal internationalism' – derived from President Woodrow Wilson's focus on international institutions as a source of peace and order – comes directly from the 'idealist' worldview (Richardson, 1997; cf. Doyle, 1997). Notably, these divides have not been associated with a particular political party, with the key debates today being between realists who have been pragmatic about the limits of American power (Bacevich, 2002; 2009), and 'moralizers' who either seek to benignly spread US values (for example through 'soft power') (Nye, 2002) or take a more vigorous militarized approach (e.g. neo-conservatives in the George W. Bush Administration) (Kagan, 2004).

A final dichotomy concerns the distinction between unilateralism and multilateralism as traditions or means of the US securing its goals. The former refers to the avoidance of alliances or any form of external restraint on US action, and the latter to the use of institutions and partners to enhance US action. Both of these positions assume internationalism, and the difference concerns *how* the US should go about its international affairs. In President Washington's

1796 Farewell Address, he noted that the US should 'steer clear of permanent alliance with any portion of the foreign world', which can be seen as an early advocacy of a pragmatic, unilateral approach. Thomas Jefferson famously extended this to have the US avoid any 'entangling alliances'. This pragmatic unilateralism was important for the US during its expansion over the course of the nineteenth century. President Woodrow Wilson's 1918 Fourteen Points, advocating a liberal internationalist approach to international relations, shifted the debate on how the US should engage with the world, focusing much more on a multilateralism based on international institutions.

Unilateralism derives from some commonly held beliefs about American power. First, that American exceptionalism gives a moral duty that outweighs the morality of the international community at large, in that the American state itself is the key source of US legitimacy, not broader commitments to the 'international community'. Second, that both international law and international institutions, while not necessarily bad, cannot tie down American power and policy goals. Overall, the unilateral approach concerns how the US follows its national interests. Unilateralists are typically critical of any arrangements that limit US power, options, or any attempts to supersede US law. For example, Condoleezza Rice argued that US policy-makers are too often guided by 'the belief that the United States is exercising power legitimately only when it is doing so on behalf of someone or something else ... the "national interest" replaced with "humanitarian interests" or the interests of "the international community"' (cited in Jentleson, 2003: 13).

Multilateralism suggests that international law, institutions, and alliances are means of enhancing US power in a way that engenders support for US policies. In this view, acting multilaterally can aid in achieving objectives. The US can enhance its power through legitimate actions, supported by allies (and international law). States often oppose US policies by bargaining, balancing or bandwagoning, and the only option from this perspective is to get other states on board. Furthermore, unfettered, activist unilateralism can lead to resentment; as prominent realist Henry Kissinger noted: 'an explicit insistence of predominance would gradually unite the world against the United States' (cited in Jentleson, 2003: 10). Overall, it is argued that a focus on multilateralism can help bridge the gap between power and influence, as if others believe in the legitimacy of particular actions, they have more support and chance of success.

While all three sets of opposing concepts have an important role in the discourse and debate on US foreign policy, they are so entangled in normative meanings and with partisan politics, as well as being historically contingent, that they have lost much analytic value. However, I would further suggest that the terms are nonetheless important in understanding debates about the relationship between the US power and the world. All the concepts continue to be used in debates about US foreign policy, and they feature significantly in the ways in which American policy-makers and commentators discuss the future role of American power in the world. Therefore, recounting these debates is not just of historical interest: the debates and policies pursued have demonstrated the contours of important conceptual concerns about the shape of the international system and the US's role within it. What remains is to broaden out our view of the US in international relations, drawing on the key insights of these debates: how can we better understand power, and what does the international system look like and what role does the US have within it?

What is power in international relations?

The most common view on power in international relations sees power in terms of the ability to achieve particular policy outcomes: that is, states have power when they are able to achieve specific goals, and especially when these goals conflict with the goals of other states in the international system. Such goals may be moderate or 'revolutionary' (or revisionist), and the amount of power required will vary in terms of the kinds of goals that are desired. However, what this means in both theory and practice is problematic, especially in terms of whether or not it tests the limits of that we can conceive of as 'power'. To use an important contemporary example, the US certainly has far superior military capacity relative to other states, but any analysis of the 'power' of the US military involvement in Iraq would question what that means in practice: while initially very successful in defeating Iraqi conventional forces in 2003, the power of the US to achieve its goals became much more limited. How can we talk of American power in this context? We can derive at least two lessons from such an example: that military power may not be fungible to other areas (such as politics); and that merely seeing power as a quantitative resource to be operationalized misjudges power. While the issues surrounding military power will be returned to in the substantive analysis that follows (in Chapter 4), the broader conceptualization of power is crucial for how we conceive of American power.

There is a need to situate American power in the rather contentious debates in the social sciences about the concept of power, and especially the debate inaugurated by Steven Lukes' discussion of 'three dimensions' of power in 1975 (Lukes, 2005). While there is not sufficient space to delve into all of the nuances of the debates, the discussion will highlight the core issues for a discussion of power in the international system (for further arguments, see: Arendt, 1970; Bourdieu, 1991; Connolly, 1993: ch. 3; Foucault, 2002; Guzzini, 1993; 2005; Hayward, 2000; Hindess, 1996; Issac, 1987; Lukes, 1986; Morriss, 1987). The distinctions made below will serve to deepen and further the argument outlined in the Introduction: that in order to understand the relative durability of American power we need to move beyond (but not discard) a focus on 'power over' and better incorporate forms of power that focus both on international institutions and structures in the international system.

Lukes' starting point was the delimitation of the concept of power by Robert Dahl in the 1950s. Dahl famously looked at power in terms of observable conflicts of interests between actors, and power was said to be at play when actor A was able to make actor B do something they would otherwise not want to do (Lukes, 2005; cf. Dahl, 1957). While there is an obvious parsimony in such a formulation, and one that chimes very much with the common perception of international relations, there are also real problems. The second dimension of power noted by Lukes (as formulated originally by Bachrach and Baratz, 1962) concerned the issue of only looking at 'observable' conflict, which serves to 'hide' other important conflicts of interest, where the interests of actor A are protected by political institutions that restrict the policy process to relatively uncontentious issues. Therefore 'non-decisions', situations where actor B is not allowed to pursue interests as they are shut out of the political process, are also exercises of power, and institutions are therefore seen as 'mobilizing bias' of their key benefactors. However, Lukes argued that both of these conceptions are too reliant on the issue of a conflict of interests, and introduced a third dimension, where power becomes the ability of actor A to shape the interests of actor B in a way which means that they are not able to see or understand their 'real' interests, which are in opposition to A's. As Lukes describes, 'the bias of the system is not sustained simply by a series of individually chosen acts, but also, most importantly, by the socially structured and culturally patterned behaviorof groups, and practices of institutions, which may indeed be manifested by individuals' inaction' (Lukes, 2005: 26). In the subsequent years, followers of the work of Michael Foucault have also added a 'fourth dimension', where power affects the constitution of subjects, the 'As' and 'Bs', in terms of their core identities (Digeser, 1992; cf. Foucault, 1980).

While this may seem a relatively abstract debate, it gets to the heart of the limits of some of the present disagreements over the future of American power. The appeal to only the first dimension of power conceals ways in which the US has embedded its interests in international institutions, as well as the ways in which the whole international system may be structured in ways that support American power, to the detriment of the interests of other states. Furthermore, in a recent update to his original argument (and in a response to criticisms from over the years), Lukes has noted that his account of three dimensions was far too focused on power in terms of *domination* (conceived broadly as 'power over'), whereas this really needs to be seen as a subset of power as a capacity for change ('power to') (Lukes, 2005: ch. 2). A better explication of power can be found in Lukes' reformulation, one reflected in Barnett and Duvall's definition in their recent survey of power in international relations: 'In general terms, power is the production, in and through social relations, of effects that shape the capacities of actors to determine their circumstances and fate' (Barnett and Duvall, 2005: 42; cf. Berenskoetter and Williams, 2007; Nye, 2011). This definition provides a good starting point for expanding our notion of what American power is and could potentially be.

However, in order to get a better sense of what these types of power mean for international relations and American power more specifically, it is helpful to turn to Barnett and Duvall's (2005) typology of power in international relations. While drawing on the 'three dimensions' argument (and with a nod to the addition of the fourth dimension), they structure the argument concerning power into two core facets. The first facet concerns where power lies in terms of the actors involved and the kinds of social relations through which power works. On the one hand, power can be seen as a resource to be utilized in the interactions between pre-given actors ('interaction'); on the other, power is exercised in terms of defining the interests or identity of the actors involved ('constitutive'). The second facet concerns the relative closeness of the actors involved: whether power is 'direct' or 'diffused' in the social system. From these two dimensions, they conceive four 'types' of power: compulsory (inter-action/direct), institutional (interaction/diffuse), structural (constitutive/direct), and productive (constitutive/diffuse).

Compulsory power is the type that is mostly referred to in the debates about American power, and it is tied closely with realist accounts of international relations. Here power is mobilized by actors to get the results that they wish over others. We see this most clearly in accounts of military power: power in its most coercive form. For example, when states threaten to use force to achieve a particular goal, this is both direct and involves two clearly defined actors. Institutional power is more diffuse, in that actors exercise power *through* institutions, rather than directly over others. This is often misconceived of as actors merely using institutions to implement direct power, but is better seen in how institutions 'mobilize bias' of their creators, but are not necessarily 'owned' by them. This description has clear overlaps with institutional analysis in IR scholarship (e.g. Axelrod and Keohane, 1993; Ikenberry, 2001), and we can see how this is important in terms of conceptualizing power in a way that moves away from the direct connection between actors, to one where institutional rules and norms reinforce interests in a much more diffused fashion. We see this kind of power at work in international relations both from international organizations (such as the United Nations), and in more diffused 'regimes' (Krasner, 1983), such as the Bretton Woods system (encompassing a series of rules about international monetary policy). In all of these cases, it is clear that power is less direct, in that the power of such organizations tends to emanate from the rules agreed in their creation, but that such rules protect particular configurations of power in the world.

The third type of power is structural, which has overlaps with historical materialist analyses of international relations (e.g. Cox, 1987; Gill, 2003; Robinson, 1996). It can also be seen in Strange's (1987) conception of structural power: here, power is accomplished not through the direct actions of agents or formal institutions, but through structural relationships which determine interests and outcomes. As Barnett and Duvall describe it, 'whereas institutional power focuses on differential constraints on action, structural power concerns the determination of social capacities and interests' (2005: 53). There are many ways in which we might see such power at work in the international system in reference to American power. For example, the US promotes an open international economy, and while such a structure benefits the US, it also shapes the preferences and interests of other actors within the international system, which makes it appear in their interest to support the system. As Barnett and Duvall note, the US (in these terms) 'has worked hard to generate consent – that is, to get those who are structurally disadvantaged because of their position in the world political economy to accept the order of things' (Barnett and Duvall, 2005: 65).

Finally, productive power goes beyond the structural in setting the actual identities of the agents involved. This can involve ways in which domestic discourses surrounding American identity (of the United States as a whole) provide a means to creating a particular subjectivity for the US in the world. The 'othering' of alternative ways of being or identities, for example turning them into 'enemies', is a clear way in which such power can operate (e.g. Campbell, 1992; Weldes, 1996). Barnett and Duvall use the example of Hardt and Negri's (2000) rearticulation of the US as an imperial power as a prominent way in which this type of power has been utilized in an analysis: 'productive power, in this way, works to produce a particular identity for the United States – a responsible and beneficent imperial actor in relation to others (imperial subjects, themselves irresponsible and in need of such help)' (2005: 66).

Barnett and Duvall claim that a number of these 'types' of power can be seen to be in operation in any given instance, and that a focus on one type as key really limits our understanding of international relations. In relation to the present debates on US decline, it is crucial to resituate the debates by emphasizing the importance of both institutional and structural power. Some scholars have done this with reference to these two types. For example, John Ikenberry's work on post-war institution-building and his discussions of the 'rise of China' debate (Ikenberry, 2001; 2008; 2011) clearly reflect an institutional position, and Simon Bromley's work on American power is much in line with the structural approach (Bromley, 2008). However, to properly understand American power, we need to further consider the interrelation of these different perspectives. The book therefore tries to bring the first three forms of power into the analysis of American power as much as possible, while alluding to the fourth as necessary, especially when discussing aspects of identity formation: while compulsory power may take prominence in many discussions of American power, the other forms may better explain the durability of American power.

Competing conceptions of American power

The power debates can obtain more clarity by linking them to the core theoretical ways US power has been examined in International Relations (IR). These approaches often frame academic analyses of the US in the world, provide a useful analytic lens for understanding US actions, and at times overlap with the worldviews of policy-makers. However, we likewise need to see these IR theories as analytic tools, to help us better understand the US in the world in light of history and policy, but additionally integrate them more clearly with the typology of power presented in the previous section. In essence, we need to show ways in which substantive theories of IR can be integrated into the power debates, as a means to better understand the ways in which the US expresses power internationally. In what follows we examine core approaches to international relations in terms of how they link to the concept of power, in terms of the compulsory, institutional and structural forms. The discussion will aim to highlight what IR theory can bring to the power debates, rather than trying to look at the matter the other way around.

Compulsory power: geopolitics and the balance of power

Much of the traditional way of looking at the US in world politics has relied on a historically 'realist' examination of the US in the world, primarily considering the US in terms of its position in relation to other states in the international system, and how it can pursue its goals – the national interest – within that context. This view mainly contends that the US follows its interests abroad, although what this means in actuality varies (and is often contrasted with 'idealism' – mainly seen as the US upholding its own values to either attempt to set an example for the world or to actively try and impose such values). It is also very much focused on an idea of a 'clash' of interests: that the US can be seen to be powerful (or as upholding power) when it can force others to follow its own interests. In this sense the realist tradition has been very much associated with the compulsory view of power. There are three reasons why the realist approach to the US in the world is significant. First, realism gives a simple and elegant means of conceptualizing US power. Second, it is an ideal starting point for a way of thinking about the role of the US and its relation to the international system that is fully focused on the role of *compulsory* power, and arguing for the primacy of this type of power. Third, it has been a core, if not exclusive, way in which US foreign policy-makers have seen the world since the Cold War period (elements of 'idealism' in the struggle between liberalism and communism were hugely important as well).

There are two broad interpretations of US power in the realist camp. First, there is the opinion that US policy-makers should mainly pursue their interests abroad in a fairly pragmatic fashion, eschewing ideology for a clear focus on the realities of power. This version of realism tends towards domestic-level explanations of foreign policy: while emphasizing the importance of the international realm for the context of US foreign policy, realism here mainly analyses the ways in which state leaders tend to (and should) react to threats to interests and secure US power. However, realism should also be seen as a pragmatic way of dealing with power and interest. As noted in the previous chapter this has been a more common theme in the history of US foreign relations than might be obvious today, especially when looking more closely at US foreign policy-making in the nineteenth century.

A second view contends that the US (like any state) merely responds to the global dynamics of power, mainly as conceptualized through 'balance of power' theory (though also through a competing idea of 'hegemonic stability'). Although this theory can mean a number of things, in this context it concerns the responses of states to changes in the material distribution of power (seen as 'capabilities') in the international system (e.g. Mearsheimer, 2001; Waltz, 1979). This form of realism views the international system as comprising particular versions of international order, based on the number of great powers. For example, prior to the end of World War II, the international system was seen as 'multipolar', in that there were a number of competing great powers, including the United Kingdom, France, Germany, Soviet Union and the United States. World War II can then be explained in structural terms by states banding together to prevent an expansionist power from dominating the international system. After World War II, the international system was often described as 'bi-polar' in that there were only two superpowers competing for influence.

This 'systemic' or 'structural' realist view sees the international system as more than just a context for state leaders to react to, or an environment to act in: the international system itself creates external pressures that lead to particular state actions. The systemic view was very influential in trying to analyse the consequences of the end of the Cold War. It was clear that the end of Soviet domination of

Eastern Europe and the eventual end of the Soviet Union itself meant that the US was effectively the only great power in international relations. As noted in the previous chapter, there was much consternation about what this would mean, both for the overall goals of US national strategy, which had for fifty years focused mainly on its Soviet adversary, and for stability in international relations. As discussed in Chapter 1, the approach to US power shared by both Presidents Bush and Clinton (and many others) saw a multilateral approach that took international institutions seriously as the best way to guarantee a more stable world. A structural view of the situation meant not avoiding the possibility that rival powers would attempt to balance and frustrate American ambitions. Structural realist approaches therefore remain salient in analysing the potential decline of US power in relation to rival powers in the present international system. In this view, the international system is mainly a fine balance between leading states who want to protect what they have, and exploit potentials to gain more power.

However, there is also an alternative realist perspective which takes a different view of the structural organization of power, looking at the domination of the international system by one key power. Referred to as 'hegemonic stability theory', this version of structural realism looks at the importance of one leading power in setting the overall terms for the maintenance of order in the international system (Gilpin, 1981; cf. Keohane, 1984). The key reference points are usually Britain in the late nineteenth century, and the US post-World War II (despite not being entirely global in its leadership). Both balance of power and hegemonic stability theories are clearly based on the predominance of coercive, compulsory power (especially on the emphasis of military power), but they emphasize different mechanisms of how the dynamics of power operate. The core link between hegemonic stability and power-balancing is an emphasis on the consequences of hegemonic decline, seen as when the likelihood of conflict, war and instability rise and are at their greatest. For differing reasons, many realists see a declining US and a rising China as a relationship with real potential for conflict (see the overview in Brooks and Wohlforth, 2008; and Layne, 2006; 2009).

While in terms of the present balance of power, the US is still clearly ahead materially, there is some consternation about the potential for rival powers to challenge American dominance (mainly through the declining relative economic power of the US, and some military competitors attempting to improve their position). In recent

years, the main 'rivals' to US power have been seen in both traditional great powers as well as emerging states. The examples of
Germany (and the European Union as a whole), Russia and China
have been especially prominent. In terms of the German and other
leading European states, there is little real rivalry in military power,
but different objectives of foreign policy goals and approaches to the
international system have put these powers in political conflict with
the US. Additionally, some foreign policy analysts and practitioners
have seen the European Union itself as a rival to the US, especially in
economic terms, though a rival that has little coherence in terms of
foreign policy or military power. Russia and China are both states
with strategic objectives and political systems that conflict more
directly with US policies and aspirations, and as such they are often
seen as potential direct rivals (these issues will be discussed in more
detail in Chapter 7).

However, despite claims about potential balancing or threats to
American predominance in the international system, there is much
debate in realist circles about what 'conflict' could mean. For realists, conflict usually involves the potential of military power being
used to coerce (or deter) action on the part of other powers, with a
real threat of war. Though some have made claims that US and
Chinese foreign policies may lead to direct military confrontation,
most are rather sanguine about this possibility. Indeed, leading realists such as Pape (2005b) and Walt (2005) have used the concept of
'soft balancing' to indicate the ways that rivals balance US power
short of the traditional building up of internal military capacity
(internal balancing) or through the formation of military alliances.
Others, such as Stephen Brooks and William Wohlforth (2008), have
argued that so-called 'soft balancing' is just international politics as
usual, and that we need to see the differences between rival great
powers for what they are: political differences that are not necessarily part of a power transition.

The realist account of US international power has been influential
in debates about the future of the US. However, it is rivalled by other
approaches, which though sometimes lacking the parsimony of the
realist approach, provide an account of other important dynamics in
international relations that potentially play a key role in understanding the US in the world. As noted above, even among leading realist
scholars, there is some difficulty in examining power in a mechanical
fashion, as the outcomes that predict conflict appear rather over-
determined at times. Though realist commentators like Brooks and

Wohlforth (2008) have managed to criticize the realist tradition from within, there is also a sense that just looking at the compulsory side of power is not enough: that the potential for a substantive conflict of interests between the US and other rising powers is obvious, but the emphasis on observable conflicts of interest (and the measure of power by capacity) rather underplays other elements of American power that are part of its international power projection.

Institutional power: strategic constraint and liberal hegemony

Realists viewed the liberal optimism of post-1990 with scepticism, seeing much of the problem of US power in the new century in potential rivals to American power, or at the very least, relative US decline. However, liberal institutionalists see the international system and the US role within it rather differently. Where realists stress the importance of US material or compulsory power (especially as backed up by military power) as the most important aspect of understanding international relations, institutionalist scholars have emphasized the importance of institutions that embed US hegemony in the international system. For institutionalists, US power is about more than just the ability to coerce, and also concerns the capacity to structure the international system in a fashion that is amenable to US interests: institutions, in essence, 'mobilizing bias' in favor of an American-led international system. Many institutionalist scholars also go beyond this, and argue that what makes such institutions and American power so robust is that they also allow other states also to reap the benefits of US leadership in the international system. Generally, institutionalist scholars focus on the role of international institutions, both formal and informal, as providing ways for the US to mitigate conflict in the international system, and more generally allow for 'absolute gains' (e.g. Axelrod and Keohane, 1993). Such views do not necessarily see the US as a benign actor in international relations, in that it is following its own interests like any other state, but suggests that there are ways of pursuing interests in a fashion that does not necessarily conflict directly with other states. International institutions can provide a focal point for cooperation, where communicating interests can help to mitigate potentially damaging conflicts.

John Ikenberry has put forward an influential version of this argument, analysing how the US managed the international order post-

World War II in a fashion that allowed it to prosper and follow its own interests, but also allowed like-minded states to share in American success (Ikenberry, 2001; 2011). The US post-war formed a 'liberal hegemony': where the leading power encourages other states to participate actively in the international system by setting limits to its own power. For Ikenberry, the US set limits by engaging in 'strategic restraint' and organizing the international system through a 'constitutional order': constraining power through multi-lateral organizations, and setting clear limits to what it was doing in international affairs. The key to constitutionalism is having clear rules that the US must also follow: the leading state is therefore not arbitrary in terms of the rules it sets, but has to commit to them (Ikenberry, 2011: ch. 2). The spread of liberal values underpinning the order – self-determination, capitalism, and pluralist democracy – was also crucial (and in opposition to the Soviet sphere of influence). The US continued to pursue its security goals with regard to the Soviet Union through coercive power, but engaged with its allies through consensus: in security matters through organizations such as NATO; in economic matters through the Bretton Woods institutions. Strategic restraint was seen as a means to allowing states that wanted to opt in a way of benefiting from an open international system, with the US as its core backer.

The institutionalist perspective provides a very different account from the realist focus on compulsory power. While the existence of superior US power economically and militarily is of course crucial for the argument (as is a focus on a particular kind of 'hegemony'), the robustness of US leadership is, for the institutionalist position, better explained by emphasizing an element of legitimacy to that power. The US plays by rules shared by its supporters in the international community, which are embedded institutionally in international organizations, and that can in principle disadvantage the US in certain situations, in order to show that it will not take advantage of its vast material superiority. For institutionalists, the post-Cold War period is therefore better explained by the expansion of American (liberal) principles, accepted to a large degree by most states, and accounting for the continued predominance of both the US and the US-led international system. For institutionalists, there is no need to explain the lack of potential conflict with a rising power such as China: China's real road to modernity is through the Western liberal order, and as such it is a potential partner not a rival (e.g. Ikenberry, 2008).

Structural power: beyond institutional hegemony

The most common way that IR theorists discuss structural power is through the concept of hegemony. IR theorists of varying theoretical backgrounds use the concept of hegemony, from realists who discuss 'hegemonic stability' (Gilpin, 1981; Stein, 1984) through liberal institutionalists who see hegemony as embedded in institutional orders (Keohane, 1984; Ikenberry, 2011), to neo-Gramscian scholars, who use hegemony still differently (Cox, 1996). To start with the commonalities, all see hegemony as a form of leadership that realizes the power of a leading state to 'enforce' the international order, though this enforcement is also enacted through some level of consent, which distinguishes hegemony from outright domination (e.g. Lebow and Kelly, 2001). Hegemony is used to distinguish 'leadership' from out–and-out coercive and hierarchical (and possibly 'imperial') relations.

As noted above, realists stress specific power capacities and potentials, especially as embodied in military spending (and other quantitative measures of capacity – e.g. numbers of soldiers and equipment) and economic measures (such as relative industrial output, productivity, and growth) – which can be used to quantify coercive capacity. Realist versions of hegemony need to be seen mainly in this light (Brooks and Wohlforth, 2008; Gilpin, 1981; cf. Ikenberry, 2011). However, it is hard to discern what differentiates 'hegemony' from 'coercion' in this context. If hegemony is just the ability to directly coerce subordinate states into conforming to the leading state's interests, then it seems little different from imperial control (cf. Ferguson, 2003; Ikenberry, 2011: ch. 2). These problems are manifest in looking at the key modern eras of hegemony: British leadership at the height of the British empire in the late nineteenth century and American leadership post-World War II. A contrast to be made between the periods is the sheer difference in relative power differentials of the hegemons and the other great powers, both in economic and military measures. For the British hegemony, there was little difference between the key great powers of the time, who all had similar levels of aggregate GDP and military spending over the course of the nineteenth century. However, for the US post-World War II, its key competitor (the Soviet Union) had a similar amount of military spending, but was much poorer in overall GDP (as noted by both Brooks and Wohlforth, 2008: 27–35; and Ikenberry, 2011: 39–47). Even using the realist measures of state capacity in their own terms, we run into a problem: how was Britain conceived of as a hegemon? For some it is merely due to the domination of liberal trading principles, that could be enforced by British naval supremacy (e.g. Krasner, 1976). Such issues raise larger questions about why other states would consent to such a system, especially when power differentials were not that great (here we might see a system more oriented towards power-balancing rather than hegemonic leadership).

Furthermore, there is a problematic relationship between coercive power and interests in the realist account of hegemony. The way hegemony is conceived in the realist perspective leaves it not much different from mere coercion. As Kupchan and Ikenberry note, 'the ability to generate shared beliefs in the acceptability or legitimacy of a particular international order – that is, the ability to forge a consensus among national elites on the normative underpinnings of order– is an important if elusive dimension of hegemonic power' (Ikenberry and Kupchan, 1990: 289). Institutionalists have dealt with the problem of consensus by looking at the centrality of institutions for setting up hegemony, arguing that there is a consensus around hegemony provided through an institutional agreement that such orders will be in the mutual interests of states that join (e.g. Keohane, 1984). Similarly, in Ikenberry's work, 'hegemonic bargains' are made where leading states agree to provide global public goods in return for setting the overall rules of international order, which are embodied in international institutions (Ikenberry, 2011). While such accounts are important for the recognition of 'institutional power', the main issue of contention is in terms of whether or not interests are easily identified by actors themselves. Elites calculate as to whether being part of the international order will serve their interests, despite trade-offs to their own international power (and a recognition of how institutions will close down options as they are formed by other states in their interests).

Why does this matter? Because it assumes that interests are not shaped by hegemony itself. While the institutionalist position generally reads hegemony through the development of robust and consensual international institutions (though not denying the way in which institutions mobilize the interests of the US), seeing US hegemony as a form of structural power (with overtones of imperialism) has been central to historical materialist thinking about international relations, as well as other critical approaches to global political economy (e.g. Kiely, 2007; Strange, 1987). We can see two versions of this:

one that stresses the importance of the transnational structure of *American* material power, the other focusing on the combination of ideas, material power and order.

In terms of the former, the material capacity and reach of American power is stressed in numerous recent accounts of US power that focus on imperialism and empire (e.g. Bacevich, 2002; Callinicos, 2003; Harvey, 2003; Mann, 2003). The second Bush Administration's approach to foreign policy, and especially the invasion of Iraq, started an increased talk of 'empire' and 'imperialism' in the media and in foreign policy circles. Such discussion went beyond what was formerly seen as a radical critique of Cold War foreign policy (though with roots in anti-imperialist rhetoric from the late nineteenth century) (see Mayers, 2007; cf. Mabee, 2004). Discussions of the US as an 'imperial' power had an important place during the Cold War, as the criticism of American imperialism associated with the radical revisionist school of Cold War historiography was very much taken on board by critics of US foreign policy, especially during the crisis of the Vietnam War.

However, imperialism as a description (or critique) of US power in the world has been used in very different ways. Often, it is just meant as shorthand for unilateralism and expansionism in foreign policy, especially when done by an actor of overwhelming power. Such views tend to see US foreign policy as overly reliant on *compulsory* power, rather than looking to multilateralism, international law and international institutions as more conducive to the US maintaining its position in the world. A more expansive version of this view is used as a way of describing US actions that encroach upon the sovereignty of other states. While such explanations have been in vogue, this has mainly been down to a critique of the perceived abuses of compulsory power. It does not really get to the heart of structural power. A number of critics have noted the difficulties the lack of real conflict between the major powers in the international system has posed towards traditional theories of imperialism (which tend to focus on the inevitability of 'inter-imperial rivalries') (e.g. Kiely, 2010; Panitch and Gindin, 2003; 2012). In order to deal with the fact of cooperation between different capitalist powers, these critical readings have focused more on the way that US hegemony makes it possible for all capitals to cooperate and profit. Such approaches conceive of US hegemony – setting the rules of the international system in a way that favors capital accumulation and the US within the international system – in a manner that forms a consensual framework between rival states, where the threat of military conflict is minimal. That is not to suggest that economic competition is absent, but that US power is maintained through its ability to materially back up the system and allow others to profit.

For example, Panitch and Gindin's (2003; 2012; cf. Bromley, 2008; Kiely, 2006) account of American empire is structurally focused on the ability of an American-led capitalism to remain preponderant in the international system, arguing that challenges to that system are few and far between due to the interests of other state elites in maintaining it. In some ways this provides a link to institutionalist approaches, which see American power as embedded in institutions where leading states 'agree' to support hegemonic power because all benefit. However, the main difference is that there is also a prominent account of the American state in Panitch and Gindin's approach, suggesting the American state itself provides a material base of specific economic power that helps to determine these outcomes. As they note:

> the interpenetration of capitals did largely efface the interest and capacity of each 'national bourgeoisie' to act as the kind of coherent force that might have supported challenges to the informal American empire. Indeed they usually became hostile to the idea of any such challenge, not least because they saw the American state as the ultimate guarantor of capitalist interests globally. (Panitch and Gindin, 2012: 11)

In this reading, the power of the state is at the heart of America's hegemonic power.

A real issue here concerns how we discuss consensus in this context. Whereas institutionalists see consensus emerging from rational agreements to signing up to institutions (and to some extent the account above is similar: that elites rationally decide their interests are with the US), scholars following a neo-Gramscian approach have provided an alternative account of consensus (Morton, 2007: ch. 5). Looking at neo-Gramscian accounts, we get a sense of interests emerging from social interaction. As Ikenberry and Kupchan describe, for Gramscian approaches, hegemony 'is the outgrowth of the intertwining of socioeconomic, political, and ideological structures, all of which are rooted in a particular mode of production. This complex set of structures limits the bounds of what is understood to be legitimate policy choice, thereby securing the continuing dominance of the hegemon' (Ikenberry and Kupchan, 1990: 289). This is an important reformulation of the concept of hegemony. On the other hand, for institutionalists and the more state-focused artic- ulation of hegemony the interests of all of the actors are internally driven, and potentially (and likely, to some degree) in conflict. For neo-Gramscians, consensus is formed by a sleight of hand: the inter- ests of the leading state are transformed into the interests of others. Robert Cox, for example, has demonstrated how US hegemony has not only been based on the material power of the US state, but is also embedded in the power of ideas that surround the material power: the broad acceptance of American hegemonic power is based on the acceptance of ideas of economic liberalism. Cox additionally argues that hegemonic ideas can be further embedded in international insti- tutions. As he states, 'institutions may become the anchor for a hege- monic strategy since they lend themselves both to the representations of diverse interests and to the universalization of policy' (Cox, 1996: 99). Not unlike institutionalists who see American power as flowing through institutions, a focus on consen- sual hegemony can also highlight the role of institutions. However, Cox warns about putting too much emphasis on institutions: 'one must be aware of allowing a focus upon institutions to obscure either changes in the relationship of material forces, or the emer- gence of ideological challenge to an erstwhile prevailing order' (Cox, 1996: 100). As such, these two approaches to hegemony take us beyond the focus on institutions and transparent interests, to show how structures can actually shape the overall idea of 'interest' within an American-led international system.

A final word needs to be said about how we characterize decline or challenges to established power in each of these conceptions. As all three views on power stress something different about the quality of the international power of the US, it is not surprising that they would have different analyses of how that power may be lost or chal- lenged. For those focusing on compulsory power, in either a balance of power version or in terms of hegemonic stability, the focus is on rising powers. Decline comes about by direct challenges to the power of the lead actor. For hegemonic stability, internal material decline (and overall relative decline) leads to hegemonic wars that upturn the international system as a whole. For institutionalists, decline tends to happen with changes to institutions: institutions can rise and fall with leading powers, and can be reshaped, or can be replaced. Finally, those focused on structural power see counter-hegemonic movements, new hegemonic orders, or fracturing into non-hegemonic systems as the core challenges to established power.

Power and international legitimacy

Approaches focusing on institutional and structural power stress the concept of legitimacy to varying degrees. An emphasis on compulsory power tends to see consensus as flowing from coercion. However, if compulsory power was all there was to international power, US power in international relations in this sense should see its superior power being easily converted into political influence: that power should mean that the US gets what it wants. However, as Reus-Smit (2004: 3) has pointed out, the frustrated ambitions of the Bush Administration and neo-conservatives have demonstrated a real paradox: that the US certainly has a preponderance of material power, but that this is not easily converted into influence or preferential outcomes for all of its desired policies. Institutionalist and structural views on power have tried to move beyond the concentration on coercion. Institutionalists understand legitimacy as the result of compromises surrounding institutionalization. Structural power contains an element of consensus that goes beyond the idea of legitimacy as something that is voluntarist. They share these emphases with constructivist scholars in IR who have focused on the concept of legitimacy as providing a core to understanding power in the world today.

We can see that institutionalist and structural approaches to power draw on classical notions of legitimate power. Max Weber saw power as legitimated in three different ways: through traditional authority (the reproduction of inherited or habitual patterns of authority), charismatic authority (that found in particularly strong leaders), and through legal-rational authority (where authority is predicated on adherence to abstract, non-arbitrary rules) (Weber, 2009a). While these forms of legitimate authority may not fit precisely with international relations, there is an importance to the idea of legitimacy, particularly that seen in legal-rational authority (e.g. Hurd, 1999). Ikenberry has also drawn on these ideas, noting that, in 'constitutional' international systems, leading powers will attempt to conform to the rules in a way that distinguishes them from imperial systems (where leading states enforce rules for subordinates, but do not necessarily follow the rules themselves).

Legitimacy crucially depends on the acceptance of others: US power is legitimate only inasmuch as the majority of other states in the world accepts it as so. Generally, acceptance has been achieved through a variety of multilateral institutions, primarily through the UN Security Council and economic institutions such as the World Bank, International Monetary Fund and World Trade Organization. For example, in security terms, the focus on legitimacy demonstrates why the UN Security Council is so important in international relations. While critics focus on the potential injustice and inequity of its make-up (and the hypocrisy of some of its decisions), this in many ways misses the point. As Ian Hurd points out, 'the power the council wields over the strong comes not from its ability to block their military adventures (which it is not empowered to do) but rather from the fact that the council is generally seen as legitimate. This legitimacy functions by raising the costs of unilateral action' (Hurd, 2003: 205; cf. Hurd, 1999). Therefore, part of the stability of international order is predicated on the legitimacy of US leadership, in terms of US backing of an order that is deemed legitimate. In this regard, problems with US power may stem from violations of the normative order that undermine legitimacy.

If legitimacy is what makes the international order and US power sustainable, it therefore also is seen as causing potential constraints on US action (Finnemore, 2009). These potential constraints can be seen as either *specific* actions which break the rules and cause increased costs for pursuing such actions, or as a more *general* breakdown of legitimacy that shifts the costs and burdens of maintaining hegemony (Brooks and Wohlforth, 2008). From this perspective the real challenge to US power in the international system therefore comes less from traditional forms of 'realist'-style power rivalries, and more from the de-legitimation of the US-led system or the potential for challengers to turn the core institutional manifestations of US power against it. Liberal critics (amongst others) viewed the George W. Bush Administration in these terms, showing that some elements of consensus were being abandoned in favor of a more assertive, expansionist and unilateral foreign policy, one that more resembled an 'imperialism' seen to be in the past. Here, the US would be open to criticism on the basis of the very principles it subscribes to via the international organizations it set up. As such, to the extent that the US moves away from international institutions, a pragmatic approach to power (gaining consent through restraint), and the idea of the rule of law as core to political order, the US would by liberal standards be moving away from a liberal hegemony, and thus more at risk from various threats to its interests, and its position in the international order (Ikenberry and Slaughter, 2006). President Obama's attempts at reconciliation with the Islamic world early in his first term were certainly consistent with a view that legitimacy and consent are important for a more successful utilization of American power

The sources of power

With the context and concept of power better explained, we need to return to the four sources of power briefly outlined in the Introduction – political, military, economic and ideological – in order to clarify how the power typology presented above will be utilized in the rest of the book. How do the four types of power in international relations relate to Mann's four sources? If we are meant to be highlighting structure and institutions – at the expense of the more coercive 'power-over' sense – what does that bring us in relation to Mann? Mann's focus on power is the organizational capacity of institutions that focus on very specific forms of power. So when we talk about the potential power projection of the US state, at least part of the conversation concerns the various ways in which these institutional sources operate, and how they relate to the forms of power– compulsory, institutional, structural and productive – described above.

Political power is mainly about the power of the state. We can always see this in two dimensions: first, in the territorial reach of the state internally, and, second, in its international relations or geopolitics. The main issue is the power of the US state as it connects to other power organizations, and especially internationally in terms of how it relates to other political units. The interaction domestically between the sources of power is important here. While the internal territorial reach of the American state is uncontested, it is also fragmented in terms of federalism, and it is also a relatively weak state in terms of its overall levels of intervention, although it allows for a great deal of access from the economic sphere. Internationally, the main question concerns the level of interference the US has with other states. While formal empire is highly unlikely (and difficult) in the current international system due to established principles of sovereign non-interference, degrees of influence through more 'informal measures' (e.g. military bases, influence over policy, dependence) are important to consider, and certainly play a role in many accounts of American power in the world (and link quite clearly with ideas about structural power and many notions of

American hegemony). The formal institutional mechanisms of international politics found in international organizations are also important in the more liberal ways of viewing power: they 'mobilize bias', but are not fully determined by their participants.

Military power is embedded in the clear networks of organizational power that comprise the armed forces themselves, and to a certain extent, their civilian masters. Power projection here is in a more straightforward sense – the power of the military is the power to coerce, and is most clearly linked to compulsory power. However, there are ways in which we can conceive of military power through the other forms of power. For example, military traditions (and militarism) can become embedded in identities which shape overall interests; the institutions of military power (i.e. the armed forces) also relate to economic power in terms of the political economy of arms production, and as such become entwined with other forms of power. Internationally, American overseas bases also provide for a 'structural' form of military power, while international alliance structures such as NATO give an institutionalization of American military power. There exist multiple ways in which we can talk about the power of the military, in terms of its potential power projection.

Economic power is mainly embedded in the multiple networks that organize American capitalism, through production, finance and labor. As these networks are fairly decentralized, and to some extent internationalized and transnationalized (especially with finance), they tend to relate in many ways to both institutional and structural power. Institutional power is provided through the creation of and membership in international organizations that govern or steer the global economy, and set rules in place that enable the smooth flow of American capital. However, as these interests are embedded in institutions it is not the simple sense that the US state or 'capitalist class' have control over them (as other states also are bound to these institutions). Structural power is found in the broader sense that US capitalism is hegemonic, in that it has an ideological hold over the possibilities of economies in the world, and that the very interests of the global economic system are predicated in terms favorable to the US (and in many ways to the elites in other states). Structural power in this sense is seen in how US economic interests come to be seen as the *common* interest of the global economy.

Ideological power mainly plays out through overarching ways of reproducing American identity, and its importance in international power projection is the extent to which such articulations help shape, maintain and potentially transform international social systems to look more like the American one (or at least allow for enough commonality to not have conflict). Here the main articulation is through a hegemonic American identity based on American 'exceptionalism' – sometimes benign, sometimes crusading – that attempts to legitimate and form the content of foreign relations; for example, through seemingly benevolently articulated policies such as democracy promotion, modernization, or through attempts to make the world look like America, and the world's attempt to resist, modify or accept such legitimations. However ideological power plays an even stronger role internally in reproducing a particular version of American identity, which influences policy by setting the limits of debate.

Taken together (and outlined in Table 2.1), the sources of power can be seen as ways of more specifically disaggregating international power, which does not necessarily privilege any particular source causally, but can indeed show that variations and different emphases are important with each source. It also highlights the importance of linking the domestic and international, as it is very difficult to see the realms as discrete (especially with a state as powerful as the US). The overall point is to use the power framework as a means to better understand how US power operates, and Mann's 'sources' as a way of distinguishing different forms of power, in order to clarify the role they play in American power projection and in the continued power of the US. Combined, they provide an analytic framework for better understanding the past and future of US power that will also be able to assess the potential for change, both internationally and domestically.

Conclusion

Throughout the post-Cold War era, through four successive presidencies, the approach to grand strategy needed to fulfil US foreign policy goals and maintain US power has been subject to much debate. Policy-makers and scholars still argue about whether the US should attempt to further enhance its power to maintain (or regain) a preponderance of power and keep the system unipolar, or (potentially conceding American relative decline) act in concert with other powers in order to maintain overall legitimacy in the international system. There are competing conceptions of power, which impact on how their holders view the US. Current debates about the future of

Table 2.1 *Sources of power and the power debates*

	Main focus	*Others*
Political	• Institutional: power of state and government to mobilize bias	• Compulsory: coercion is at the heart of state power
Military	• Compulsory power: direct coercion	• Institutional: institutionalized military alliances; • Structural: global basing, military training, arms sales • Productive: militarism
Economic	• Structural: the international role of the dollar; global norms of openness; the free-market economy	• Institutional: global governance structures • Compulsory: weight of economic power in direct conflicts of interest
Ideological	• Structural power: internationalizing American exceptionalism	• Institutional: the embedding of values in global institutions • Compulsory: imposing values internationally through 'hard' power • Productive power: identity formation and its relation to international power projection

the US tend to be framed from these differing points of view, which vary both in their overall positions on the future of US power, but also in terms of what the US should do, in policy terms, to maintain its current position.

It was argued here that a better understanding of US power through an increased focus on institutional and structural international power is especially found in a discussion of how power relates to international legitimacy. While there are differences in how alternative approaches to US power (and IR more generally) conceive of these aspects of power, it will add analytic depth to look at them more or less discretely in order to see the ways in which different dimensions of the domestic sources of US power complicate and enrich our understanding of both the US in the world and the future of US power. In light of US power capacities and its role as the leading state in the international system, conceptualizing US power in terms of hegemony provides an important way of critically conceptualizing US power internationally. However, to get a better purchase on how hegemony relates to power in the argument presented in the book, we need to link these ideas up more robustly with structural power, rather than just seeing hegemony in terms of compulsory or institutional power. Structural power has a clear focus on hierarchy in understanding relations of power internationally, while also bringing in the significance of both consent and coercion to the discussion of such hierarchies. There are similarities between this view and the institutional view described above, in that both see US power in the world being legitimated through some sort of consensus. However, here there is a more critical component to the idea of consent: interests are not just mobilized through international institutions in a rational fashion, where interests are clear and recognized, but the terms of *which* interests comprise and are actualized by the hegemon itself. This is where power lies. It is a means for the powerful to set the context for deciding what an interest is, rather than just trying to prevent debate over particular interests. What this brings us is a broader sense of how American power can situate the overall 'rules of the game' in international relations, through its sheer material power, but also in terms of how that power creates a realm of consensus about what is desirable in international relations.

In the next four chapters, we will examine the political, military, economic, and ideological power resources of the US in order to gain a deeper understanding of US power and to further answer the core questions about the future of the US.

Chapter 3

The Power of the State and the Foreign Policy Process

The political power of the American state provides a focal point for American power, and therefore a discussion of its dynamics is crucial. The purpose of the present chapter is to look at political power within the US state in order to investigate the potentially fragmented character of political power and how it impacts on US power projection. Here we will open up the 'black box' of the state in order to better understand how decisions about foreign policy are reached and the different dynamics that help to define the kinds of actions the US takes internationally. The chapter delves into the connections between the American state and power by looking at a theory of the American state, both through its formal institutions and broader powers. Accounts of US foreign policy-making make a distinction between the impacts of international relations and the domestic decision-making context. As stated in the Introduction, the view taken here is that *both* are crucially important. The international level sets a crucial context, in terms of the broader array of relations the US has, the material balance of power, and sets of international institutions that provide the limits and potential for expressions of US power. However, the domestic level provides many core explanations for the expressions of material interests, the style of US foreign policy, and the actual power bases that the US draws upon.

The present chapter will also look at the connections between domestic society and the state, and additionally examine the formal and informal powers of government to influence foreign policy-making. It seeks to understand American power domestically in terms of the political power of the state, through both the broad powers of the American state and more narrowly in the domestic formulation of foreign policy. While this does lead us into rather conventional accounts of the policy process, it is also crucial for understanding the possibilities for American power in a state that is defined by pluralism. Here we will mainly discuss different actors' access to the policy process, while not ignoring the broader context of social relations within which political power exists. The chapter will detail these inputs into the policy process, examining domestic contestation over US foreign policy and power projection, emphasizing how a variety of interest groups and non-governmental sources of power shape American power in the world, and the content of foreign policy itself.

But how do we see power in the foreign policy process itself? One way is in terms of which actors have the ability to control outcomes. Does the president have the final say in a given situation, or is this given to some other actor or group of actors? A second way is to look more broadly at the structures that facilitate the foreign policy process. How are decision-making structures organized; what kinds of limits are there on individuals to 'make a difference'? A third way involves branching out to look at the state as a whole: rather than just focusing on the government, looking at a broader array of social forces that structure, shape and provide both limits and opportunities for the expression of power. None of these is mutually exclusive, and all need to be involved in an analysis of power in the institutions of government. The chapter will therefore examine all three issues – the kinds of powers different actors have within the foreign policy-making process, and how these roles can be constrained by broader structural factors – with the main theme concerning the rise of executive branch power, and what that might mean for the future of American power. Broader social forces will be discussed in terms of the influence of the media, interest groups and public opinion.

External observers of the US political system often deride the influence of 'outside' groups on the legislative process, particularly the way it becomes skewed by various organizations 'lobbying' for influence or for their groups to be given favorable treatment of some sort. While there are certainly problems with this influence, it is also part of the pluralism of the US system, which is a core reason why it is difficult to change the role of lobbying. In foreign policy terms, the role of lobbying has come to the forefront in recent years, especially regarding the role of business in pushing foreign policy, and the very controversial issue of the influence of the purported 'Israel lobby', seen as skewing US foreign policy towards support of Israel. Additionally, the growing role of potentially unlimited campaign funding is also changing the potential for moneyed interests to influence the electoral process, with possible effects on foreign policy.

While such influences do exist, their actual power is in many ways difficult to measure, and the discussion below will take a critical view on how we can conceive of influence. Overall, the chapter argues for the importance of seeing the development of foreign policy as a contested process, and one that is heavily imbricated by other sources of power.

The power of the American state: contexts of US power

A core question in International Relations (IR) concerns where foreign policy comes from: what are its sources; what is its context; how is it made? While numerous theories of international relations have been constructed that avoid a theory of foreign policy, preferring to focus on systemic explanations of international relations, many have continued to want to open up the state in order to better understand the ways in which specific foreign policies are made, implemented and affected. A core way that US foreign policy (and other states' foreign policy) has been explained is through Kenneth Waltz's (1959) classic understanding of three 'images' of international relations: the international; the domestic; and the individual. For Waltz the key question concerned the *best* level for explaining international relations: can we infer international relations from human nature, from the nature of specific regime types, or from the nature of the system itself? While Waltz settled on the final idea, we can also use his framework as an analytic device. Which level should we look at to understand a particular foreign policy problem? Understanding the power of the US undoubtedly involves all three levels, but I will argue that examining the interaction between the domestic and international is crucial.

While the international system and specific international relations impact on the context that policy is made in, and provide core constraints for policy-makers, the content of foreign policy is also shaped by *internal* forces, which requires understanding the state itself. Foreign policy decisions within the US are made by elites within the US government, in a relationship between the executive branch and the Congress: the formal structures of government, in terms of which people are allowed to make foreign policy decisions, and the balance of power in government are therefore essential to understanding where foreign policy comes from. Though the relationship between the executive and Congress is somewhat complicated in practice (and will be returned to later), the foreign policy elite are mainly represented by the president, his foreign policy team, and civil servants within the executive departments that deal with international issues. Congress affects this through various committees dealing with international issues, its power over funding the executive, and the Senate's power to ratify treaties and confirm executive branch appointees.

However, we need to further detail the internal structure and power of the US state. The easiest starting point for an explication of the American state is by looking at institutions and traditions. When thinking about foreign policy, the state is frequently associated with particular state officials, especially the president, often seen in the succession of presidential foreign policy 'doctrines', rarely named after anyone other than the president, or perhaps the Secretary of State. While we need to be cautious about putting too much weight on individuals in understanding power and policy-making, examining who makes decisions over foreign policy does lead us into interesting places in thinking about state power (e.g. Allison and Zelikow, 1999; Dumbrell, 1997; cf. Neustadt, 1990). First, it asks the question of where power is located. If it is mainly with presidents and their foreign policy teams, we can see where power is concentrated within the formal apparatus of the state. However, if we expand out to look at the interactions of this core with other groups – within the institutions of government (cabinet, Congress) and outside (business leaders, the media, other groups) we start to see foreign policy as being influenced by a much broader range of sources. Second, looking at the decision-making process can also challenge the idea that particular individuals or groups have a broad scope to radically alter foreign policy making. Individual policies towards specific issues certainly do change, but there also exists an overarching ideological consensus that shapes foreign policy-making, and as such the overall expression of American power internationally (e.g. Hartz, 1991; Hunt, 1987). Additionally, American involvements in international relations – war, trade, diplomacy and expansion – have all had an effect on the institutions of the state itself (Katznelson and Shefter, 2002).

Much more will be said in Chapter 6 regarding the ideology or values behind the American state and its role in the international power of the US, but we do need to briefly look at core values in order to understand the particularities of the American system. The development of a national state in the US was infused with republican ideas about balancing power within the system and the expression of the 'will of the people' (Madison et al., 1987; cf. Foley, 2007). Power-balancing was especially important in order to prevent concentrations of power or the overall domination of the system by individuals (they especially wanted no more influence from kings). The system was deliberately set up in terms of 'checks and balances' on power. The US was to have a separation of powers between three branches of government – the executive branch, the judiciary (the Supreme Court) and the legislative (the bi-cameral Congress) – each of which would also in turn have powers to ensure that the other branches did not abuse their powers. To start with the Congress: the legislative branch has the power to make laws, to consent to appointments made to both the judicial and executive branch, to consent to treaties signed by the executive branch, the power to regulate commerce, broad powers to initiate taxation and spending, declare war, and, importantly, the power of impeachment of officials in both of the other branches. The executive can make treaties, appoint officials, has broad powers over the command of military forces, and can also veto legislation proposed by the legislative branch. The judiciary has the broad power of review of legislation to ensure its constitutionality. Of course, all branches have more powers (and the procedures and histories of all three are more complex than made out here), but this gives the basic sense of the relationship and balance between the various branches, and demonstrates in practice the concerns of the founders (see e.g. McKay, 2009; Singh, 2003). As will be discussed below, foreign policy can be seen as a struggle between all three branches (but primarily between Congress and the president), although foreign policy-making has been increasingly deferential to presidential prerogatives.

The system was also set up as a representative democracy, based fairly firmly on republican ideas (e.g. Madison et al., 1987; cf. McKay, 2009; Singh, 2003). The system was anti-monarchical, and intended to have an executive leader that was more a figurehead than a president with a large amount of power. The main business of governing was intended to be through the Congress (the Constitution lists the Congress first in terms of the make-up of the government), and the Congress was to be split into two chambers: the Senate (upper) and the House of Representatives (lower). The two chambers were imbued with different ideas of representation, with the Senate to represent equally the states of the union (with two senators each, serving longer terms of office), therefore protecting states' rights within the union; and the House consisting of a representation of the population at large, in effect the 'people's house'. The manner of election has changed over time, but the spirit of the two chambers lives on, with the Senate currently consisting of 100 members, two representing each state elected for six-year terms of office (currently, every two years a third of the Senate is up for election). Representatives for the House are apportioned by the population of each state, so more populous states have greater numbers of representatives (the present total for the House is 435 – these numbers also provide the proportion of Electoral College votes allocated to each state in presidential elections – which adds up to 538 Electoral College votes in total when the Senate figures and three extra for Washington, DC are added in).

The breakdown of representation between states and people shows the continued importance of states within the context of the union (Grodzins, 1966; Gerston, 2007; cf. Brinkley et al., 1997). Today it is sometimes forgotten that the initial premise of the union was to have united *states*, which accounts for the much greater sense of federalism in the system than in other sovereign states in the world. Each state of the union has a similar structure to the US federal government – executive, legislature and supreme court – which also enact laws and public policy. Over time the federal government gained in its power and (especially) in its size and overall capacity, however, the level of autonomy of the now fifty states is still rather high in numerous areas (for example, public safety and education), and accounts overall for the continued articulation of 'states' rights' within US politics.

The formal institutions of US politics do not tell us all about the American state. Many studies of US foreign policy tend to examine these formal institutions (and sometimes a range of other actors with access to these institutions, such as interest groups and the media) exclusively. However, anti-statist and other tendencies have left the US much more open to other informal influences. As Mead has noted, 'The United States' tradition of a relatively weak and decentralized state combined with an unusually well-organized and dynamic civil and commercial society means that the policies of the state reflect only a small part of the activity of the society' (Mead, 2009: 140). Furthermore, as will be discussed at length in Chapter 6, we also need to see the worldviews of policy-makers and others as embedded in deeper ideological currents within the US.

To further this point, it is helpful to link our ideas about the US to a theory of the US state. We can see the state as composed of the formal institutions of government (as described above), the bureaucracy of the civil service, and the legal apparatus backing up these institutions; this gives a good sense of the scope of state power, both foreign and domestic (cf. King and Stears, 2011). This aspect corresponds broadly with Mann's conception of political power (Mann, 1993; cf. Weber, 2009a; Giddens, 1987; Tilly, 1992). The institutional apparatus of the state extends authoritative power over a delimited territory, and as argued in Chapter 1, this expansion has been important in terms of how the US state itself has extended across the American continent. The state also embodies the core institutions of formal government, as well as other aspects such as the development of laws and a legal system that backs up the state's authority. The formal process of government in terms of elected offices has been discussed earlier. However, the civil service of government also plays an important role in the American state (as with most modern states) (Wilson, 1989; cf. Beetham, 1996), as a set of unelected and theoretically non-partisan bureaucrats help to run the government. In the executive branch, these start in a pyramid fashion from the secretaries of various departments, down the chain to various other officials with experience. Why is this important for understanding power? These officials are paramount in carrying forward the interests of the state over time, not just in an idealized sense that they represent the interests of elected officials (and proxies for the people's interest, or implementing the people's interests), but they also provide continuity to the institutional identity of the different executive departments, and help to consolidate and reproduce the interests of those organizations. In essence, an emphasis on bureaucracy helps to reinforce the idea that states can have their own interests that may not coincide with those of society at large (e.g. Evans, Rueschemeyer, and Skocpol, 1985). The legal apparatus is important in defining the scope of the state, but also provides the legitimation of the state itself. We can see this by drawing on Max Weber's definition of legal-rational authority, where states have legitimacy through their reliance on abstract laws that are universally applied, therefore demonstrating a sense of fairness or at least a lack of arbitrariness (Weber, 2009a).

In the US context, the president has the final authority over foreign policy decisions, but due to the checks and balances of the American political system, he is constrained. However, in addition to this formal organization, the executive branch bureaucracy also has much influence on the president's decisions, and such organizations are not necessarily acting in the national interest, but have their own agendas and rivalries. Finally, powerful individuals are also influenced by the positions they occupy: the Secretary of Defense will often give advice that prioritizes the military. All of these factors have to be taken into account when discussing specific foreign policy decisions. For example, the decision to invade Iraq in 2003 was made, at least partially, through competing departments within the executive branch. It is well known that State was keener on traditional diplomacy, while Defense was more inclined towards invasion. These distinctions were partly to do with traditional inter-departmental rivalries, but also due to the specific individuals playing those roles, and the character and beliefs of the president.

However, the influence at the state level goes further than this. While some conflate the 'domestic' level and the 'state' level, it is important, especially in states with largely autonomous civil societies, to take into account the role of broader domestic-societal influences. While there is much debate in political science about the make-up of the state (e.g. does that state act in consensus with society as a whole, or is it in conflict?), the state is a receptacle of a broader culture of society, even where this culture is contested. These cultural attributes could be the broader values of society, from a fleeting cultural identity to the influence of public opinion on the state. Additionally, cultural influences can be seen in the broad influence of actors within civil society, be they interest groups, economic actors, or citizens voting. We can expand on these issues by looking further at the influence of economic and military power on the state (having discussed ideology previously). While theories of the state tend to make a distinction between state and society – which has the result of seeing societies as the other side of the state – we can see the state as attempting to contain various actors within its reach, all of whom have degrees of autonomy, and also to a certain extent, linkages that go beyond the state itself.

The economic sphere produces and forms the interests that develop out of market relations, and also social stratification through the formation of social and economic classes. The importance of the economic sphere is particularly pronounced in the US state, in the main due to the particular self-understanding of the US as a 'commercial republic', and the emphasis placed on a relatively unconstrained version of capitalism. The long-term success of

American capitalism, first through industrial production and then in a post-industrial stage, with dual emphases on services and finance, has given a real weight to the importance of economic interests and power which has tied them ever more tightly with the state (Berry, 1989; McConnell, 1966; Vogel, 1989). This can be seen in the importance in the American system of 'access' to the political process, where organized interests (with resources) find it easy to push agendas in the formal realm of government. The 2010 Supreme Court decision *Citizens United v Federal Election Commission* allowing unlimited donations from corporations to political campaigns has only increased the potential influence of economic power in the political realm (Mann, 2011). Economic power is thus critical for power projection more generally, as it not only links economic interests and the state, but also gives much weight to American power more generally. Importantly, economic power is crucially international and transnational – in the domination of American capitalism, through the importance of American firms internationally, international trade, and American finance.

Military power has great importance to the US state. While some theorists of the state – particularly Marxist theories (e.g. Jessop, 2008: 62–65; cf. Balakrishnan, 2005) – have tended to bracket off military power, or see it more as an extension of economic interest, many neo-Weberian approaches see it as integral to understanding state development (e.g. Tilly, 1985). Weber defined the state as 'a human community that (successfully) lays claim to the *monopoly of legitimate physical force* within a given territory' (Weber, 2009a: 78), indicating an important coercive backdrop to state power. However, and in some ways conceding ground to critiques of the strict Weberian position, sociologists such as Giddens and Mann (Giddens, 1987; Mann, 1993) have both stressed the need to under-stand military power as an autonomous institution, as militaries have their own organizational autonomy. The emphasis on military power is on coercive means, and it is usually characterized by tightly cohesive institutional structures that are in various degrees of auton-omy, and sometimes contestation, within the state. That is to say that militaries have their own organizational structures, which are very hierarchical and focused on discipline, and in terms of policies not always congruent with those of the political classes. The tradi-tions in the US have been profoundly anti-militarist, and the US state has tried to maintain (at least until about 1950) a smaller standing army (though a larger navy, helpful in protecting commercial interests and trading routes) and very tight civilian control of the military. While the US military has grown bigger, civilian control is still seen as very important (Bacevich, 2006; Desch, 1999). While some of this balance has been challenged during the Cold War, it has very much stayed on the side of the civilians. It is still worth seeing military power as an institution in its own right, not least due to the fact that as a professional force, it remains relatively isolated and distinct from the rest of American society, despite being the focus of much patriotism and nationalism (Weigley, 2001); and of course, due to the particular logic of coercive power, focused as it is on the use of deadly force. As an expression of power, it is meant to be a deterrent to those wishing to use military power against the US homeland, but is at its most pronounced in its defense of US interests abroad, to the extent to which American military presence (through bases, training, invasions, humanitarian missions) has been a crucial extension of overall US power, and has much to do with questions about the legitimacy of American leadership in international relations, and with questioning the purpose of force (e.g. Bacevich, 2002; C. Johnson, 2004).

We can see that the structure of the US state and its relationship to other forms of power help to better understand the relationship between the US and the world, in terms of how interests are formulated, how traditions are articulated, and how institutions relate to one another. With this broad understanding of the structure and power of the US state, we can move on to examine the particular relationship between core actors and forces in the policy process, which will help illuminate the contest over power within the American state, and which gives rise to specific policies and attention to the goals of American foreign policy and its international power projection.

The powers of Congress and President over foreign policy

The analysis of the political power of the US to organize for foreign policy has tended to place a great deal of emphasis on the role of the president. While no one would sensibly claim that this one individual (or one institutional role) is the *only* key to understanding US political power, the president provides an important starting point. Although the president has taken up more and more centrality and power in the foreign policy process over the course of the twentieth century and beyond, it is wrong to think that the office has complete unfettered scope for action. As noted above, the US Constitution provides a clear separation of powers between the three branches of government in the US, and the organization of foreign policy-making was understandably done on similar lines.

The judiciary does have major powers to set the context of what legitimate action is on the part of the executive branch, and therefore plays an important if infrequent role in resolving constitutional and legal disputes about the scope of foreign policy powers. The Supreme Court has only very rarely become involved in disagreements over foreign policy. However, the cases it has taken up have been very important for future interpretations of presidential and congressional authority. A prime example is the 1936 case of the *United States v Curtiss Wright Export*. In this case, the final decision of the Supreme Court indicated that the president has powers over foreign policy that are not specifically enumerated in the Constitution, and that Congress does not need to delegate such powers. While the ruling, along with the sweeping statements about presidential power, has been controversial, and not entirely accepted, the language has often been invoked to indicate presidential prerogatives over foreign policy.

Other Supreme Court Decisions in the past fifty years have also had an important impact. For example, the Court's 1971 ruling in favor of the *New York Times* in publishing the so-called 'Pentagon Papers' was important for protecting freedom of expression over national security matters. The papers were a long (some 47 volumes of material), secret Department of Defense study of the course of the Vietnam War, seen as indicating a number of deceptions committed by the Johnson Administration, and therefore in the public interest. In its ruling, the Court sided with lower court decisions, demonstrating that the publication of the papers was in the public interest, and therefore demonstrating limits to government secrecy, even in times of war (Sheehan et al., 1971). A more recent case of importance can be seen in the 2004 decision of *Hamdi v Rumsfeld*. Yaser Esam Hamdi was an American citizen who was captured in Afghanistan, and subsequently declared an 'enemy combatant' and detained in a military prison at Guantanamo Bay. The case before the Supreme Court regarded the ability of the federal government to indefinitely detain 'unlawful combatants', especially those that are American citizens. The decision decided in favor of Hamdi (5-4), that the government does not have the right to hold a US citizen indefinitely without access to due process; however, it upheld the right to detain 'unlawful combatants' without charge, a ruling that has been seen as an infringement on civil liberties, through an overstretched definition of a 'combatant' (Savage, 2007: 321–2; cf. Goldsmith, 2007; Niday, 2008).

The powers of Congress

The Constitution, in Article I, Section 8, enumerates the main formal powers of Congress over foreign policy. The basic powers provided include: the power to provide funding to the armed forces, the power to regulate trade, the right to declare war, the confirmation of executive branch appointees, the approval of treaties, and crucially, passing legislation that enables Congress to enact those duties. In fact, this is a rather remarkable list of powers considering how much emphasis is put on the executive branch today. It is worth briefly looking at each in turn to determine exactly what they entail.

The power to provide funding is one of the most crucial powers held by Congress. This power is not limited to foreign policy: the 'power of the purse' is vested in Congress more generally, as it controls the budget of the federal government. All appropriations must be fed through the House before both chambers approve. For foreign policy, this mainly means providing funding for programs in specific executive departments, particularly those of the Departments of Defense and State. For example, Congress approves funds for military actions, and if they disapprove of a particular action, they can deny the funding. For example, in the early 1970s Congress passed a variety of amendments to conditionally stop funding the war, which was a direct way of stopping the president from pursuing the war in Vietnam. Congress must also approve all issues to do with international trade. Though some of this power is tied up with the power to approve treaties, the Constitution gives Congress clear powers over commerce (often referred to as 'The Commerce Clause', Article I, Section 8, Clause 3).

One of the most controversial areas of congressional power is the scope of the 'war power'. The Constitution gives Congress the power 'to declare war' (Article 1, Section 8, Clause 11). However, despite the numerous wars and military actions that the US has been involved in, there have only been five formal declarations of war by Congress in the history of the US (The War of 1812 against Britain; The Mexican-American War of 1846–48; The Spanish-American

War of 1898; World War I in 1917; and World War II in 1941). The reason behind the lack of formal declarations has been a series of problems with interpreting the war power. Ostensibly, the power over war is shared between Congress and the president, where Congress declares war and the president acts as commander-in-chief of the armed forces. However, it is not entirely clear whether this necessitates a formal declaration of war (which was much more common in international relations in the eighteenth and nineteenth centuries), or if an authorization of the use of force is enough. Alternatively, it also appears that the president is allowed to use force in extreme instances, and the question remains as to how expansive the president's powers are in interpreting when Congress needs to be consulted before using force in these extreme cases. While Congress certainly has the power to declare war, the ability of the president to engage in military conflicts without authorization has not often been contested on constitutional grounds. The seeming imbalance in authority over this power grew in the 1960s, leading Congress to enact the 'War Powers Resolution' of 1973, which placed further limits on presidential powers over war, and will be discussed at greater length later.

The final two powers are given as part of the Constitution's granting of presidential power, often referred to as the 'Advice and Consent Clause' (Article 2, Section 2, Clause 2), which gives the president the power to both make treaties and appoint officials, with the advice and consent of the Senate. This means that the Senate has historically taken the power to approve presidential appointments for a variety of foreign policy-related positions, including ambassadors and heads of executive departments such as the Departments of State and Defense. The Senate can block appointees for various reasons, particularly due to concerns about appointees' qualifications and background, or more often, concerns about their stance on particular issues.

The Senate also has the power to approve (or block) treaties negotiated by the president. The Senate has not given consent to approximately twenty treaties in US history (while consenting to around 1,500) (see United States Senate, n.d.). Notably, the Senate rejected the 1919 Versailles Treaty negotiated and signed by President Wilson, including key provisions such as the establishment of the League of Nations. The Treaty of Versailles was mainly rejected by the Senate due to the body's exclusion from the process of making the treaty: the 'advice' role was ignored by President Wilson, and the

Senate punished him for it (the Congress was additionally concerned about sovereignty over decisions to go to war) (Fisher, 2004: 81–4). There has additionally been an increasing trend towards 'executive agreements', treaties that derive only from the president's authority without the need to have Senate approval (and some controversy about whether this is just expedience, or a means of extending executive power) (see Krutz and Peake, 2009; Congressional Research Service, 2001).

However, one reason why treaties rarely are rejected is that presidents are usually keen to avoid embarrassments caused by problems with ratification in the Senate, and will often alter wordings in line with what powerful senators want, in order to see their easy passage. For example, the Chemical Weapons Convention (signed by President Clinton in 1993) was kept from vote until it conformed to Chair of the Senate Foreign Relations Committee Senator Jesse Helms' wishes (he had thought the original terms were unverifiable and potentially infringed on US sovereignty), and was eventually ratified in 1997. There have also been attempts to use 'fast track' legislation to avoid congressional debate over trade bills. As trade bills that are signed by the president are still subject to ratification by the Congress, they can often be changed substantially in ways that alter their initial terms. Fast track legislation allows bills to be passed by Congress only on the terms given. However, such legislation has proven unpopular due to the restrictions it places on Congress.

Finally, Congress, as the legislative body, is given broad powers to pass legislation in order to fulfil its duties. It is formally given powers over the organization and maintenance of the armed forces, and powers to create rules for these forces. The 'necessary and proper' clause additionally gives powers to create laws to help support Congress in executing the powers that it is given. Broadly speaking, Congress now organizes many of these powers through its committee system, where specialized committees deal with key areas of foreign policy. Committees are often the place where the main business of foreign policy is done, prior to being brought before the full Congress. Powerful committee chairs can often be core 'veto points' over legislation and particular policies (as noted above in the example of Jesse Helms and the Senate Foreign Relations Committee). While committees such as foreign relations are the obvious places to look for power over foreign policy issues, other committees such as appropriations, armed services, intelligence and homeland security are also important.

The capacity of Congress to examine the programs and proposals of the executive branch through independent means, coupled with its grip on the purse strings, makes it a very powerful branch of government, in terms of its potential impact on foreign policy-making. At the same time, Congress is often in line with the executive branch, which can derive from the sharing of a broader political culture (to be discussed in Chapter 6). Foreign policy is also rarely high on the agenda of voters, and as the next election is always looming, especially for members of the House, the domestic policy agenda is often seen as more pressing.

The powers of the president

Congress was granted particular powers over foreign policy in order to prevent domination by the president. While the framers of the Constitution were keen to ensure that the newly established national government would be able to protect itself and the states from foreign incursions, they were also eager to avoid concentrations of power within government itself, especially those that would resemble the monarchy that they had just freed themselves from (e.g. Madison et al., 1987). However, as the commander-in-chief of the armed forces, the president was mandated with power to appoint executive officials (such as diplomats, ambassadors, and cabinet heads) and the power to make treaties, with the advice and consent of the Senate. The added limit was that Congress would control the funding of these activities, and had the power to declare war, so there would have to be negotiation with Congress over important foreign policy decisions.

The role of commander-in-chief was granted to give focus in times of national crisis. However, such authority was deliberately limited in terms of declaring, funding and possibly entering wars. As Alexander Hamilton stated in *Federalist No. 69*, comparing the president's power with the British king (and presumably queen as well):

> The President is to be commander-in-chief of the army and navy of the United States. . . . It would amount to nothing more than the supreme command and direction of the military and naval forces . . . while that of the British king extends to the *declaring* of war and to the *raising* and *regulating* of fleets and armies – all which, by the Constitution under consideration, would appertain to the legislature. (Madison et al., 1987: 398)

The role of the president is therefore intentionally circumscribed. However, as will be noted later, there is some ambiguity in this role. Does the president, as commander-in-chief have the right to use force in emergencies without congressional approval? Does the president have the authority to use force in situations that are not classified as 'wars'? The problems with the distinctive powers of the Congress and president over the use of force have always been apparent, but became especially controversial with the rise of presidential power after World War II, with repeated attempts by presidents to extend the reach of their authority over military power.

The other two major powers of the president have been described above, as they form part of the 'advice and consent' role of Congress, surrounding the power to appoint officials and to sign treaties. While these roles can become controversial and politicized, with a few exceptions, they have not become quite as contentious in the foreign policy realm as in some other areas (particularly recently in the case of the appointment of Supreme Court Justices).

Legal and political disputes over the control of foreign policy

The ambiguity in the Constitution about the final word over foreign policy (and particularly the use of force) has been subject to many debates. As legal scholar Harold Koh has noted, 'one cannot read the Constitution without being struck by its astonishing brevity regarding the allocation of foreign affairs authority among the branches' (Koh, 1990: 67). As such, there has been real contestation over the actual powers and prerogatives in each branch. This has been particularly acute with the rise of presidential privilege in foreign policy, particularly with regard to the use of force.

For some, the increase in power of the president is a good thing. Much of this view stems from the idea that foreign policy requires decisive action, and that the president and the executive have a much clearer mandate to initiate such activities. The Cold War provided the impetus for such views. For example, in 1951 Dean Acheson (then Secretary of State), speaking to the Senate Foreign Relations Committee, claimed that 'we are in a position in the world today where the argument as to who has the power to do this, that, or the other thing, is not exactly what is called from America in this very critical hour, and if we could all agree on the fact that something should be done, we will perform a much greater role in the world, than by quarrelling about who ought to do it' (quoted in Fisher, 2004: 112; cf. Madison et al., 1987: no. 23). For others, the emphasis on presidential power in the early Cold War led to an 'imperial presidency' (Schlesinger, 2004), very much against what the founders intended, and also limiting the powers of a sovereign Congress. The Vietnam War and the Watergate scandal of the 1970s helped to put the centralization of presidential power under critical scrutiny, if not killing it as an ideology.

Recent presidents have increasingly articulated the view that presidents and the executive branch are both better placed and constitutionally entitled to take broad powers over foreign policy, both by specific foreign policy actions and by actual statements concerning presidential power. The approach to governing focused on executive authority described above was renewed with some vigour during George W. Bush's Administration, particularly under the influence of his powerful vice-president, Dick Cheney. As Savage describes Cheney's approach:

> He wanted to reduce the authority of Congress and the courts and to expand the ability of the commander in chief and his top advisors to govern with maximum flexibility and minimum oversight. He hoped to enlarge the zone of secrecy around the executive branch, to reduce the power of Congress to restrict presidential action, to undermine the limits imposed by international treaties, to nominate judges who favored a stronger presidency, and to impose greater White House control over the permanent workings of government. (Savage, 2007: 9)

Despite criticism of the Cheney approach, it is difficult to 'scale back' institutional roles once new powers have been taken on board, and presidents have been unwilling to give up roles and powers that their predecessors have previously taken up. For example, while ostensibly different in character from those in the Bush Administration, President Obama has claimed similar presidential authority over military action, both in the case of the intervention in Libya (with some protests from Congress over the lack of consultation or authorization) and in the use of drones in counter-terrorism policy (J. Mann, 2012: 295–7; Savage and Landler, 2011).

However, much of the contestation has been derived from the real ambiguity in the Constitution about the exact powers of each branch. While Congress is enumerated with particular powers, the president is given very few *specific* powers, and what is obvious is that power over foreign policy was meant to be shared. The legal arguments, while very important, mask the intensely political nature of these debates, and for some legal scholars, the legal debates really need to give way to the *politics* of foreign policy. Instead of fixing the exact limits as prescribed by the Constitution, the shared powers mean that there will always be arguments. For example, Jefferson Powell states that: 'the Constitution allocates authority along sequential lines: exclusively legislative power to create and maintain most of the tools of foreign policy followed by independent and generally exclusive executive authority to formulate foreign policy and pursue it, followed by the legislature's capacity to review, criticize and, within limits, forbid' (Powell, 2002: 140). This view shows a more dynamic interaction between branches as the ideal, that Congress sets limits through legislation and funding, the executive pursues its policies within these limits, and Congress reviews and provides oversight. Such a view is further reflected in Koh's statement: 'outside of that realm [of enumerated powers] governmental decisions regarding foreign affairs must transpire within a sphere of concurrent authority, under presidential management, but bounded by the checks provided by congressional consultation and judicial review' (Koh, 1990: 69).

While the formal powers of the president as enumerated in the Constitution seem quite limited in many ways, the president has been able to use the increasing power of the presidency over the course of the twentieth century to take a commanding role in leading and implementing foreign policy. Much of this was of course attenuated by a series of international crises that only served to highlight the need for focus in foreign policy, as well as enabling the powers of the presidency. World War II, the Cold War and 9/11 have created enduring legacies in the articulation of presidential power over foreign policy in relation to Congress that led to many perceived problems in the current system. As such, the formal powers of both Congress and the president are significant for understanding the legal basis for the control of foreign policy, as well as how the newly created republic envisaged foreign policy as part of a broader political philosophy of divided government. However, the ambiguity in the Constitution about presidential powers, their role in the modern world, and the transformation of the US from a small new state to a global superpower do not give us the full picture of how the US arrived where it is today.

Congressional–executive branch relations

While the details and controversies concerning congressional and presidential powers over foreign policy are important, they do not exhaust the ways in which foreign policy is actually formulated, or the more informal processes and powers that have developed over time. A number of factors have led to the increasing power of the president and executive branch to conduct foreign policy, and a decreasing willingness within Congress to challenge presidential power.

The rise of presidential power

As Lewis Gould (2003) describes, at the turn of the nineteenth century, the presidency was very much seen as an equal partner to the Congress in all areas. Presidential activism was generally deplored. The first half of the twentieth century saw the expansion of the presidential staff, the reinterpretation of the powers of commander-in-chief, and the political role of the president in relation to the 'permanent campaign'. Many scholars see Franklin D. Roosevelt as the first 'modern' president (though Gould makes a case for McKinley: Gould, 2003: ch. 1), who not only had a large staff, focus on the media, and an eye to campaigning, but also brought a large expansion of the remit of the federal government. In foreign affairs, this can be seen particularly in the rethinking of the organization of national defense that started during World War II.

The increasing size and influence of the Office of the President in the twentieth century saw successive presidents stake out foreign policy as their own. While some of this was down to the broader societal changes connected to urbanization and industrialization (also see Gould, 2003), there was also an increasing prominence of presidents to stake their claims over foreign policy. A number of examples demonstrate this tendency. President Wilson perhaps started the trend with his push to get the US involved in World War I, despite general public and congressional disapproval, and finally ratifying the Treaty of Versailles without prior congressional consultation, resulting in its rejection. President Truman pressed presidential authority even further by committing troops to the Korean War in 1950, on the basis of United Nations Security Council authorization. The Korean War may well represent a turning point in presidential–congressional relations in terms of foreign policy: an exceedingly large deployment of US military forces (a war by any definition) was done without congressional approval (either through a declaration of war or even an authorization). The increasing use of covert action as a means of using force but getting around congressional oversight also became a major part of presidential power during the Cold War (Callanan, 2009; Kinzer, 2007; Treverton, 1988) (the use of unmanned drones today involves similar issues – Miller, 2011; Singer, 2009). However, the increasing readiness of Congress to conduct oversight post-Vietnam War could indicate a change in the scope for presidents to unilaterally control foreign policy. For example, the Church Committee was formed in 1975 to investigate problems with the intelligence services in the wake of the Watergate scandal, and increasing public evidence of potentially illegal activities both home and abroad. Other examples include Congress's non-ratification of the SALT II treaty (signed by President Carter in 1979), and the rather close margin by which the 1991 Gulf War authorization was passed through Congress (Rosati and Twing, 1998: 39).

There are several reasons behind the president's ability to pursue foreign policy more vigorously from the White House and executive branch, mainly to do with informal powers provided by the office. First, although Congress and especially the House of Representatives are meant to be the voice of the people, the president as a single individual representing the country as a whole has an ease of visibility that confers substantial power in speaking on certain issues. President Theodore Roosevelt ably described such visibility as a 'bully pulpit': the office provides an opportunity to speak with a single voice on important matters that may not have otherwise been heard. This is especially true in the case of important foreign policy issues. While Congress speaks with many voices, the president is known to all.

Second, the rise of the presidency has also coincided with the huge expansion of the executive branch departments. The president has control of the two most important foreign policy bureaucracies: the Department of State and the Department of Defense. The president can therefore command these departments to do things within the bounds of the budget and mandated authority. The creation of the national security bureaucracy in 1947 was really at the heart of a shift towards presidential power. Previously, the Departments of State, War and the Navy ran their own programs and policies with little coordination. The two military departments were seen as preparing for war, rather than part of a substantial peacetime military program, premised on providing 'national security'. However, as further discussed in Chapters 1 and 4, World War II and the development of the Cold War put such notions to rest, with President Truman arguing for the development of a much more substantial peacetime military-security program, with a centralized structure for dealing with the broad provision and coordination of national security. The 1947 National Security Act finalized this point of view by unifying the Departments of War and Navy into a single Department of Defense, and also created an array of other foreign policy-related organizations, which remain to this day, such as the Central Intelligence Agency (CIA) and National Security Council (NSC).

A third, related, development has been the substantial institutionalization of foreign policy making *within* the White House (Destler, 1981; Zegart, 1999). Prior to World War II, the key outlet for foreign policy was the Department of State, while after World War II, the creation of the NSC gradually allowed a great deal of foreign policy work to be done within the White House. This not only allowed the president to have greater control over policy-making, but concentrated power within the White House: as Daalder and Destler note, 'since then, presidents have given less priority to making the overall government function with maximum effectiveness, and more to having a White House staff that is loyal to them alone' (Daalder and Destler, 2009: 7). The position of National Security Advisor, originally created as a staff secretary to the NSC, gradually became one of the most powerful positions in the foreign policy establishment. However, as a White House staff position, it is not subject to the advice and consent of Congress. While not all National Security Advisors have played a prominent public role, a number have been seen to run foreign policy out of the White House, giving presidents another strong advantage in leading foreign policy (see Daalder and Destler 2009; Rothkopf, 2005). For example, National Security Advisors such as Henry Kissinger were extremely powerful, Kissinger in fact taking a lead role in foreign policy, often over that of the Secretary of State (and Kissinger himself taking on both roles from 1973 to 1975). More recently, these tendencies were prominent in the George W. Bush Administration, and continued in the Obama Administration. While having a quite noticeable and successful foreign policy representative as Secretary of State (Hillary Clinton), President Obama has still relied on a tight circle of insiders from both the NSC and his own Senior Advisors in the White House for foreign policy (J. Mann, 2012).

Congress resurgent?

The increase in presidential power during the Cold War was in some ways unsurprising: despite some concern in the late 1940s within Congress about the centralization and militarization of defense policy, there was a development of a gradual consensus over foreign policy matters, which meant less overall contention between the president and Congress. While it would be too simplistic to say that there was an enlightened consensus (Johnson, 2005; Reichard, 1986), especially during the time of anti-communism, there was still little opposition from Congress during the 1950s and early 1960s to the foreign policy activities of the president.

The event that challenged this unity was the onset of the Vietnam War. Congress later regretted authorizing the American military build-up in Vietnam with the 1964 Tonkin Gulf Resolution, especially as the war went on with no clear end in sight. The Tonkin Gulf Resolution was seen as giving a blank cheque to the Johnson Administration to do whatever they wanted. This regret, combined with mounting public concern about the war, led Congress to slowly push back against Administration policy. The Senate in 1969, led by Senator William Fulbright, passed the National Commitments Resolution, which reaffirmed the right of Congress to be properly consulted on actions taking the country to war. The Resolution confirmed the Senate's belief in constitutional principles regarding war powers (Fisher, 2004: 139). Concerned that presidents had become too powerful in taking the nation into armed conflicts without sufficient approval from Congress, Congress passed the War Powers Resolution in 1973 (vetoed by President Nixon, but overridden by Congress). By the terms of this joint resolution, the president must consult Congress about the use of force, defined as bringing US armed forces 'into hostilities': the president is required to inform Congress about the deployment of troops within 48 hours, and after that is allowed 60 days, by which time congressional approval must be granted, or troops must be withdrawn (although the president may be granted up to an additional 30 days). The approval of the War Powers Resolution showed that Congress was serious about asserting its authority over the use of force.

However, for a number of reasons, the Resolution has been rather ineffective. First, it has been seen as unconstitutional by a number of scholars, and most presidents have looked on it with some disdain. There are a number of reasons why there are problems with its constitutionality. For one, the War Powers Resolution defines rather narrowly the powers of the president in a way that goes against many readings of constitutional powers, and it would likely need to be put into force through a constitutional amendment. Furthermore, a 1983 Supreme Court decision in the case of *INS v Chadha* indicated that a key provision of the Resolution, where Congress could terminate a conflict by a concurrent resolution, would also be unconstitutional (in that it would allow Congress to enact law without the consent or legislative veto of the president) (see Baker and Christopher, 2008; and Fisher, 2004: ch. 6). The Resolution has not been very consistently utilized by presidents, who have sometimes formally engaged in the process, sometimes not, and sometimes acted in accordance with the principle without bothering to go through the formal mechanisms (Fisher, 2004: 149–51).

Second, Congress has not seriously utilized the War Powers Resolution as a way of controlling military adventures since 1973. Presidents have submitted 172 reports on the use of military force between 1975 and 2007, but only twice has the 'time limit' of 60 days been specifically utilized. Once it was mentioned in a report from a president (by President Ford in 1975 announcing the use of the military to reclaim the merchant ship *Mayaguez*). Congress initiated the second instance in authorizing President Reagan's use of force in Lebanon in 1983 (Fisher, 2004: 150; Grimmett, 2008). Third, despite being seen by many as a way of increasing congressional authority, a number of critics who support the spirit of the Resolution have noted that it has only served to *strengthen* presidential prerogatives in pursuing the use of force without consulting Congress. The provision to grant up to 90 days before congressional authorization is needed has been seen as giving free reign to presidents to use force for up to 90 days (Fisher, 2004: 150; Koh, 1990). Finally, the use of the term 'hostilities' in the resolution makes it rather unclear what exact kinds of situations it is meant to be regulating.

Finally, despite the War Powers Resolution and the oversight role, Congress post-Vietnam War still seems more likely to defer authority to the executive over the use of force, and to foreign policy issues more generally. While presidents are constrained by what Congress will support, especially financially, there is still little effort by Congress to *initiate* foreign policy. Despite claims to reassert authority, much of the real work that Congress has done for both foreign policy and the use of force has in fact been reactive, in the form of committees exploring decisions after they happen. Ad hoc review commissions (such as the Church Committee in the 1970s and the Tower Commission in the 1980s), have had an important oversight role, and may provide means to stop undesirable actions from occurring in the future. In some ways, these reactions to presidential actions do allow Congress to play a 'balanced' role in the foreign policy process, following presidential prerogative in foreign affairs with oversight. However, there is more plurality in the system that only increased with the end of the Cold War. Since then, there have been problems with presidents gaining a consensus on overarching strategies for foreign policy as, outside a crisis, public opinion has increasingly focused on domestic affairs.

More recently, this 'reactive' system of congressional oversight of executive branch action has been criticized as rather lacking. Thomas E. Mann and Norman J. Ornstein (2007; 2012) have been trenchant critics of the decline of congressional oversight, particularly when it comes to foreign policy and military actions. They attribute this to a number of problems, but mainly in an overall decline of Congress as an institution and the rise (and assertion) of executive power. Since the 1990s (and especially the Republican Congress elected in 1994), there has been an overall decline in oversight committees. They note that in 2003–04, there were only 37 oversight hearings, as opposed to 135 in 1993–94 (Ornstein and Mann, 2006: 71). The executive under President George W. Bush also displayed an arrogant attitude towards Congress, in terms of a lack of compliance, contempt of congressional oversight, and withholding information.

Congress also developed an increasing partisanship, which meant that the Republican-controlled Congress was frequently seen as supporters of the Republican president, rather than as the body keeping the executive in check. Partisanship was further fueled by broader changes in American politics. For example, the expansion of cable television (and the decline of national news broadcasting) and internet punditry allowed for the development of niche news outlets that were exclusive to party-political extremes. As Mann and Ornstein describe, 'there is a reinforcement that the only dialogue in the country is between polarized left and right, and that the alternative is cynical public relations with no convictions at all' (Mann and Ornstein, 2012: 71). Additionally, the gerrymandering of congressional districts through the re-districting process (where changing demographics require new electoral boundaries) has meant increasing difficulty for meaningful challenges to incumbent members of Congress (though probably overstated as a cause of growing polarization) (Mann and Ornstein, 2012: 143–7). An increasing partisanship had also begun to see Congress more as part of a national movement rather than a group representing individual constituencies, contributing to Congress losing its identity.

The dictates of electoral politics are also impelling members of Congress to spend more time campaigning and less time doing potentially harmful or irrelevant oversight activities ('harmful' or 'irrelevant', that is, for their electoral futures) – a magnification of the 'electoral connection': an approach to congressional behavior stressing the predominant focus of congressional members as being on re-election (e.g. Mayhew, 1977). Along these lines, foreign policy was never an area that meant much for the electoral prospects of members of Congress, seen in how the congressional committees involved with foreign policy issues were rarely where the power was. Committees such as Appropriations – dealing with expenditures and budgeting – have been more influential for the members' re-election prospects.

Finally, the problems of filibustering (where a 60-vote majority is required to stop debate over an issue) in the Senate have reached a point where almost every controversial vote needs a 60-vote 'supermajority' to pass. The character of the filibuster had also changed, in that the majority of these actions have been done as *threats* to filibuster, rather than the now old-fashioned practice of talking for hours on the Senate floor as a means of stalling a vote on an issue (Klein, 2013). The result of these practices has been a growing inability to get anything done in the Senate. Overall, despite the attempts of Congress to regain its relevance in the 1970s and 80s, shifts in politics had made it increasingly negligent.

However, other observers think that such a case is overstated. Howell and Pevehouse (2005; 2007) argue that partisan politics has always been the crucial factor explaining robust congressional oversight: that when an opposition party is in the majority in Congress, more oversight and contestation occurs. They further argue that this has consequences for controversial actions, such as the use of force: presidents use force 45 per cent more often during periods of unified government (Howell and Pevehouse, 2005: 222). Lindsay (2003) has further noted that 'deference and defiance' in Congress tends to be directly related to the existence of external threats, arguing that Congress is most deferential to the executive when the nation sees itself as being threatened externally. Lindsay therefore provides a complementary explanation for the Republican Congress' support for Bush policies: not just partisan politics, but also the context of 9/11.

Overall, despite the president's resources, there still remains a balance in the control of foreign policy. While presidents get the most attention (for both failures and successes), Congress is still crucial in setting the context for what presidents are able to do, and has the ability to monitor the results of policy. Overall, power remains dispersed to a certain extent, despite the increasing presidential power over foreign policy. It is increasingly difficult to get business done in Washington (especially with a divided government), and the ability of Congress to curtail initiatives by the White House is a fundamental factor in understanding American power in the world.

The Foreign Policy Bureaucracy

The relationship between Congress and the president in the making of foreign policy is further structured by how policy gets made and implemented. The policy-making environment has important ramifications for understanding the powers and limits of particular actors in the foreign policy process. As many have argued (e.g. Allison and Zelikow, 1999; Clapp, Halperin and Kanter, 2007; cf. Wilson, 1991), foreign policy is made in circumstances that are highly constrained by pre-existing bureaucracies with their attendant staffs and ways of working, as well as the heads of agencies and committees who tend to argue for the interests of their organizations. The broader constraints of bureaucratic power need to be accounted for when looking at the foreign policy process.

While the president's control of the main foreign policy bureaucracies in the executive branch is a substantial source of power, it also has limitations. The analysis of foreign policy-making within the US has long noted the limits set by bureaucracies. While incoming presidents select staff at the top level of the executive branch (mainly for cabinet heads and assistants), underneath this thin layer exists a vast bureaucratic staff. While the hope is always that the staff of executive branch bureaucracies will be loyal to whichever president is in charge, the fact is that presidents only have limited influence in shaping the cultures of large bureaucracies (Allison and Zelikow, 1999: ch. 3; cf. Welch, 1992). For example, the

Department of Defense is a large organization that is resistant to change, not necessarily for partisan political reasons, but because those working there have particular traditions and operating procedures that they have utilized for a long time, which means that even the most radical new secretaries struggle to impose change from the top. Such problems can be seen in Secretary of Defense Donald Rumsfeld's attempt to 'transform' the military, which turned into a battle within the department, particularly over the conduct of the Iraq War.

Such cultural differences can also create real tensions between departments. For example, the Departments of State and Defense have very different views of the world, and on how the US should respond to threats. These tensions can cause difficulty for the president, especially if unclear about what the best approach might be to a specific issue, or even an overall grand strategy. For example, in the 1962 Cuban Missile Crisis, the military advocated invasion (with Secretary of Defense Robert McNamara in favor of a blockade) and State diplomacy, with the military trying to push President Kennedy towards more aggressive options. Such tensions also occurred in debates about the war against Iraq in 2003, with Secretary of State Colin Powell arguing against military action, and other figures (e.g. Vice-President Dick Cheney, Secretary of Defense Donald Rumsfeld) making the case for military action. More recently, the Obama Administration has had internal fractures over what to do about Iranian attempts to obtain nuclear weapons, the support of rebel forces in Libya, and in regard to the raid in Pakistan which killed Osama bin Laden (J. Mann, 2012; Singh, 2012). However, bureaucratic views are not always constant, or not always what they might appear. While one would expect the military to be more prone to military options, post-Vietnam War, the military has been reluctant to use force where interests are not at stake (or not clear), or where war is not clearly winnable.

In addition to having their own particular cultures, heads of bureaucracies can also have their own political agendas, particularly when funding or preserving their distinct identity is involved (Allison and Zelikow, 1999: ch. 5). For example, the plans over defense reorganization after World War II were contested by the Department of the Navy, because they thought centralization would affect their tradition of independent thought, while the army (as part of the Department of War) saw centralization as desirable, as they would become more central to the structure of decision-making.

There were additional battles over who would control the newly developed airforce, and, later on, clashes over the share of the defense budget (Hogan, 1998). These debates were not primarily made in terms of what would best serve the national interest (though of course such notions were part of the broader debate), but rather premised on organizations fighting for turf (e.g. Zegart, 1999). Department officials also maintain and develop their own links with Capitol Hill and outside government, further complicating their relationship to the president. The 'iron triangle' – links between bureaucrats, law-makers and lobbyists – and the 'military-industrial complex' (to be discussed in Chapter 4) are often accounted for in this context, demonstrating other dimensions of power that influence foreign policy-making from within the US state.

The NSC adds a further dimension to issues of inter-bureaucratic and intra-executive branch relations. The NSC was set up in 1947 to better integrate civilian-military planning of security matters. It is made up of three key groups: statutory principals (president, vice-president, Secretary of State, Secretary of Defense); statutory advisors (Chairman of the Joint Chiefs of Staff; Director of the CIA); and a professional staff that provides policy documents and serves the council. The 'National Security Advisor', who oversees the direction of the council, ties all of this together. While originally just intended as a secretary to oversee the smooth running of the council, over time, as presidents used the council to do more and more, the position took on great significance. The formal council itself was meant to be a non-partisan place to coordinate national security, with the staff drawn from an inter-departmental pool, providing non-partisan information. However, over time, this changed, as the formal council decreased in importance, while the staff became an in-house foreign policy-making advisory body within the White House itself (meaning the Office of the President) (Destler, 1981; Nelson, 1981).

The people who have filled the role of National Security Advisor have also helped to push the NSC in various directions, from a minimal approach in its early years, to being more thoroughly engaged with policy formulation (e.g. McGeorge Bundy, Henry Kissinger, Zbigniew Brzezinski), to profoundly interventionist (Robert McFarlane, John Poindexter), and back again (Sandy Berger, Condoleezza Rice) (Daalder and Destler, 2009). Despite the prominence, both public and institutional, of the National Security Advisor, Amy Zegart (1999) has argued that the institutionalization of the NSC Staff as a key source of foreign policy-making advice has been of far more importance than the degree of advocacy taken by particular National Security Advisors. The staff is like other elements of the civil service, and often carries over from previous administrations. The rise of the NSC should be seen as one way in which successive presidents have brought foreign policy making power directly into the White House, and much more under their control than if it was all done through negotiations with State and Defense. As such, the power of the president over foreign policy-making has been enhanced through these efforts of centralization (and perhaps getting around some of the checks and balances intended by the founders).

Overall, the bureaucracy that gives the president large power resources can also be a source of inertia and conflict for reaching or even deciding on foreign policy goals. Chapter 4 will look further into the ways in which national security has taken up a prominent role in US foreign policy since 1945. Even within government, the Department of Defense has strong institutional power for pursuing its agenda, through the budget and links to Congress and industry. The final point also highlights the importance of outside sources to US foreign policy, to which we now turn.

Societal influences on foreign policy-making

While the formal processes of foreign policy-making are important parts of political power, broader societal influences also matter. While the contours of military, economic and ideological power crucially intertwine with the political in setting contexts and limits for foreign policy-making (as outlined in the first section), there are also other factors that are to some extent particular to the American political scene. The perceived pluralism or openness of the US system has allowed for other access points to policy influence. While organized interest groups were long seen as important to policy formation, increasing emphasis has also been put on the role of the media and public opinion as important for thinking about policy-making.

During the Cold War, the rise of presidential power and a broad consensus on foreign policy meant that there was little scope for influence from outside sources. Though the Vietnam War somewhat fractured this consensus and made the policy-making environment more complicated for presidents, the power that the executive branch had still made foreign policy resistant to outside sources. However, the end of the Cold War and the end of a clear consensus on main US foreign policy goals increased the possibility for outside influence. When combined with an increasing potential for Congress to influence the foreign policy process through shifts in procedure and greater use of congressional review, the longer-term goals of foreign policy were seen as being potentially more and more influenced (if not dominated) by outside forces (McCormick, 1998).

Interest groups

Organized interest groups play a prominent part in American politics and American foreign policy. Such groups are basically groups of citizens who organize themselves into pressure groups (e.g. Berry, 1989). These groups conform to ideas about the 'pluralism' of the American political system, meaning that the system has a variety of inputs, not all of which come from the direct elections of politicians. Departments of the executive branch regularly meet with groups to help formulate positions on various issues, and they also impact on election campaigning through financing. Similarly, interest groups have been very influential on Congress, through campaign funding and lobbying over legislation. Interest groups dealing with foreign policy issues come from a variety of different areas. Many emerge from business interests, and they seek to influence various aspects of trade and energy policy, or from defense contractors who want to guide specific defense procurement decisions (which are related to foreign policy and defense goals). Many of these groups straddle the international/domestic divide, in that it is not always clear which sphere their influence is meant to fit into. For example, pro-business lobbying organizations, such as the Chamber of Commerce, try to influence foreign economic policy regarding free trade, but they also deal with many domestic policy areas, like taxation and business regulation. Much of the recent attention to interest groups in foreign policy-making has been focused on so-called 'ethnic' lobbies, and it has been highlighted that such groups can potentially influence decision-making within Congress.

A core question of the interest group literature has been how those groups actually influence foreign policy. While it is clear that factors such as the strength of their organization, their insider status, and the specific kinds of lobbying engaged in are all important, the actual causal influence is harder to establish (Paul and Paul, 2008; cf. Smith, 2000). Furthermore, while interest groups have a large impact on the formulation of domestic policy, their impact on foreign policy is much more debatable. Even in relative financial terms, it can be seen that the money put towards domestic policy lobbying dwarfs foreign policy lobbying. In 2010, lobbying organizations spent $193,652,793 combined on issues clearly related to foreign policy (this figure, derived from data from the Center for Responsive Politics, combines the defense sector and single-issue groups focusing on Israel, human rights, and foreign and defense policy – OpenSecrets (2012)). In comparison, the health industry spent $508,584,334, and the US Chamber of Commerce alone spent $132,067,500. While this shows us that other interests spend more on lobbying, this does not tell us much about the level of influence.

A key problem when discussing lobbies concerns how we can measure influence. Is it the case that certain foreign policy positions are taken up just because of lobby pressure, or because lobbies are already 'pushing against an open door', in that policy-makers were already inclined towards the policy, and lobbies just helped push it along? However, it has also been argued that interest groups need a way to actually access the government, or as Haney and Vanderbush put it, they 'must be able to find the door, whether it is open or not' (1999: 345). Access is therefore important, and developing links with Congress is vital for lobby groups to have any sort of influence. Furthermore, what the literature has fairly clearly established is that lobby influence is greater when protecting the status quo: it is much more difficult to change policy than to push for the continuation of an already existent policy (Paul and Paul, 2008: 9).

To illustrate these issues, we can examine two prominent 'ethnic' lobby groups: the Cuban American National Foundation (CANF) and the American Israel Public Affairs Committee (AIPAC). Both groups have very strong and influential organizations designed to put their views forward to members of Congress, as well as provide funding for election campaigns, amongst other efforts to secure influence. CANF provides an excellent example of how such organizations can be influential in foreign policy, but also shows the complications in mapping influence. Was CANF an outside group that managed to shift the policy preferences of government, or was its role more convoluted? Haney and Vanderbush (1999) note a real influence of the Reagan Administration on the actual creation of CANF, which points to not only the existence of an organization that supported a policy shift (though part of a grand strategy of containment) that Reagan was trying to push through, but also the creation of a civil society group to support that policy. While the group was very successful in the 1980s, it also points to the problematic legacies of such groups: that as they gain power, they become very hard to dislodge from the policy process, even when governments may desire change. The Helms-Burton Act of 1996, which formalized a long series of presidential embargos on Cuba, is often seen as a strong example of the influence of the Cuban–American lobby, in that despite the post-Cold War context, a Cold War-style policy continued against Cuba (additionally, the law, signed by President Clinton, was seen as a way of Congress asserting its power over Cuba policy). However, the limited role of CANF in drafting the actual policy, and the ways in which various provisions were undermined by presidential prerogatives (often with the support of Congress) also show that the influence of interest groups is not always clear (Brenner, et al., 2002). Though the Cuban–American lobby is still influential through congressional representatives that represent large constituencies of Cuban-Americans (particularly in Florida), the decreasing strategic importance of Cuba and increasing influence of economic foreign policy has created a growing fragmentation in support of an embargo on Cuba.

AIPAC is probably both the best-known foreign affairs lobby group, and often seen as the most influential. Since the 1980s, AIPAC has become one of the largest lobbying groups in Washington, and US military aid to Israel is the largest for any country, presently at around $3 billion per year. AIPAC is particularly influential, most obviously, in attempting to shape US policy towards the Middle East, and especially policy towards Israel, including military aid and initiatives regarding Palestinian–Israeli relations. AIPAC's policy has mainly been to ensure that the US supports Israeli policy (and Israel more generally), but it has been seen (by some) in recent years to be more and more consistent with more intransigent elements of the American (and Israeli) right (examples in Edsall and Moore, 2004). In fact, some have taken this to demonstrate that AIPAC itself is a peculiarly *American* political movement that lines up with numerous elements of neo-conservatism (and its support of Likud policies), and rather badly reflects the diversity of foreign policy debates within Israel itself (e.g. Levy, 2006). As such, like CANF, AIPAC should not be seen as consistently conforming to the beliefs of all American supporters of Israel, but has a set of views that has become fairly narrowly in line with particular US and Israeli policies (and potentially in conflict with other US pro-Israel interest groups that advocate different policies;

which groups such as the Israel Policy Forum and Americans for Peace Now have in the past).

The recent publication of the article and book 'The Israel Lobby' by International Relations scholars John Mearsheimer and Stephen Walt brought the controversy of AIPAC (and beyond) back into prominence (Mearsheimer and Walt, 2006; 2007). The fundamental point of the piece was about the effectiveness and pragmatism of US policy towards Israel. The authors contended that the US gets little in return for its support of Israel, and that policy-makers had allowed the national interest to be twisted by lobbying, and as such skewed the possibilities of a more rational and realistic policy towards Israel and the Middle East. Mearsheimer and Walt's piece raised important questions (and a very heated debate) concerning the influence of lobbies on foreign policy-making, both in terms of how they actually operate and, to the extent that they are effective, how they may potentially adversely affect US foreign policy.

In terms of the former issue, many have criticized Mearsheimer and Walt for their account of lobby influence (e.g. Lieberman, 2009; Mead, 2007), especially for overstating the cohesiveness of the lobby and for their account of causality. Leaving the former issue aside by exclusively focusing in AIPAC (therefore also conceding the accuracy of the critique), we can see that the critics raise an important general question about how lobby groups actually influence government. Like the example of CANF above, in terms of causal influence, the question of whether or not AIPAC is pushing against an 'open door' is important. Furthermore, explaining lobby influence needs to be able to explain variation: i.e. are similar policies followed in the absence of lobbying? The US has seen support of Israel as an important strategic goal since the late 1960s, especially since the 1967 Six Day War. Lieberman (2009) has also noted that it is difficult to explain other pro-Israeli policies (such as the recognition of the state of Israel in 1948) that were initiated when AIPAC did not even exist. It was noted above that lobbies tend to be more effective in protecting the status quo, and that is precisely what groups like AIPAC attempt to do. As James Lindsay notes, 'The Jewish [sic] lobby succeeds partly because it is pushing on an open door – it advocates policies that most Americans favor on the merits. Israel is a stable, pro-Western democracy in a region where governments are often unstable, autocratic, and anti-American' (Lindsay, 2002). Lobby groups tend to be quite effective when the issue is one that has an obvious resonance with American symbols, and Lieberman (2009:

242) has noted that American public opinion, though fluctuating in line with individual events, had in the main been very supportive of Israel.

Questions about influence can also be raised when examining interest groups that are not given as much attention in the political science literature. For example, despite wide-ranging claims of the importance of the oil industry in influencing the decision to go to war in Iraq in 2003, very little of the political science literature on interest groups has examined the link (or links between business and foreign policy-making more generally). However, it is clear that business lobbies that focus on petroleum and energy have long petitioned Congress for influence. In terms of lobbying money, energy and natural resources lobbies spent $434,906,114 in 2010 to promote their interests to government. As with ethnic lobbies, it is hard to find the exact causality between influence and policy outcomes in this case, especially in a domestic environment explicitly structured to be pro-business (in terms of the ideals of economic growth and competitiveness). As Ran Goel has noted, 'whereas the executive furnishes the political, military and, to a lesser extent, economic elements necessary for the industry's international oil exploitation, production and transportation functions, the US oil industry is a foreign policy stalwart due to its technology, capital and long-standing submission to foreign policy objectives' (2004: 482). The oil and energy industry does not need to just spend money to influence, as there exists a broader interest in supporting the desires of industry, inasmuch as it aligns with both strategic goals and the desires of a broader domestic constituency, such as the desire of automotive manufacturers to keep up consumption rates and for consumers to lead lifestyles that support consumption.

All of this suggests that the relationship between interest groups and foreign policy is more complicated than it may seem, and difficult to measure outside the broader context of foreign policy-making and American political culture. Well-organized and financed lobbies seem to be potentially successful in keeping interests on the agenda and preventing policy reversals, and, once created, are hard to dislodge from the policy process unless strong competing interests develop. As noted above, interest groups often reflect broader cultural trends, and are not easily ascribed to lobbying influence. The real question may be whether or not interest groups can ever go beyond a broad consensus in American society (and culture) in advocating particular policies. The influence and existence of lobby groups demonstrates both the importance of the pluralism of the American state and the entwining of economic power and the political.

The media, public opinion and foreign policy

In the US (as in other liberal democracies) the media has been seen as crucial in its role as a watchdog of government. A free media was part of the vision of American pluralism, with the freedom of the press enshrined in the First Amendment of the Constitution. In the 1990s, the advent of 24-hour cable news changed the perception of what news media could do: from the role of CNN and other outlets potentially setting government agenda (the so-called 'CNN effect'), to the decline of objectivity found in Fox News' coverage of the Iraq War, the media had become much more influential as a mediator and creator of ideas, rather than just as a check on government power (e.g. Kull, Ramsay and Lewis, 2003/04). Starting with the first Gulf War, the 1990s and beyond have also seen tighter and tighter management of the media by presidents: from press conferences to embedded media in war.

Changes in the character of the media still leave us with a fundamental problem: how can we analyse the influence of the media on US foreign policy making and American power? Robinson (2008; cf. Jacobs and Page, 2005; Baum and Potter, 2008) has helpfully categorized theories of media influence into two main groupings: pluralist theories versus elite theories. Pluralist theories are those that broadly acknowledge the role of the media as a critical force in US politics, which provides a way for the public to receive information about the world unmediated by government influence. As such, the media in this view has the potential to influence public opinion in ways that potentially make government more responsive to criticism and alternative perspectives on policy. This is not necessarily to say that independent media influence always provides the best policy options, but that an independent media can have real influence that needs to be responded to by policy-makers. By contrast, the elite model sees the media as constrained by broader structural forces in the American state. Here, the media is seen to support the views of the elite, either by reflecting a broad social consensus of appropriate action at the elite level, or in the sense that journalists themselves are part of an elite consensus on foreign policy, and must report the variety of view provided by elite opinion. This view is not that elites necessarily consciously set the agenda, but that there are structural impediments to dissent (Herman and Chomsky, 1994; cf. Hallin, 1986).

However, there is also a need to situate the media more broadly in US society. As with thinking about the role of interest groups, it is not clear how analytically useful it is to separate the media from other debates about the sources of US foreign policy (Jacobs and Page, 2005; Baum and Potter, 2008). As Herring and Robinson (2003) note, the academic literature is fairly consistent in demonstrating that the pluralist model does not hold up to scrutiny. As such, we do need to situate the media's power in the broader dynamics of power within American society. Herman and Chomsky's manufacturing consent model, though not without problems, situates the media's influence over government policy within the issue of corporate concentration of the media and its role as an industry; i.e. that the media can shut out critical voices which would upset advertisers. It therefore contextualizes the media in a broader framework of power relations within society that are crucial for understanding foreign policy and the internal dynamics of US power more generally.

An argument can be made that all of the theories rather underestimate the public. Both sets of theories see the public as an entirely passive register, as if people believe everything they hear, and are uncritical of the information that they receive. The role of public opinion in foreign policy making is therefore in many ways the 'flip side' of looking at the media's role. While theories of the influence of public opinion as examined by political scientists tend to be isolated from that of the role of the media (Jacobs and Page, 2005; Baum and Potter, 2008; cf. Knecht and Weatherford, 2006), public opinion does play a crucial mediating role between the public at large and the government, and as such is important in thinking about the links between the media, public opinion and policy-making. In elite foreign policy circles, there is still a sense that foreign policy is too important, and too complicated, to be left to the 'average' citizen. While election campaigns and other major policy-making events are heavily scrutinized by the media and constant polling (by both the media and government) to see how issues will play out politically, foreign policy has often been shielded from such scrutiny. However, it is obvious that foreign policy is also not entirely absent from the whims of public opinion, especially clear in terms of public dissatisfaction with American military engagements abroad, which have consistently been difficult for policy-makers (Kovach, 1996; Sobel,

2001). For example, public support for the Vietnam War waned over time, as the possibility of anything resembling a victory for the US declined, and the numbers of American soldiers being killed and wounded increased. The 2003 Iraq War has come under similar scrutiny, and was certainly an important factor in both the 2006 midterm elections and the 2008 presidential election (Baum and Potter, 2008).

Overall, these broad societal influences on the policy process need to be seen in a larger context. They form a part of the pluralism of the US state, but such pluralism is heavily mediated by other sources of power, and particularly the economic and military. While the ideal of pluralism opens up the government and state, the possibilities for action are constrained by the limits of formal government power over foreign policy, entrenched elite interests, ideology (that will be further examined in Chapter 6), and the influence of economic and military institutions (further discussed in Chapters 4 and 5).

Conclusion

Control over foreign policy is a contested power within the American state, shaped by governmental actors to be sure, but including a variety of other interests and structures that shape, constrain and influence the making of foreign policy. In sum, understanding the resources the president can draw on through the prescribed constitutional powers of the office, and through the bureaucracy that exists within the executive branch, as well as the constraints that these very same institutions give, is essential to understanding US foreign policy and American power in the world. However, the variety of actors, the structures of power, and discourse within the state, also limit and give context to American power and the specific foreign policies that presidents formulate.

It is clear that there are difficulties for the future of political power in projecting US interests. The fracturing of elite consensus has been seen both over the long-term problems of the wars in Iraq and Afghanistan, and in the fallout from the 2007/08 financial crisis. Furthermore, shifts in the political landscape have meant that the contestation over these and other issues have begun to impact on the ability of presidents and Congress to agree on anything, much less create new policy and laws. The long-term effects of these issues are hard to determine, as the US has faced such crises before, but perhaps will be leading to some sort of realignment of political power. The election of Barack Obama to the presidency in 2008 was certainly one part of this, but the reaction in the congressional elections of 2010 was further partisanship, and a presidential-congressional relationship that looked even more fractious than the previous Congress. The rise of the 'Tea Party' movement as an important faction of the Republican Party was a major part of the increased partisanship in 2010 (and a real part of the success of the Republicans in taking back the House of Representatives), but has also led to more division in American political culture. The tense relationship between the re-elected Barack Obama and the 2013 Congress (and especially the Republican-led House) demonstrates that these relations will be an important issue in the future of American power.

Chapter 4

The Evolution of Military Power: An American Way of War?

American military power is a crucial part of its global reach. The US has the largest military spending of any country in the world, outspending the next ten biggest spenders combined (IISS, 2011). The defense budget for fiscal year (FY) 2011 was approximately $687 billion, including some $160 billion for 'overseas contingency operations' (OCO), mainly for the wars in Iraq and Afghanistan. The FY2012 budget was down to $645 billion, due to the decreased funding to such operations (with the FY2013 request down even further to $613.9 billion – with OCO down to $88.5) (White House, 2012a; cf. United States Department of Defense, 2012a). This spending goes not only to staff costs, but also to arming and equipping what is by far the most technologically advanced military in the world. That the US has managed since the start of the Cold War, when high peacetime military spending and a permanent large peacetime military was first established, to do this while only spending between 5 and 10 per cent of GDP on defense also shows very starkly the interlinking of economic and military power.

That such preponderance in military power has been a crucial part of US power and influence in the world is undisputed, but there is much contention over the actual role of US military power. Military power is probably the most distilled sort of compulsory power, as in its essence – the ability to use and threaten the use of violence – it is about power *over*. The controversy about the use of military power therefore certainly stems from the perceived abuses of American military power. The relationship between the US and military power is one of much fascination, that is often hindered by a simplistic view of America as a peculiarly militaristic nation. While it is certainly true that the Cold War placed an increasing emphasis on military power as a key aspect of national security (and an increasing institutionalization of militarism in the state), such a focus was contentious at the time, as US republican political traditions had been against both the centralization of power and the existence of standing armies in peacetime, which were seen as potential enemies of liberty.

However reluctant the US has been in embracing a more militarized state, the use of force has been a long entrenched part of US foreign policy, and its development as the pre-eminent international power after the Cold War has been a part of this tradition. The 'imperial' adventures of the US during the late nineteenth and early twentieth centuries demonstrated little hesitation to promote US interests abroad through the use of force (but use of economic power to coerce, through policies like 'dollar diplomacy' was also pronounced), a trend continued in many ways by various Cold War overseas interventions and beyond. However, much of the supposed continuities belie changes in the purpose behind the use of force, and the actual efficacy of military power itself. As US policy-makers have found, it has become very difficult to convert military power easily into political goals (adding to the problems found in examining only the compulsory side of US military power). For example, while the US military very clearly holds an overwhelming deterrent function against other states (there is little likelihood of a serious interstate attack on the US homeland), the US military has been surprisingly ineffective at 'winning' wars against presumably weaker opponents in Iraq and Afghanistan.

The use of force to defend the homeland as opposed to the use of force abroad also has developed very different normative connotations in the international system (especially the de-legitimation of offensive war as a justifiable form of foreign policy), which further makes the use of force a challenging political issue. One of the key trends in international relations post-World War II has been institutionalizing norms of non-aggression and limiting the potential abuse of military power in the international system, institutions of which the US has been a key backer. The measure of power in military terms therefore should not just be seen in quantitative or qualitative comparisons between national militaries, but also inherent in the kinds of political goals that militaries are meant to have. If the projection of military power is mainly seen as a way of protecting US homeland security (however defined), it has tangibly different goals from efforts at nation-building. The conceptualization of military power therefore links up with the general debates about US power discussed previously. For realists especially, US preponderance in military power should lead to real compulsory power for the US in international relations, but various problems have beset the actual use of force for expansive political goals.

We need also to further entrench military power in the power debates, looking at ways in which it also is embedded institutionally in the international system, but also at the structural role it plays in backing US power. Additionally, military power has played an important constitutive role domestically, and what also needs investigation is how the militarization of US society and politics has often led towards military solutions to political problems, an overselling of the potential of military force, and the role of the civil–military relations in causing potential difficulties for the future of US power. While the use of the military abroad will be discussed, the domestic organization and constitution of the armed forces and military power is important for understanding both the history of US military power and the internal dynamics which better explain the specific characteristics of US military power. The chapter examines the development of military power in the US, highlighting the persistent theme of anti-militarism, and especially how such traditions were effectively abandoned in the Cold War period. The international role of military power in the Cold War is also covered in-depth, especially focusing on military interventions, as well as highlighting the institutional and structural dimensions of military power. Finally, the chapter examines civil–military relations in more detail, highlighting the impact of military power on domestic society. The chapter concludes with some reflections on the future challenges for US military power, especially in light of the Obama Administration's move away from the interventionary wars of the Bush era.

The development of military power

National defense is one of the most important goals of US foreign policy. However, in the development of military power, the US is by no means special: the establishment of national militaries has been a constant in modern states in the international system, both for reasons of defense, and potentially for the 'usefulness' of coercive power outside their borders. The means by which the national defense is undertaken can vary, and has also been contested by domestic social forces. American use of military power abroad has been a prevalent feature of US foreign policy. From the 'Undeclared' Naval War against France starting in 1798 to the 2011 intervention in Libya and continuing 'drone' attacks in Pakistan, Somalia and

Yemen today, the US has never been reluctant to use force when it seemed appropriate to achieve its goals. The variety of military engagements the US has had is very important, and it should be noted that a list of such uses of force over the past two hundred years would be very long indeed (see Grimmett, 2010). However, the circumstances of these different uses of force are also significant, both in terms of the international context and the goals of these interventions. Nevertheless, while particular interventions are important in their own right, what is the most interesting factor in military *power* concerns the domestic sources of this power, especially for thinking about the role of military power in American society and its influence on power projection more generally.

When the War of Independence ended in 1783 the Continental Army and small Navy were disbanded in accordance with a belief against standing armies. This initial move was characteristic of the anti-militarism that was to become a core theme in US political history. However, it also left the new nation under the Articles of Confederation powerless to have an effective national defense. At least part of the rationale behind the 1787 Constitutional Convention concerned national defense, including some sort of national military. However, despite the strong arguments provided by federalists like Alexander Hamilton (the *Federalist Papers* have some particularly good articulations of these arguments: see e.g. Madison et al., 1987: no. 23), the eventual ratification of the Constitution in 1788 did not lead to any substantial expansion of the armed forces. The continued distrust of military institutions, added to the financial weakness of the US, left little ability to plan for extensive military operations (Weigley, 1977). The Congress authorized the creation of a small navy and army (and the Departments of War and Navy, in 1789 and 1792 respectively), and the construction of forts on the frontiers of the US. State militias supplemented the army, and privateers supplemented the navy.

However, the relative peace of the 1780s was disrupted by the end of the decade by the French Revolution, which threatened war between the great powers of Europe that could again potentially envelop the North American continent. France and Britain would also increasingly threaten American interests, as would the Barbary Pirates in the Mediterranean. Native American tribes on the Western frontier of the new state also posed a perceived military threat. Due to the threats facing the early US and it own limitations, early military strategy was much more premised on defense, and even by the time of the Napoleonic Wars, not much had been done to think of military power in grander terms. As Weigley notes, 'the military policy of the United States prepared the country for little more than a strategy of passive defense against any adversary stronger than the Indian tribes' (1977: 46). The War of 1812 against Great Britain began to change American attitudes to military power. While the US was successful in preserving the status quo (no mean feat against one of the world's great powers and the premier naval power), it suffered a series of defeats that also made its leaders rethink the role of the military. As Porter argues, 'the War of 1812 and the War with Mexico exposed similar systemic weaknesses of the American state: sectional cleavages, an ill-prepared military force, a weak national Administration unequal to the task of mobilising forces or governing its vast territory when violence threatened' (1994: 255).

The reasonable success in the War of 1812 did help to galvanize the nation. It showed that the US was capable of defending itself against the predations of Europe, and also saw the end of a period of intense European interference with the US (Herring, 2009: 131–3). The US then embarked on a more aggressive foreign policy, mainly focused on western expansion. Though much of the westward expansion was done through savvy diplomatic and financial dealing, it also had a crucial military side, in continued wars with the Native population and Mexico. As discussed in Chapter 1, the Louisiana Purchase, completed with France in 1803, gave vast swathes of land in the center of the continent, and additional acquisitions were made for Florida (ceded by Spain by 1819, partially due to US military adventurism), Texas (annexed in 1845, which was a key cause of the US–Mexico War of 1846–48), the Oregon territory in the northwest (in 1846) and the territories from the west of Texas to the Pacific coast as a result of the war with Mexico (completed in 1848). By 1850, the US claimed possession of lands stretching from the Atlantic to the Pacific.

The latter half of the nineteenth century saw two major wars that each in their own way transformed the character of US military power. The first and most crucial was the American Civil War of 1861 to 1865. The war was a transformative moment in US politics and state-building, not only changing the internal dynamics of the state – ending the slave economy in the South – but also consolidating national power, which had been still very much in the hands of the various states (see e.g. Bensel, 1990; Foner, 1988; Skowronek, 1982). In many ways the war solidified US military power, through a post-war strengthening of the state, showing the potential for massive state intervention into society, and through the experience of what was one of the first truly industrialized wars. The substantial mobilization of men and materiel for the war, the Union side alone fielding 1 million soldiers, up from a peacetime level of 16,000 in the US Army, showed the dramatic potential of US military power through state mobilization (Porter, 1994: 258). As William McNeill points out, the war eventually was seen as a precursor to World War I, 'as the first full-fledged example of an industrialized war, in which machine-made arms dictated new, defensive tactics, while railroads competed with waterways as arteries of supply for millions of armed men' (McNeill, 1982: 242). Although the military was demobilized rapidly at the end of the war, the increase in state power and military experience was important for the future of US military power.

The second major event was the war with Spain in 1898. While the war was not nearly on the level of the Civil War, it began an era of increased expansionism and calls for (and some protests against) a more direct imperialism. The war also saw an increase in direct intervention in the affairs of other states in the Americas. While certainly not unprecedented, these interventions became much more allied with a sense of empire, resulting in continued military interventions in Cuba, Nicaragua, the Dominican Republic, Haiti, Honduras, Mexico and further afield in the Philippines and China. As such the reluctant militarism of the early republic had been succeeded by a more aggressive and expansionist America, in many ways seeking to emulate its European predecessors and rivals. However, it should be noted that there were strong debates within the US about the uses and abuses of US military power abroad – mainly in the guise of an anti-imperial rhetoric – to the extent that they even impinged on the 1900 presidential elections. William Jennings Bryan, the Democratic candidate (and later Secretary of State for Woodrow Wilson), ran on an explicitly anti-imperialist platform, critical of the US war in the Philippines (Mayers, 2007: ch. 8).

While the early part of the twentieth century prior to World War I was defined by William McKinley and Theodore Roosevelt's more aggressive and militaristic nationalism, US entry into World War I changed the image of US military power. The 'style' of military engagement during the war became much more predicated on the liberal internationalist values of President Woodrow Wilson. The US was drawn into the war by the increasing intransigence of Imperial Germany, particularly seen in the sinking of the Lusitania in 1915 (an unarmed passenger ship) which turned many Americans against Germany, and the move by Germany to unrestricted submarine warfare in the Atlantic and the 1917 Zimmerman Telegram (a German proposal asking Mexico to make war with the US). President Wilson was able to set a pretext for US involvement: that World War I would be a war to end all wars (or as Wilson put it, a 'war to make the world safe for democracy'), and the result would be a change to the balance of power politics that had preceded it (see e.g. Knock, 1995). The use of US military power in this instance had a goal beyond just protecting immediate US interests: it was a plan to remake the world.

The US intervention was highly successful in bringing the war to an end, demonstrating the growing importance and effectiveness of US power. The legacy of war for the military as an institution was not dissimilar to the aftermath of the Civil War. The war again proved the capacity of the American state to mobilize for war, but again demobilized soon after. As Sherry notes, 'just as impressive as the speed with which Americans plunged into World War I and divined its meanings was the rapidity with which they discarded much of its legacy' (1995: 9). The interwar period began to see the start of debates about the organization of American military power that would become influential after World War II. The organization of the Departments of War and Navy in separate Cabinet Departments, along with a Department of State dealing with foreign affairs, meant there was little coordination between departments. As war was seen as an aberration that the US would mobilize for when needed (other than for 'minor' imperial adventures), the lack of coordination over peacetime strategy was ignored for many years. However, the inter-departmental strategy never worked effectively, and military and political decisions often reached the White House separately, and the president ended up having to weigh the differences between political and military objectives in order to form some sort of coherence. Though experiences in World War I and reforms to all three executive departments increased some desire for consultation, much proposed went nowhere (May, 1955).

If the pursuit of WWI was itself a success, the resulting peace conference was less successful. President Wilson's core proposal for a new, peaceful international system, embodied in the League of Nations, was left ineffectual due to the lack of US involvement: the US Senate refused to ratify the Versailles Treaty, partially due to traditional partisan politics, but also to do with real concerns that the treaty would override Congress' right to declare war in favor of that of an international organization (Fisher, 2004: 82–3). The result was a more inward-looking US: that despite growing power in the world, the US was still affected by traditional anti-militarism and a lack of interest in being involved in what were seen as European problems. The onset of economic crisis inaugurated by the 1929 Wall Street crash only increased such tendencies. However, the inwardness can be overstated. The US also was active diplomatically in numerous attempts to put limits on international militarism, such as through the Washington Naval Conference of 1921–22 (which helped end the naval arms race between the great powers) and the signing of the 1928 Kellogg-Briand Pact outlawing aggressive (i.e. non-defensive) war. As Sherry has further noted, the US obsession with both private initiative and technology led to an *alternative* arms race, that was led more by Americans' fascination with developing new technology and reflecting on how that technology would insulate them from war: 'in that fashion, the progress of American armaments between the world wars seemed indicative more of bygone virtues and peace-loving impulses than new terrors and challenges' (Sherry, 1995: 11).

The obsession with technology can clearly be seen in the increasing focus on airpower as a key instrument of war. While aircraft had been used in WWI, the interwar period saw much debate and fascination with the potential for airpower. Airpower was seen as being a potentially devastating strategic weapon that would be able to single-handedly stop war through wreaking havoc on cities. It also had the advantage (as seen by both the US and Great Britain) of being more cost-effective than having large standing armies and more in line with traditions of anti-militarism (Biddle, 2002). Such ideas became prominent in the US through crusaders such as aviator Billy Mitchell (drawing on ideas of Italian theorist Guilio Douhet), and eventually provided some inspiration for the doctrine of the US Army Air Corps, and the background for American strategic bombing in World War II (MacIssac, 1986).

However, the event that dramatically changed the ideology and organization of US military power (and US power more broadly) was the onset of another global conflict. Imperial Japan's invasion of China in 1937 and Nazi Germany's invasion of Poland in 1939 resulted in a global conflagration that the US could not avoid, much as a reluctant public and Congress tried. President Roosevelt was an internationalist with much sympathy for aiding allied democracies such as Great Britain, but could not attempt overt assistance (mainly due to the series of Neutrality Acts passed by Congress in the 1930s), until the isolationist Congress began to soften its stance (the passage of the Lend-Lease agreement in March 1941 was probably the clearest end of US neutrality). The Japanese attack on Pearl Harbor naval station on 7 December 1941, was a pivotal moment in the history of US foreign policy. In the immediate term, it gave President Roosevelt a reason to get directly involved in the war, and it more broadly shattered the complacency that geographical isolation could insulate the US from the power politics of the rest of the world (e.g. Gaddis, 2004: ch. 3). It also turned the US from a minor military power (at least in comparative terms) into the most powerful state in the world at the end of the war. In 1914 the US had about 31 per cent of the military personnel of Great Britain, and 18 per cent of that of Germany (though its gross tonnage of naval forces was much closer to the other great powers); in 1937 it was spending only 1.5 per cent of GNP on the military, as compared with Germany at 23.5 per cent; the British Empire at 5.7 per cent; and Japan at 28.2 per cent (derived from figures in: Kennedy, 1989: 261 and 429). By 1945, The US was spending some 37 per cent of GDP on the military (White House, 2012b): and while this would go down dramatically, it would never return to the old levels. The use of atomic weapons by the US against Japan also brought a new power and new form of warfare that would fundamentally shape the dynamics of international relations for years to come (Brodie, 1946; Jervis, 1989).

While much could be discussed regarding the operational history of World War II (e.g. Murray and Millett, 2001), in terms of the development of military power other factors are of greater interest. First was the war's demonstration of the potential for liberal capitalism to engage in industrialized total war. The US went from having a military ranked eighteenth (in terms of overall size) in the world in 1941 with an airforce of 1,700 aircraft, to having 47,000 aircraft produced in 1942 (to the Axis powers' 27,000). In 1942 for every one naval vessel produced by Japan, the US produced 16. By 1944 the Ford 'Willow Run' aircraft plant in Michigan was producing one bomber every 68 minutes (Overy, 2006: 233–41). In essence US victory in the war was a demonstration of the latent power of the US and the synthesis between industrial power and military power. It was also important that the US was very focused on the problems of logistics, and gained a real superiority here which in essence helped to win the war (see e.g. Overy, 2006).

Second, like the legacy of the Civil War and World War I, World War II left a vastly powerful state, that had organized the war effort from above, if in a particularly 'American' way. As noted in Chapter 1, wartime production was coordinated through a number of organizations, including the War Production Board, the Manpower Commission, and the Office of War Mobilization (Koistinen, 2004). The organization of central production planning reflected the dominance of private enterprise, and industry leaders became key figures in the management of the war economy (Sherry, 1995). Coordination mechanisms for the economy were also reflected more broadly in military planning, where President Roosevelt had devised a 'Joint Chiefs of Staff' system for the coordination of military policy. Overall, World War II saw the development of an expanded state bureaucracy, particularly in the military sector and the direct involvement of the state, led by the business community, into the economy: through price controls, labor mobilization, and the direction of production. The legacy of the war also left the US society with a vast wealth of military experience, from combat, to leadership, to the production of arms.

The Cold War and the military establishment

The post-war environment left the US in a difficult position. There was an increased recognition of the needs of military power in a world of total war, where weapons technology was breaking down borders, and where surprise attacks would not allow for ad hoc mobilization arrangements. However, plans to mobilize permanently went against US traditions of anti-militarism and anti-statism. While demobilization of the armed forces happened rapidly (from about 12 million in 1945 to 1.5 million in 1947), the aftermath of the war led to a great debate about the future role of the military in American political life. Much of the debate became folded into a variety of issues: the legacy of and responsibility for the attack on Pearl Harbor (and the results of a government commission looking into the disaster), a political debate about the best way to organize for defense (found in the congressional debates surrounding the 1947 National Security Act), and the rising power of the Soviet Union (especially in terms of how this former ally was beginning to be seen as the US's greatest threat). The discussion especially surrounded the issue of 'preparedness', pitting those committed to a new willingness to have peacetime planning for defense against those who saw a creeping militarism.

In the end, a compromise of sorts was struck, which can be seen in the key institutional impact of World War II that would have lasting effect on the organization of US military power: the passing of the 1947 National Security Act. The Act substantially changed the organization of the armed forces, and also the role of national defense within the US. The Act created a civilian-run National Military Establishment (NME), the National Security Council (NSC) and Central Intelligence Agency (CIA). The NME consolidated the Army, Navy and Air Force within it, replacing the separate Departments of War and Navy, as a means to providing better coordination between the services and better civil–military coordination across the executive branch. The NME lasted only a few years until institutional reform left the organization looking much as it does now: in 1949 the Secretary of Defense was given a much stronger role, the military secretaries were demoted from their cabinet status (and their positions on the NSC), and the NME was transformed into an independent, civilian-led Department of Defense (DoD). The DoD became one of the largest and most important actors within the US government, even outside the foreign policy arena. Its budget has consistently been one of the biggest government expenditures (now only second to Social Security and Medicare and Medicaid). The NSC over time became the crucial place for foreign policy formulation, and with the eventual creation of the role of 'National Security Advisor' (officially titled 'Assistant to the President for National Security Affairs') in 1953 as a recognizable head. The National Security Advisor became, especially from the 1960s onwards, an identifiable and important part of the foreign policy establishment. Finally, the CIA fairly quickly became not just a coordinator and provider of intelligence, but an active participant in international affairs through covert action (authorized early on in June 1948 by NSC 10/2).

If the National Security Act was the institutional foundation of the Cold War state, 'containment' was to be its core manifestation in foreign policy. George Kennan, an American diplomat in the Moscow embassy (and later Director of Policy Planning in the State Department in the late 1940s), formulated the basic principles of containment in two core documents: the 1946 'Long Telegram' (Kennan, 1946), a diplomatic cable that roughly outlined the motives of the Soviet Union and the American response; and an anonymous article (signed as 'X') in the policy journal *Foreign Affairs*, which more clearly outlined containment as policy (Kennan,

1947). Containment, as originally articulated by Kennan, was seen as the only response to an expansionist, power-seeking Soviet Union: 'in these circumstances it is clear that the main element of any United States policy towards the Soviet Union must be that of a long-term, patient but firm and vigilant containment of Russian expansionist tendencies' (Kennan, 1947: 575). The idea was to put counter-pressure on any Soviet attempts to gain advantage. Although Kennan's original articulation was much modified over the course of the Cold War, its basic ideas in terms of Soviet motives and American responses became a blueprint for Cold War strategy (Gaddis, 2005: ch. 2).

The National Security Act provided the institutional backdrop, containment the policy, but the real shift in terms of size came with the creation and implementation of NSC-68 – the 1950 classified report of the NSC – which became the ideological and strategic plan of the Cold War American state. While NSC-68 was in many ways built upon previous statements about US post-war strategy, it codified them in a way that not only framed them as urgent, but was also an ideological and moral call to arms against the Soviet Union. It also stressed more intently the military character of the core problems, rather than Kennan's more political focus (also shared by his colleagues at the time – see Leffler, 1992: 179–81). Written in the aftermath of the 1949 Soviet testing of the atomic bomb and the communist victory in the Chinese revolution, it saw the Soviet Union as inherently dangerous and expansionist, and called for the full-scale mobilization of economic and military power (with an added internationalization through alliances) to put a halt to Soviet power (Hogan, 1998: 295–302; May, 1993). It stated that 'in a shrinking world, which now faces the threat of atomic warfare, it is not an adequate objective merely to seek to check the Kremlin design, for the absence of order among nations is becoming less and less tolerable. This fact imposes on us, in our interests, the responsibility of world leadership' (United States National Security Council, 1950: 29).

NSC-68 linked 'total war' and Soviet Communism and together these were what provided the US with a new 'mission'. The threat of the Soviet Union was not just seen as something that could be kept at bay through the old policies of diplomacy and a more limited military: the US would need to engage with the world. NSC-68 did much to codify this new mission and its necessary sacrifices. Though some have stressed its adoption as leading to a qualitative difference in

Cold War policies, Leffler has emphasized the continuities, in that many of the pronouncements were already seen in various influential documents in the period 1946–49 (for example, seen in NSC-20/4, the first comprehensive overview of national security policy – United States National Security Council, 1948). All it really did was ask for more: higher taxes, lower domestic expenditures and higher military spending (Leffler, 1992: 356). The conclusion to NSC-68 stated that the only option for the US was 'a more rapid build-up of political, economic, and military strength and thereby of confidence in the free world than is now contemplated is the only course which is consistent with progress toward achieving our fundamental purpose' (United States National Security Council, 1950: 71).

One area where war was certainly seen to have changed was in the development of nuclear weapons. Although in 1950 when NSC-68 was released the 'nuclear balance' was very much in the favor of the US, Soviet acquisition of the atomic bomb in 1949 led planners to embrace nuclear weapons as the key to their geopolitical strategy. They immediately planned to develop a more powerful hydrogen bomb (made a reality in 1952) – and thus began not only the arcane and secretive planning for nuclear war (or for deterrence), but also a growing reliance on nuclear weapons as a core part of US military power. President Eisenhower's 'New Look' defense policy (of 1953) placed an increasing emphasis on nuclear weapons and away from 'manpower' solutions. Not only did that play more readily into American traditions, but it also suited the American preferences for technological solutions to war. The focus on strategic airpower (and especially through the creation of Strategic Air Command in 1946) was seen as one way to solve the problem of large standing armies. As noted earlier, the emphasis on strategic airpower drew on a long-standing infatuation that the US (and its liberal ally the United Kingdom) had developed in the interwar period and through the strategic bombing campaigns of World War II: that airpower could provide a technological means for winning war (Biddle, 2002; Mahnken, 2008; Overy, 2006: ch. 4; cf. Rosenberg, 1983). The focus on nuclear weapons as a strategic weapon was therefore not just about fiscal restraint, but drew on a longer tradition of focusing on technology as a way to not only win wars more effectively, but also as part of historical anti-militarism.

As the character of war and security were seen to have changed, from an era where wars happened sporadically to a nuclear era where permanent preparedness were to be the norm, a fragmented foreign policy was seen as a disaster waiting to happen. Permanent preparedness was to be provided through a civilian coordinated national security strategy, institutionalized in what has been recognized as a 'national security state' (Hogan, 1998; Stuart, 2008; Yergin, 1977), meant a real shift in US priorities. Thus, the new institutional apparatus and the policies that were a part of it were also fused with a way of thinking about national security that, as Michael Hogan has described, provided a new 'discourse' of national security, or a 'national security ideology' (Hogan, 1998: ch. 1; cf. E. Rosenberg, 1993a): that total war created real national insecurity, necessitated total preparedness, and saw in the Soviet threat a long-term geopolitical struggle which reinforced the other factors, necessitating American leadership in the world (in a kind of modified version of nineteenth-century Manifest Destiny). As Hogan noted, the necessity to counter the Soviet Union in terms of a threat to freedom 'seemed to leave the American people with little choice but to defend their own security and their own liberty by defending peace and security everywhere' (Hogan, 1998: 14).

While some certainly saw this shift as a necessity, a specifically American response to external aggression (e.g. Friedberg, 2000), others were more critical. C. Wright Mills' durable critique focused on the concentration of power in a small military elite, who had a 'military mindset' therefore seeing in the world a real military necessity that belied the pursuit of peace. As Mills described it:

> for the first time in American history, men in authority are talking about an 'emergency' without foreseeable end. During modern times, and especially in the United States, men had come to look upon history as a peaceful continuum interrupted by war. But now, the American elite does not have any real image of peace – other than as an uneasy interlude existing precariously by virtue of the balance of mutual fright. The only serious accepted plan for 'peace' is the fully loaded pistol. In short, war or a high state of war-preparedness is felt to be the normal and seemingly permanent condition of the United States. (1956: 184)

Overall, in a 150-year period, the US went from being a small state with a limited capacity for armed force, with a guiding ideology of anti-militarism, to a 'superpower' with one of the most technologically superior fighting forces in the world, with permanent peacetime preparedness and organization.

The shifting priorities, purposes and capacities of the US military through history have also pointed to the problems of the initial conception of 'anti-militarism'. While there were criticisms of this in the early Cold War period from radical critics like Mills, republican anti-statists, represented well by individuals such as Senator Robert Taft, also made similar arguments, combining a desire for a more isolationist foreign policy with a concern about federal spending and state control. However, a dramatic intervention came from a more conventional source from within the US political system: the president. In a remarkable Farewell Address in 1961, President Eisenhower (who was also a five-star General of the Army and Supreme Allied Commander in Europe during World War II) declared that the US faced an internal threat from militarization due to the development of the 'military-industrial complex'. As President Eisenhower (1961) stated:

> This conjunction of an immense military establishment and a large arms industry is new in the American experience. The total influence – economic, political, even spiritual – is felt in every city, every State house, every office of the Federal government. We recognize the imperative need for this development. Yet we must not fail to comprehend its grave implications. Our toil, resources and livelihood are all involved; so is the very structure of our society.
>
> In the councils of government, we must guard against the acquisition of unwarranted influence, whether sought or unsought, by the military-industrial complex. The potential for the disastrous rise of misplaced power exists and will persist.

Eisenhower's concern over the undue influence of military industries and the 'military establishment' touched on a real tension between the traditional anti-militarism of the US and the massive expansion of military power in the Cold War period (cf. Ledbetter, 2011). Despite Eisenhower's vast experience in dealing with the military, he found that even he struggled to keep the military complex in check, and despaired about the prospects of a president with less military experience.

How can we judge the overall influence of militarism in the US state? The increased costs of military power are one place to look for its overall influence on the US state. Until the early twentieth century, military spending outside of wartime was only a tiny

Figure 4.1   *National defense share of the budget (outlays) and economy (GDP)*

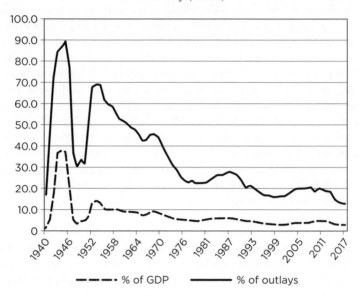

Source: White House, Office of Management and Budget, 2012b.

proportion of GDP, only accounting for 0.4–0.9 per cent of economic output; it did account for a large part of government spending (20–25 per cent) but was tiny as a proportion of the economy overall (Sherry, 1995: 5). As Sherry notes, 'in sum, well into the twentieth century national defense claimed only a minor part of the nation's resources. War imposed enormous burdens, but defense as an ongoing activity did not' (1995: 6). The new Cold War climate and the rise of the 'national security state' changed this dynamic. The compromise made between advocates of the new preparedness and anti-militarist Republicans tended towards a technological fix to military power. Permanent preparedness would be maintained through capital investment in the military, and not 'manpower' (Hogan, 1998). Nonetheless, defense budgets began to soar compared with previous levels. After a substantial dip in spending as part of post-World War II demobilization, defense spending went on the rise with increases associated with the Korean War (1950–53), which allowed President Truman to implement the recommendations of NSC-68. The amount of spending shrank somewhat from that initial stage, spurred on by Eisenhower's (and Congress') desire to cut the defense budget and the end of the Korean War, and from that point to the end of the Cold War, defense spending remained between 5 and 10 per cent of GDP, though it became a decreasing part of the overall national budget in terms of outlays (see Figure 4.1) (Fordham, 2007: 378).

While the rises in defense spending and permanent preparedness were important shifts in the US, the figures also hide some important aspects. First, the shrinking proportion of defense spending to GDP (and government spending) was only partially to do with cuts in defense spending after the initial Truman surge. They also reflect the phenomenal growth of the US economy and overall government spending, where defense outlays remained fairly constant post-Eisenhower (apart from real increases during the Reagan Administration), but took up a smaller proportion of the national economy (and especially after the expansion of government spending in the 1960s, with Social Security and Medicare/Medicaid taking up bigger portions of the federal budget). Second, they also showed the political limits to defense spending: even where permanent preparedness was accepted, that there was not to be a trade-off between 'guns' and 'butter' (Fordham, 2007: 376–9; cf. Hogan, 1998: ch. 3). The complicated picture presented by the political economy of defense shows the rather remarkable post-war position of the US: due to political restraints and economic dynamism, it was able to spend vast amounts on defense without it affecting the economy overall (and in the 1980s and beyond, by utilizing the power of the dollar to enable rather extravagant deficit spending).

However, the influence of defense did come at a price. The increasing power of both defense industries in terms of lobbying, and defense practitioners of foreign policy matters, did mean a real militarization of US foreign policy. Ernest May has argued that the early Cold War fundamentally altered the architecture of government, putting defense at the forefront of government activity (May, 1992). Whereas pre-World War II, executive departments like the Department of Labor and the Department of Commerce were the most prominent cabinet positions, when the Cold War was in full swing, the Secretary of Defense, National Security Advisor and other 'security' related positions were most prominent. With the rise in importance of military-security matters, 'the main business of the U.S. government had become the development, maintenance, position, exploitation and regulation of military forces' (May, 1992: 227).

Concerns about militarization have continued to play an important role in critiques and analyses of contemporary US foreign policy post Cold War. A number of critics have emerged, particularly since the 2003 Iraq invasion, to criticize the continued militarism of US foreign policy (e.g. Johnson, 2004). International relations expert and former US Army Colonel Andrew Bacevich has done much to popularly revive the theme of militarism, but also to give it due analysis in the current context. In his 2006 book *The New Militarism*, Bacevich cited a number of trends that demonstrate that the Cold War militarism still has consequences today. Particularly surprising is the overall demise of anti-militarism in the US political system and society more generally: military power is seen as important in its own right, with little dissent from that position. That there are no more anti-militarist republicans (or very few, for example libertarians such as Ron Paul) in either political party is a major shift, and a likely consequence of the demands of militarization over time. As Bacevich has stated, 'few in power have openly considered whether valuing military power for its own sake or cultivating global military superiority might be at odds with American principles' (2006: 14). A related trend compounded by the previous is a normalization of war: war is seen as one policy option amongst others, one that is often sensible, and that war is no longer seen as a failure of policy. Both of these trends add up to both a broad acceptance of war as policy (much as Mills feared – Mills, 1956), but also a context that sees war as not only a legitimate option, but one from which the US should not shy away. As Fordham notes, 'continued high levels of military spending purchased capabilities far beyond what was needed to defend the United States and its allies. Activists of many different political stripes, both in and out of government, clamoured to put those capabilities to work' (2007: 376). It remains to analyse this problem in two further dimensions: first, how military power expressed itself internationally, and second, what impact the rise in militarism had on American society and its approach to defense and military policy.

Military power and power projection

The changes in the Cold War state also necessitate considering the projection of military power abroad. Direct uses of force occurred a number of times in the Cold War period, but probably most consequentially during the wars in Korea (1950–53) and Vietnam (1965–

73). While much has been written about both conflicts, and especially the second (as it led to a cultural and political divide that has been prominent in American politics and society ever since), a brief summary of the impact of both will be given. With the Korean War, it was the first use of force post-World War II, legitimated by the UN Security Council voting to stop the aggression of North Korea (the Soviet Union was boycotting the UNSC at the time over the non-representation of the People's Republic of China on the Security Council) (see e.g. Cumings, 1990; Halberstam, 2007). The US was eventually successful in restoring the original division in Korea. However, despite being seen as the 'forgotten war' (Harbutt, 2002: 81; cf. Cumings, 2011), it was one with long-standing effects. First, the US military has been ensconced in South Korea ever since, upholding the dividing line with the North. Second, the Korean War enabled President Truman to implement NSC-68, and increase military spending and heighten the overall military posture of the US. Third, while the Korean War is almost forgotten in terms of its domestic effects, it was important in the various oppositions to it at home: Congress was critical as it had not mandated the war, and there was real overreach on the part of the Truman Administration in terms of economic mobilization (for example, the Supreme Court decided against the government in the case of the 1952 nationalization of the steel industry). Additionally, there was also civil–military friction between Truman and General Douglas MacArthur, who was eventually relieved of command by Truman for contradicting the Administration's policies. However, as Sherry has argued, the war did not have a huge impact on American society at large – there was limited participation, and there was still much obsession with the 'red scare' at home. As he notes, 'war remained shadowy, its issues agonising but its presence elusive' (Sherry, 1995: 186).

However, the war in Vietnam proved more controversial, and has been part of the American cultural and political imagination ever since. American involvement was essentially advisory at first, taking over from the French in its former colonies. Here again Vietnam was separated by a communist North and democratic South, and was seen (even more emphatically) as another Cold War battleground. When the US naval ships the USS *Maddox* and (two days later) the USS *Turner Joy* were (seemingly) attacked by North Vietnamese forces in August 1964, this was used as a reason to step up American involvement into a full-fledged military intervention. While international approval was not forthcoming, President Johnson did seek congressional approval for military action, through the 'Gulf of Tonkin Resolution', which authorized the use of force. At its peak, there were 500,000 American military personnel in Vietnam, and the ground war was complemented by the escalation in bombing of North Vietnam. As the war dragged on without resolution, outside the destruction it was causing to the region, it also became a larger political issue within the US itself. The military presence became increasingly contested by the populace at large and the military leadership increasingly critical of civilian interference in military planning (see e.g. Anderson, 2005; Herring, 1996; Young, 1991).

The turning point for much of this contestation was the 'Tet' Offensive of January 1968, a massive offensive by North Vietnamese and South Vietnamese guerrilla forces on major urban targets. While in tactical terms the US and South Vietnamese forces were successful in repelling the attacks, in the US, it was seen as a real defeat, a sign that the war was still ongoing, dangerous, with no end in sight. It became integral to the presidential election campaign of 1968, with Lyndon Johnson eventually withdrawing from the Democratic primaries in the face of strong challenges from anti-war Democrats such as Eugene McCarthy, and with Republican candidate Richard Nixon offering vague promises for 'peace with honor' (Anderson, 2005: ch. 4). The final withdrawal of American military personnel was only accomplished some five years later in 1973. The Vietnam War had many long-lasting effects. For one, it fed into perceptions of American decline in the early 1970s, with the US essentially defeated militarily by a smaller (and communist) state. Additionally, military spending only exacerbated the economic problems the US faced in the 1960s with its international economic position. The war also increased the tensions in an existing cultural divide, here expressed between conservative critics who saw the defeat (or in some instances even *talk* of defeat – debate continued as to whether the war was 'unwinnable' or not) as endemic of a kind of moral decline within the US and liberal opposition to the war (see e.g. Sherry, 1995: chs 6 and 7). It was also a real blow to the pride of the military, vilified by many domestically, partially due to the lack of success, but also due to the social alienation (amongst other problems) of returning soldiers (many conscripted into service) (see Sherry, 1995: 300–1). In addition to the societal divisions, there was also a newfound political problem with the use of force, the so-called 'Vietnam syndrome', which related to the political problems of using force when key interests were not clear, and that an easy military victory was not assured. The Vietnam War had an impact on a generation of policy-makers, one that only now seems in abatement with the Obama Administration (see J. Mann, 2012).

Though these direct military confrontations were of great import, there are also aspects of American military power that relate to institutional and structural power that have not been fully developed, which can be seen in a variety of practices that extended American military power throughout the world. The first (which can also be viewed as a form of institutional power) is the institutionalization of US military power in international organizations. NATO provides a particularly good example in this regard, as it not only provided an alliance structure in which the US could push forward its favored policies (and thus enhancing its military power institutionally) but also provided a complex structure for the US to enforce a particular way of thinking about military power, based on its own material capacities. As Deudney and Ikenberry describe it, 'the NATO alliance went beyond the traditional realist conception of an ad hoc defense alliance, because it created an elaborate organization and drew states into joint force planning, international military command structures, and established a complex transgovernmental political process for making political and military decisions' (Deudney and Ikenberry, 1999: 183). NATO therefore reorganized the structure of force within the alliance, and also had a long-term synthesizing of strategic objectives, and issues such as inter-operability of forces became an important way of transmitting American ideas of 'best practice'. Additionally, the 'nuclearization' of Europe only increased such internationalization (cf. Trachtenberg, 1991). Nuclearization also led to issues to do with the command and control of nuclear weapons, as even though the ultimate authority over nuclear weapons in the alliance remained with the leaders of the United States and Great Britain (France having withdrawn from the integrated command structure in 1966), the multinational character of the alliance made arrangements more complex (Gregory, 1996) and increasingly brought all of the states into a direct 'dependence' on the US (Davis, 1982).

Additionally, over the course of the Cold War, internationalization was further embedded through the transmission of American military practices and equipment: through arms sales to client states and military training (see e.g. Berrigan and Hartung, 2005; Pierre, 1982). The American military took an increasing presence globally, through its 'blue water' navy capable of operating in every region of the world, but also through a complex series of basing arrangements, whereby the American military maintained itself (and continues to) in a variety of locales across the world. Such arrangements are surely part of a more hegemonic sense to American military power, which some critics have even decried as 'imperial' (e.g. Johnson, 2004: ch. 6), but are also part of what Barry Posen describes as having 'command of the commons', the core areas of sea and space outside US territory, meaning that the US 'gets vastly more military use out of the sea, space, and air than do others; that it can credibly threaten to deny their use to others; and that others would lose a military contest for the commons if they attempted to deny them to the United States' (Posen, 2003: 8). However, we can take the hegemonic sense of American military power further. With the development of nuclear weapons, direct conformation between the US and the USSR became more and more unthinkable, in terms of the potential for escalation. As Barkawi and Laffey note, 'the enforced nuclear peace meant that the local forces of clients and proxies became more important instruments for conducting superpower competition. The periphery took on a central importance of the site of armed conflict. The *nature* of war changed – policymakers found other ways to use force as an instrument of policy' (Barkawi and Laffey, 1999: 410). In instances where relationships were more asymmetrical, direct control of armed force was replaced with varieties of indirect control. The integration of the CIA into national security planning also meant that covert operations were also a way of extending US coercive power in varied ways that were often outside the means of traditional military power. As noted earlier, the use of covert operations was recognized as plausible policy very early on by President Truman, and has been utilized extensively by administrations ever since. The coups against the Iranian government in 1953 and the Arbenz government in Guatemala in 1954 were both covert actions utilizing the CIA (Kinzer, 2007; Nelson, 2007), and various important activities continued through the Cold War and after, from supporting the coup in Chile in 1973, in Afghanistan and Nicaragua in the 1980s, and continuing in the 'War on Terror' today (see Weiner, 2008).

Civil–military relations and the 'American way of war'

The increasing use of force internationally was not without domestic consequences, and discussions of militarism and military power need to be further placed in the context of civil–military relations in the US. The continued and increasing separation of the military from society – in that the military today as an institution has little direct link with the experiences of most Americans – and the expectation of easy victory, that American superiority in technology can make war virtually 'risk free', compound the previous elements. This leads us to a consideration of where the military fit more broadly in American life, and how an 'American way of war' can be discerned. The US Constitution very deliberately divided control over the military between the Congress and the president: Congress (the Senate in particular) would have the power to declare war, while the president would be the commander–in–chief of the military. This separation was to ensure not only the control of military power by the deliberative body, but also the maintenance of civilian control of the military. Though the foundation of the US state was partially premised on the grounds of national security (i.e. that it would be easier to provide for national defense if the thirteen colonies were unified), the founders also feared concentrations of power, particularly that found in a permanent peacetime military. Although the Cold War changed the relationship to militarism as well as the balance between Congress and the president and the 'war power' (discussed in detail in Chapter 3), such civilian authority has still been seen as important. In fact, the model for US civil–military relations is seen in Samuel Huntington's (1957) idea of 'objective control' where civilians cede autonomy to military professionals over tactical and operational issues, but the military defers to civilians for overall strategic planning (e.g. Desch, 2007).

However, since World War II and the rise of the national security state and associated increase in size of the peacetime military, there has been an increasing 'civil–military gap': the lack of understanding of the military by civilians is becoming increasingly large. The period between World War II and Vietnam War saw decreasing numbers of serving military personnel, despite the continuation of the policy of 'selective service' (i.e. the draft). Much of this has to do with a number of processes, but the eventual development of the All Volunteer Force (AVF) in 1973 created an entirely professional military force, and, as a consequence, less chance that a broader array of the US population would serve. Ironically, the creation of the AVF did turn the military into a much more diverse institution than previously, as women and African-Americans (and other minority groups) seized the opportunity to take up service as a profession, with all the benefits it conferred (see Bailey, 2009; Burk, 2007).

The civil–military gap is mainly a cultural gap, between American individualism and a military service that demands obedience, hierarchy and conformity to a group (Weigley, 2001). But there is also a further gap between the general civilian population and those that have experienced the realities of combat (or even just military service), found in an increasing disjuncture between service and citizenship (Shaw, 1991). The careers of Vice-President Dick Cheney and President Bill Clinton's experiences show some of the problems at work. Cheney stated in a 1989 private response to the *Washington Post* regarding his lack of service in Vietnam: 'I had other priorities in the '60s than military service' (see Seelye, 2004). Such a statement from someone who prominently advocated the use of force sits oddly with notions of service. Similarly, Bill Clinton was criticized heavily during the 1992 Democratic presidential primaries for his efforts to avoid the Vietnam draft. Journalist Hendrik Hertzberg (2004) similarly contrasted the two Republican candidates standing together in the 1988 election, George H. W. Bush and Dan Quayle, as a demonstration of 'the moral decline of the American ruling class': Bush after his high school graduation in 1942 had volunteered to serve in the Navy Air Force in World War II, flying 58 combat missions and receiving a Distinguished Flying Cross; while Quayle had avoided the Vietnam draft for four years by attending college, and eventually contrived a spot with the Indiana National Guard through family connections. Bill Clinton and George W. Bush were the first presidents without any military experience at all since Franklin Delano Roosevelt, and increasingly, service became rather irrelevant to a candidate's election potential (e.g. that John Kerry could lose so readily against George W. Bush on the issue surrounding military service in Vietnam speaks volumes about such a shift; as does the lack of reference to John McCain's service as opposed to Barack Obama in 2008). The decline in service from the political elite shows an increasing gap between those who shape strategic policy and those who implement it. This gap is not necessarily problematic: as Mills argued, it is in fact surprising that a state with such historical resistance to military professionalism has been so inclined to have leaders with professional military experience, even including those in the higher ranks of the military (Mills, 1956: 176–7). However, when a militarized political elite with little military experience combined with a wholly professional armed forces it makes the military increasingly separate from society at large and the political class as a whole. As Bacevich notes, 'having dissolved any connection between claims to citizenship and obligation to serve, Americans entrust their security to a class of military professionals who see themselves in many respects as culturally and politically set apart from the rest of society' (2006: 29–30).

Such a shift is important, as it came concurrent to the changes within the military and its relation to politics as well. The military was held in high regard after World War II, and retained some of its distance from politics. However, the Cold War militarization had expanded military influence a great deal, and the military began to have fractious relationships with presidents. Early examples include General Douglas MacArthur's clashes with President Truman over the Korean War strategy, and the so-called 'Admiral's Revolt' of 1949, where senior Navy officers orchestrated a secret media campaign to stop the Secretary of Defense's cancellation of a new aircraft carrier. Such relations really came to a head during the Vietnam War, where not only did military commanders resent the micro-management of military strategy by civilians (particularly Secretary of Defense Robert McNamara's corporate style), but also blamed the eventual 'defeat' on civilian interference.

The increasing politicization of the military was also countered in society by an increasing criticism of the military (especially in the anti-Vietnam protest movement). The response from the military was highly political. General Creighton Adams played a crucial role in restructuring military doctrine so that the reserve forces were a major part of any war strategy, called the 'total force policy': as such, any future major deployment of force would necessitate the calling up of reserve forces, and thus require a very big political commitment. The idea was that the government would not so easily take the military to war again. A second lesson derived from the Vietnam experience was to avoid any sort of counter-insurgency warfare (it should be noted that this was limited to the US Army: the US Marine Corps maintained counter-insurgency or 'small wars' doctrine throughout the period). The US military for most of the 1970s and 1980s therefore focused on conventional land war as its core commitment (particularly on a Soviet–US war on the European continent), thus further avoiding any possible future 'Vietnams' (Bacevich, 2006; Desch, 2007). However, these types of wars were still supported by proxy, especially clear in US support for anti-Soviet forces in Afghanistan in the 1980s, as well as series of conflicts in Latin America (Coll, 2005; McClintock, 1992; cf. Brands, 2010).

These views were further codified in the Weinberger and Powell doctrines (named respectively after President Reagan's Secretary of Defense Caspar Weinberger and Chairman of the Joint Chiefs of Staff General Colin Powell). The Weinberger doctrine relied on five key tenets: that force should only be used when US national interests are clearly at stake, when there is clear public and congressional support, where there are clear objectives, when there is a clear intention of winning and when the use of force is a last resort. Colin Powell expressed these as a series of questions that needed to be answered before force could be used, adding the need for an 'exit strategy'. Although these guidelines were not accepted by all, they gave a clear articulation of the post-Vietnam War approach to force from within the military: that overwhelming force with clear objectives and public support was paramount for the military to support involvement.

Overall, the Cold War (and Vietnam War) experiences turned the military into a viable political force that had almost superseded civilian control by narrowing down the terms of the use of force so much that it was almost impossible to find situations where it would be useful. Additionally, activist military leaders, such as Colin Powell in his term as Chairman of the Joint Chiefs of Staff, tended to be more than just advisors to the president, and also vigorously advocated military policy. The success of the first Gulf War was precisely because it so neatly fitted the parameters of the Weinberger doctrine, and further rebuilt the military's premier place as an exemplar of US values, a real shift from the final years of the Vietnam War. The institution of the military, as Bacevich argues, became 'highly esteemed, lavishly supported, rarely used' (2006: 51).

However, the military's position did not last through the 1990s. While 'supporting the troops' retained an important place in civic nationalism, the Clinton Administration saw the beginnings of change, as battles over the use of force in the post-Cold War era began. A series of military interventions – in Somalia, Bosnia, Haiti, Kosovo – that in many ways violated the Weinberger/Powell doctrine led to increasing civilian authority being reclaimed, for better or worse. A rival 'Albright doctrine' – named after hawkish UN ambassador and later Secretary of State Madeline Albright – became prominent; as Albright asked: 'what's the point of having this superb military that you're always talking about if we can't use it?' (Isaacson, 1999). The de-linking of service and citizenship also meant that the political class has had much less experience with the military, seen in the rise of 'armchair generals'. The culmination of these changes was seen in the Bush Administration and the 2003 Iraq War: the military became one of the biggest sources of dissent on the need for and efficacy of using force in that context. For example, in the build-up to the war, Army Chief of Staff Eric Shinseki stated that they would need several hundred thousand troops for the campaign; however, Assistant Secretary of Defense Paul Wolfowitz dismissed the figures (Ricks, 2006: 96–100). That Wolfowitz won shows how much the balance between the military and civilian leadership had become skewed. Ironically, the big tension became that between the hawkish civilians and reluctant soldiers (Desch, 2007).

The impact of the wars in Iraq and Afghanistan has allowed some changes to occur within the military itself. Despite the accuracy of projections such as Shinseki's, there was also resistance to thinking through new doctrines that would support the goals set by policymakers. In that context, a number of individuals in the armed forces were able to find a niche for reintroducing counter-insurgency doctrine into the US Army's overall doctrine, which was perceived as a way to better succeed in Iraq. Led in particular by General David Petraeus (who also commanded the 101st Airborne Division in Iraq), a new approach to the war in Iraq was seen in a counter-insurgency doctrine that focused less on destroying the enemy and more on gaining domestic legitimacy. The new doctrine was codified in the Counterinsurgency (COIN) Field Manual, released in 2006 (see Ricks, 2010: chs 1 and 2; and United States Department of the Army, 2007). The switch to COIN represented an important change in the US in terms of the focus of military power. However, COIN is also very costly, demanding a large and sustained military presence, which may strain domestic society's willingness to support such endeavours (cf. Merom, 2003). The Obama Administration has already started to rethink the policy. While encouraging a 'surge' of troops in Afghanistan in 2009 (Obama, 2009c), the most recent articulation of the Administration's defense policy (United States Department of Defense, 2012b) advocates a move away from sustained nation-building operations, and towards a more streamlined defense policy, focused on Asia. Overall, the major evolution of American military policy has been back to emphasizing technology as part of a counter-terrorism strategy: the use of drone attacks and smaller operations with special forces (J. Mann, 2012; Singh, 2012: ch. 4).

All of which ties into the particular form of militarism that characterizes the US. Michael Mann (1987) has conceived of the Cold

War militarism that liberal polities developed in two forms: a rarefied 'deterrence-science' militarism, with elites focusing on the abstract (if frightening) calculations dealing with nuclear strategy, out of the public eye; and 'spectator sport militarism', the consequence of professionalization, with the public cheering on of military adventures abroad, rather divorced from direct participation. If the former has somewhat abated with the end of the Cold War, the latter continues to play an important role in how militarism infuses the political system in the US. Furthermore, Martin Shaw (2005) has noted that the separation of Western societies from military institutions, seen in the trend in the West towards ending conscription and the subsequent use of small professional armed forces (and foreign proxies), creates societies much less inclined to accept military casualties as a 'worthy sacrifice'. As a consequence, strategies of 'risk-transfer war' push risks away from Western soldiers, and towards non-Western civilians, as a way of bracketing war off from Western societies. War for Western states is to be completely removed from the home state: soldiers will not die, economic life will remain constant, and politics will continue as usual.

The dynamics of militarism and civil–military relations therefore also play into current American expectations about what war looks like (or should look like). While it would be an over-generalization that there is a singular 'American way of war', there are certainly historical tendencies for Americans to make assumptions about what US forces at war should look like, what expectations there are of military power, and what kind of power is glorified. From a broad societal perspective, it is clear that Americans have expectations that the technological and qualitative superiority of the American military should lead to victory. This provides many problems when American military forces have been deemed unsuccessful, ignoring as it does the broader politics of war, in that the goals set by policymakers are hugely important in the conduct of war.

The military have long held different views. As Russell Weigley (1977) has argued in his influential survey *The American Way of War*, American military commanders have mainly been focused on winning 'wars of annihilation' that focus on the importance of mass and decisive battles to achieve victory. Although US military forces have fought many other kinds of wars in the past (e.g. in the Philippines, Vietnam and Iraq), the wars that have focused on unconditional surrender of the enemy and massive mobilizations of soldiers and firepower have been the most consistently won and celebrated. The claiming of the veterans of World War II as the 'greatest generation' is one popular manifestation of this (which is also fed into by the positioning of World War II as a necessary and virtuous war), but this American way of war is also expounded in the Weinberger doctrine, and its emphasis on winning through mass. The other side of this focus is the need to avoid counter-insurgency and attritional warfare – derived from experience. A technological fixation has also long been associated with American approaches to war, which see war as a technical problem to be solved (Mahnken, 2008). The focus on nuclear strategy during the Cold War (as opposed to large conventional armies), and the 'Revolution in Military Affairs' in the past twenty years show core examples of these tendencies (Freedman, 2003; Latham, 1999). Recent reliance on unmanned drone attacks is a further extension of such technological solutions (Singer, 2009).

Presently, the military system that remains is one that is still skewed by militarism, but one that is pervasive on both sides of the civil–military divide, bolstered by an enormous peacetime military establishment, with a political class and broader public that still has a fairly sanguine notion about the efficacy of military power. Even after the problems and crisis of the Iraq and Afghanistan wars, there seems little possibility of challenging the role of military power within the US, seen not only in the repeated calls for military action against Iran over the potential development of nuclear weapons, but also in debates about cutting defense (Lepore, 2013). The solidity of militarism within the US political system can easily be seen in that anti-militarism is no longer a credible position, even for the Republican Party that used to espouse these ideals.

The future of US military power

The history of US military power has seen a fundamental transformation over the course of 200 years. Whereas it is clear that the US, from the birth of the republic, has been willing to use force to protect its interests, like any other state, it was also for the first hundred years or so of its existence infused with a very particular anti-militarist tendency. While this did not prevent the US from expansionism or intervention, it did demonstrate clear political limits to what Americans were willing to tolerate in terms of military power. However, the rise of American power in the twentieth century, combined with the changing character of war, led to a shift in

American preparedness. While the US would never become completely dominated by the military, the end of World War II and the beginning of the Cold War saw a shift in priorities of the US state, towards higher military spending and a focus on defense and national security. While some saw this as a necessity, it was still seen as developing real problems for the future of the US in terms of the influence of military power within the polity itself, and also dangerously skewing US foreign policy-making towards military goals.

While the US continues to spend enormous amounts of money on military power, the wars of Afghanistan and Iraq have also shown the limits of the military power. While the US was easily able, in both cases, to topple militaries and states with relatively weaker armed forces, it was not entirely able to convert military power into the political goals it set out to achieve in either case, partially due to the lack of coherent political goals wedded to military objectives, but also due to the impossibility of the military easily achieving goals like state-building. The military itself went through a huge upheaval in those years, at first protesting against the imposition of unsustainable military actions, but then by re-conceiving US military doctrine in a fashion that would enable it to achieve a broader purpose, through a revised and comprehensive approach to counter-insurgency. To some extent the policy shift has been a success. However, it is not without further costs: that counter-insurgency requires long-term, large-scale commitment is without question, and the ability of the US to sustain such commitments is highly questionable. The recent report demonstrating a rethinking of American military and defense policy in terms of a 'pivot' towards Asia (United States Department of Defense, 2012b) is part of coming to terms with some of these problems. The report, 'Sustaining Global Leadership', calls for a need not only to reduce spending in a time of economic austerity, but also to face up to new global realities. Mainly the report indicates a move away from costly stability operations, to an emphasis on reducing costs, and a move towards focusing defense and security on Asia. As such the real challenges to American military power are dealing with the overall efficacy of military power, potential shifts in the balance of power, and the ability of the US to pay for its extravagant military. The next chapter links into this issue by focusing on the future of US economic power.

Chapter 5

The Rise (and Fall?) of American Economic Power

The economic power of the US is a prime source of its hegemony and influence in world affairs. The future of US economic leadership in the face of relative decline is potentially the most critical issue for the future of American power. Key rivals such as Brazil, Russia, India and China (the so-called 'BRIC' economies – though now expanded as 'BRICS' to include South Africa), as well as economically robust states such as Germany, continue to have strong growth and a (seemingly) relative immunity to recent economic problems. While US military power is unrivalled (if not necessarily as fungible as is sometimes thought), economic power is not. However, there remain important questions that need to be addressed to understand the present state of US economic power. First, there is a fundamental issue concerning how US economic power is expressed. Like military power, economic power should not be seen merely in terms of relative material measures such as GDP or GDP growth (as important as these are). The institutional and structural power of the US in the global economy is equally important, and understanding the various ways that this power can be analysed is crucial for answering other important questions on the future of US of power. Second, with a better understanding of the character of US economic power, we can move on to the relative durability of economic power, and whether US economic power is in terminal decline. While these issues are related, they should be seen as analytically distinct. The former tends to involve the extent to which the US can maintain leadership or hegemony over the global political economy. The latter has more to do with the mounting set of domestic crises and challenges that the US economy faces. Obviously, these are interlinked, but they do not necessarily presuppose one another.

The chapter addresses all of these issues by charting the gradual, spectacular rise of US economic power through the nineteenth and early twentieth centuries, especially focusing on the guiding ideas of national political economy that were developed, and how they influenced later policy and ideology. The chapter then examines the domestic side of American political economy. While most discussion of US foreign policy and power focus on the international dimension of economic power, the domestic dynamics can provide a number of important insights. First is the extent to which the national interest is skewed and contested by regional divides in political economy. Second is how specific domestic dynamics express themselves internationally. A core aim of this part of the chapter is to clarify the role of economic power within the broader contours of American power: the US remains a highly dynamic capitalist state, and the relationship between civil society and government, and the broader domestic dynamics of American economic power is an important part of understanding the future of American power.

The chapter then moves on to examine the US-led global economic system that was developed post-World War II. Here we can see the institutional features developed in part (but backed materially) by American policy-makers, along with their British counterparts. While these institutions did not initially have a truly global reach, and shifted in purpose over the course of the Cold War, they remain fundamentally important in backing US institutional and structural power over the global economy, and with the end of the Cold War did become global. Finally, the chapter addresses core problems with American economic power, mainly in terms of the domestic economic challenges the US faces, but also to do with expanding 'competition' globally. Overall, the main argument of the chapter is that while US economic power is clearly in relative decline, the main issues it faces concern its actual hegemony (or leadership) in the global political economy in the context of the rise of other states and the series of domestic economic crises that are becoming increasingly difficult to solve.

US economic power in perspective

In comparative terms, the extent of US economic power is obvious. The US (as of 2011) has the largest GDP in the world at 15 trillion US dollars, with its closest competitor, China, some way behind at $7.3 trillion, and other competitors at about a third of that (World Bank, 2013). Figure 5.1 notes the comparative overall wealth of (usually noted) key competitors of the US in terms of economic power from 2000 to 2011. Looking at the figures over time it is clear that China has been catching up with the US in its overall wealth and this measure becomes even closer if measured at Purchasing Power Parity (PPP) – with China at $11.3 trillion, and the US at just under $15 trillion (though there is some contention in using PPP to measure relative power – see Brooks and Wohlforth, 2008: 40–45). China's catch-up has mainly been due to the remarkable growth rates that China has managed over the past decade (see Figure 5.2). However, even here, the greater per capita GDP of the United States ($47,199 in 2010) compared with China ($4,428.46 in 2010) also shows a greater potential to convert economic power into state power – through taxes and overall surpluses that are available for investment (see Figure 5.3) (Ikenberry, 2011: 44; Beckley, 2011/12). The comparative indicators do also show the strong growth of India and Brazil, but still behind the US overall – China is clearly the state that is 'catching up' the most rapidly, with estimates predicting between 5 and 20 years, dependent on growth levels. The other developed economies remain fairly static, with growth rates that

Figure 5.1   *GDP in trillions current $US, 2000–11*

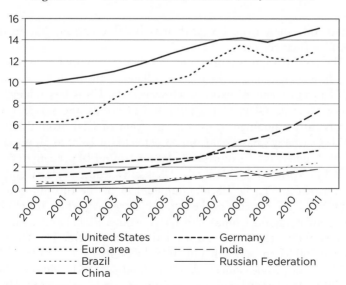

Source: World Bank, *World Development Indicators*, 2013.

Figure 5.2   *Annual GDP growth, in percentage, 2000–11*

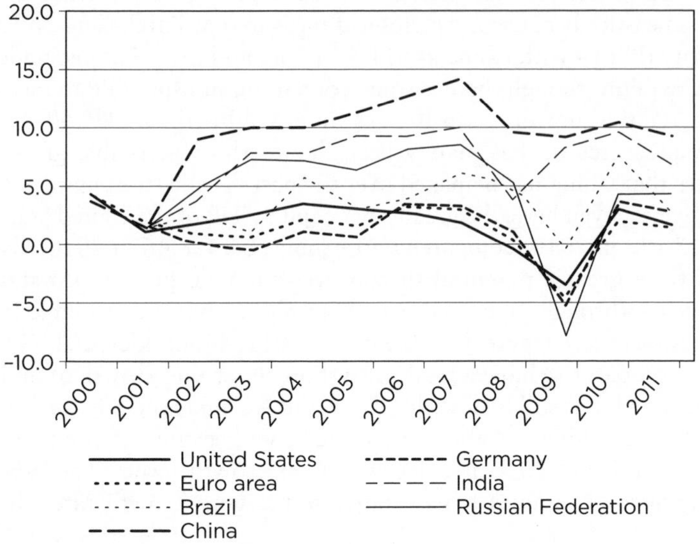

Source: World Bank, *World Development Indicators*, 2013.

reasonably match the US (with massive fluctuations due to the 2007/08 financial crisis.

   The US still imports more than any other state (with China closing in); however, it is increasingly challenged by both China and Germany in terms of exports. However, the US is less reliant on exports for its GDP: China's exports of goods and services has consistently amounted to over 30 per cent of GDP from 2000 to 2011; Germany's has risen from 33 per cent in 2000 to 50 per cent in 2011; whereas US exports account for around 14 per cent of GDP in 2011 (World Bank, 2013). The US is still a leader in global corporations. In 2011, the US maintained 133 of the top 500 global companies (26 per cent of the total) (by revenue), where the closest competitor (again China) had 61 (Fortune, 2011). As with the figures above, there is again a relative decline here. The Fortune Global 500 list indicates that in 2005 the US had 176 in the top 500 (35 per cent), while China had only 16 (and Japan 81). Finally, while the 2007/08 financial crisis had an influence on liquidity in the US, it has had little impact on one of the sources of US financial power: its ability to maintain debts and current account deficits while not

Figure 5.3   *GDP per capita, in current $US, 2000–11*

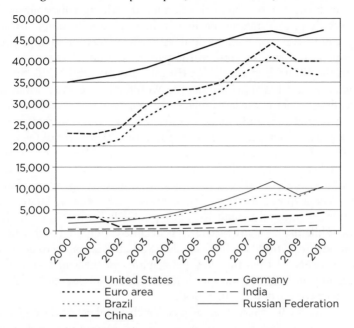

Source: World Bank, *World Development Indicators*, 2013.

incurring the normal financial penalties (Germain, 2009: 685–6; Mastanduno, 2009; Schwartz, 2010). While much of this is predicated on the use of the dollar as an international reserve currency (and more will be said about this later), it is also due to the ability of the US to retain remarkably low rates of government borrowing, and willing investors at home and abroad.

Looking at these trends over time, it is clear that the US is facing a relative decline in its economic power, if examined through the measure of material resources. Measuring growth, output and levels of international trade all show some degree of relative decline. Furthermore, the ongoing economic crisis within the US – both through the recession caused by the 2007/08 financial crisis and the ongoing fiscal crisis – has put in place potential competitors to US economic hegemony; a view that is shared to some extent by a number of commentators (e.g. Zakaria, 2009) and to a certain degree the Obama Administration (J. Mann, 2012; Singh, 2012). However, this view is mainly based on a material picture of power capacity, and is thus most closely related to the 'compulsory' view of power. First, even relying on these figures describing a distribution of power, despite the relative decline of the US, it is still comparatively more powerful economically (and militarily) in relation to other peer competitors than any state in the past two hundred years – other than the US itself in the 1950s (Brooks and Wohlforth, 2008: 31; Ikenberry, 2001: 43). As Brooks and Wohlforth note, even Britain as a leading power in the late nineteenth century was outspent militarily by both Russia and France, and its economy was only marginally larger than either, each accounting for about 20 per cent of the total GDP of the six leading great powers (Brooks and Wohlforth, 2008: 30). When looking at the position of the US today (as of 2009), it accounts for some 60 per cent of the total military spending of key 'rival' great powers today (China, France, UK, Russia, Japan and Germany), and still around 40 per cent of GDP (Ikenberry, 2011: 42, 45). While the US share of GDP has declined compared with where it stood after World War II (Kennedy, 1989), this is mainly to do with the recovery of the other key participants in the war (especially Germany and Japan), and the rising economic development of Asia and parts of the developing world.

Second, as Ikenberry has argued, such numbers mainly give a picture of the distribution of power in the international system in terms of the key 'peer competitors' of the US, but 'that is all. It is not a description of the political formation that is built on and around those distributed capabilities' (Ikenberry, 2011: 46–7). Just looking at power distributions tells us little about how order is maintained and, as such, a mere focus on aggregate material power (or potential power) does not tell us everything. While these measures indicate the US is clearly in *relative* decline (from a rather high benchmark), it is still the world's largest economy, and has other attributes that need to be taken account of in order to better conceptualize both power and decline. As Susan Strange (1987; 1988) has noted, the obsession with American economic hegemony in terms of *capabilities* rather than *relationships* has long been problematic. Does the size of an economy equate to power? As Kagan (2012) has pointed out, China had the biggest economy in the nineteenth century in terms of overall size, but this did not give it international pre-eminence; rather it was the victim of repeated predations of the great powers. This, of course, points to the importance of institutional and structural power.

In terms of the former, we can see a number of influential institutions that are linked to US leadership in the global economy, which has been based since the post-World War II period on international institutions that 'govern' the global economy. Institutions such as the World Bank, International Monetary Fund (IMF), and the World Trade Organization (WTO) are all based on US principles in terms of the desire for an open international economy, which have a broad acceptance in the international realm: all are crucial institutions for providing mechanisms of governance, and also guiding ideologies for global capitalism. These views see US economic power in terms of a broad 'multilateralism', as open, in terms of both international trade and overall international economic integration, and that the core international economic institutions have been promoted by the US as a means to embed its interests in a liberal international economic order for collective benefit. That's not to say that the US has done it selflessly – in fact most scholars who take this viewpoint see it as a way of enhancing US power – but that by promoting US leadership in an open international economic system, all will gain (Ikenberry, 2011).

It should be stressed that these institutions, while certainly led by the US, are also relatively autonomous in that they do not always uphold direct US interests. We should see them in another way, in terms of the institutional notion of power: they mobilize the bias of upholding American-led capitalism, rather than just the direct inter-ests of the US state itself. Since these two sets of interests mostly coincide, it has always been beneficial for the US to keep involved with all of these institutions. Additionally, as Ikenberry has argued, they also provide a way for other states to be part of the American-led system, while having some assurances that the US will not domi-nate everything. This can be well illustrated examining the rise of China in terms of institutional power. Ikenberry (2008) has argued that China's rise is best seen in how it has prospered through its gradual integration into the Western (and US-led) economic order, not through opposition. Although Ikenberry is not saying that further integration is preordained; it is the case that conflict can potentially be mitigated by the further promotion of liberal interna-tional order – an important point when considering the future of US power (economic or otherwise). As such, the real issue here in terms of decline is whether or not US leadership and legitimacy is being challenged in relation to this architecture, or if other architectures are taking over (which will be analysed further in Chapter 7).

In terms of structural power, the US has managed to maintain this power through a series of important structural and institutional initiatives that had their origins in the immediate post-war period, and have continued on to the present day (Wade, 2003). Susan Strange relied on four sources of structural power (security, production, finance and knowledge) to conceptualize this order (Strange, 1988: ch. 2; cf. Konings, 2009), and drawing loosely on these we can see that American structural economic power is well embedded in the international system today. As discussed in the previous chapter, the US is by far the biggest spender on defense in the world, and even though it does not have a relative advantage in terms of numbers of personnel, its spending on capital investment and technology gives it the most qualitatively superior military force in the world, with the ability to project power globally.

American firms, in terms of innovation and production, still have real advantages in the international system, and while American firms are relatively weaker in terms of the their global market share than in the past, they still have much overall weight in the world (Germain, 2009; Schwartz, 2010). As Germain notes, 'while the global economy is now receptive to an unprecedented degree to the globalizing activities of companies from emerging market economies, it is no less receptive also to the global operations of American firms, which continue to maintain a strong position in many older industries such as defense manufacturing alongside newer high-tech industries, high-end service industries and of course cultural industries' (2009: 684). The US also retains a real dominance in technology, as seen in its relative weighting in terms of high-technology production, its investment in research and design as well a higher education in science (Brooks and Wohlforth, 2008: 32–3; Beckley, 2011/12).

In terms of finance, the US maintains a central position in the global economy through the use of the US dollar as a global reserve currency (Germain, 2009; Schwartz, 2010; Wade, 2003). The dollar continues to be heavily utilized as the main foreign exchange holding by foreign governments, and additionally used to price key commodities – such as oil – in the global market. The global use of the dollar allows the US to maintain a number of structural advantages. First and foremost, it allows the US to run large trade imbalances and deficits simultaneously, while not succumbing to the normal pressures such imbalances normally give. While such power is not uncontested, and not unchanging through time, the US has been remarkably adept at maintaining dollar hegemony through a number of crises of adjustment that have occurred over the past fifty years (Eichengreen, 2011; Mastanduno, 2009). Additionally, leading states such as China that continue to hold large dollar reserves have not attempted (and might find it hard to attempt) to leverage such holdings into coercive economic power (Drezner, 2009; cf. Cappaccio and Kruger, 2012). To the extent to which major states in the global economy as well as markets retain confidence in the dollar and US debt obligations, and additionally see the importance in maintaining the US as the center of the global economy, the dollar will retain its power, with all the benefits it accrues (Helleiner, 2009; Kirshner, 2008).

Overall, while it is clear that there is a relative decline in US economic power (one that has been going on for quite some time), the US still has a number of structural advantages that work in its favor. This is not to say that these are not under threat, or will not be challenged in the future, but they are important for understanding the position of the US in the present. While more will be said about the structural problems and weakness of US economic power today, as well as the institutional and structural dimensions of US economic power, attention to the historical development of US power is also crucial to understanding its future.

The development of economic power

The US did not start out as an economic powerhouse. As with the rise of military power, the US only came to the level we now associate it with later in the nineteenth century. The development of the US as an economic power was significant in providing an extra-European source of economic power in the nineteenth century, and its early growth and increasing status in maritime trade clearly demonstrated its potential (Kennedy, 1989: 120–1). However, the importance of the US was also in terms of its specific founding ideology, which went hand in hand with US economic power: the idea of the US as a liberal, commercial society. As so much of present US power hinges on its economic capacity, it is important to discuss its background: as in the field of military power, much of the priorities of the US domestically and in the world rest on previous institutional developments. From an agrarian society to an industrial power in the late nineteenth century, to the industrial and financial center through the twentieth, the economic power of the US and its attendant ideology has become preponderant in the world at large.

The commercial and economic potential of the US goes further back than just the creation of the independent republic, as much of the idea of early America was about the freedom that the land represented. The early agricultural development of the US was very important for what was to follow. As Seavoy notes, 'the successful transfer of English institutions that induced commercial agriculture was one of the principal legacies of colonial governance that contributed to the rapid industrialization of the United States in the nineteenth century' (Seavoy, 2006: 8). The commercial and industrial revolution that had recently developed in England was therefore something that had been exported in principle to the US, and underpinned much of the thinking about the American political economy: limits for the role of the state and an emphasis on private property and individual liberty.

The founders of the republic were in a precarious position after the revolution. The US was primarily an agricultural economy that focused on the export of raw materials, particularly cotton and tobacco, but was also a developing industrial power (Kennedy, 1989: 121). However, there was also obvious potential to develop an even bigger manufacturing capacity as a part of national development. The battle of ideas between a 'Hamiltonian' and 'Jeffersonian' vision of American economic development became a prominent way of thinking about the development of the US over the course of the nineteenth century (and as Lind has noted, in some ways has affected the contours of economic thinking in the US ever since) (Lind, 2012: 12–16; Seavoy, 2006: 82–3). Early on, Alexander Hamilton, the first Secretary of the Treasury, in his famous 'Report on Manufactures' of 1791, emphasized the need to develop indigenous industry through protectionist measures and a program of improving national infrastructure. Hamilton's views, which became relatively dominant in American thinking about creating and improving economic capacity in the nineteenth century, highlight the importance of a development strategy devised around economic nationalism (Earle, 1986). The Hamiltonian vision focused on a state-led programme of development, with the state taking the lead in promoting the expansion of industry, infrastructure, and the creation of a national bank to control monetary policy.

Jefferson, on the other hand, promoted the individual virtue of yeoman farmers: the rise of an industrial working class was seen as being against the American republican tradition. For Jefferson, the promotion of industry (especially through tariff barriers) would lead to an unhealthy relationship between government and business, and also to the harmful expansion of cities and an industrial working class (Seavoy, 2006: 84; cf. Jefferson, 1993). Seavoy additionally notes that much of Jefferson's views were also an apologia of sorts for slavery – a practice which he publicly derided, but continued by holding slaves until his death – as the Southern plantation economy negated the possibilities and disruptive potentials of free labor (on the concerns of 'free labor', see Foner, 1995); Lind further notes that in retirement in 1816 Jefferson had hoped for the industrial north to split off from the south (Lind, 2012: 44).

While the tensions between these early visions of political econ- omy were real, when Jefferson became president, he and his succes- sors did see the rationale in Hamilton's proposals, and, as Lind points out, 'by the 1820s, a consensus on the need for infant-indus- try protection, internal improvements, and a national bank had coalesced' (Lind, 2012: 47). While conservative politicians today often look back at the US as being a vanguard of commercial capital- ist virtues – which in some ways it certainly was (the 'Model Treaty' described in Chapter 1 was certainly revolutionary in this sense – though also a pragmatic solution to the problem of relative American weakness) – the nineteenth-century reality is more on the Hamiltonian side. The American agricultural and industrial econ- omy was famously protected from outside influence. Although farm- ers did need export markets, the import of goods was prohibited through high tariffs. Even the development of manufacturing was predicated on this policy – despite the Model Treaty's emphasis on free trade, Hamilton and his followers saw a real need for a protected American economy. Similarly, infrastructural develop- ment in transportation – mainly in steamboats, turnpikes, canals and railroads – was also developed through the national state, seen as crucial to national economic improvement (Seavoy, 2006: 101–5).

All in all, these two visions probably should not be seen as entirely competing, but relatively contradictory trends that were in tension throughout the nineteenth century, and underpin in many ways the debates surrounding the size (and purpose) of the state against the liberty of individuals that have been occurring since, though under different circumstances. Despite the consensus between early democrats and federalists, the election of Andrew Jackson in 1828 saw a renewal of anti-government and anti-industrial sentiment, part of Jackson's populist movement against moneyed interests and the domination of corporations (Howe, 2007: 500–501; Lind, 2012: 108–9). This had real impacts on the future of a national bank and national-led infrastructure projects. In many ways the rise of Jacksonian populism also brought out into the open the somewhat submerged battle between the increasingly important industrial northwest (and western 'free soilers') and the agricultural economy of the South, and also in the South's continued reliance on slavery, a rift that would eventually lead to all-out war between the regions (Stephanson, 1995: 31–2; cf. McPherson, 1990). Despite the rise of populism, the importance and influence of industrial power grew and grew, and the US by 1830 could be considered the sixth industrial power of the world (Kennedy, 1989: 121).

American economic development up to the Civil War saw an ever-increasing importance of industry, and according to Kennedy's figures, between 1860 and 1900, industrial production went from being 7.2 per cent of world output to 23.6 per cent (Kennedy, 1989: 190). The US was beginning to live up to its potential as a great economic power. However, the divisions described above that eventually led to the Civil War in 1861 also demonstrated the pronounced developmental divisions between North and South (Ashworth, 1995; McPherson, 1990). The North was able to muster all of the industrial and financial might of an industrialized power, while the South was unable to contest a drawn-out war with an agricultural economy and had no real way to finance war (see Kennedy, 1989: 228–34). The North's victory was in some ways a victory for the Hamiltonian program; as Lind notes, 'even before the war ended and the period of Reconstruction began, the remaking of the United States by northerners was well underway' (Lind, 2012: 141).

In the twentieth century, politicians increasingly saw a need to intervene in economic matters, mainly to do with a variety of recurring economic crises, such as the Panic of 1893, the biggest recession the US had yet seen. The public debate at the turn of the century became fixated on the problems of the gold standard, with Democratic presidential candidate William Jennings Bryan railing against the evils of the gold standard, and promoting the virtues of 'bi-metalism'. The presidencies of Theodore Roosevelt, William H. Taft and Woodrow Wilson, again subject to numerous depressions and recessions, increasingly saw the need to find ways of stabilizing the economy and finding a way of dealing with the increasing problems of industrialization. Drawing on the 'progressivism' of the time, Roosevelt was at the center of an era (lasting until about 1920) that focused on government regulations to stabilize the economy and make it 'fairer' overall (Hofstadter, 1955; cf. Jenkins, 2012: ch.

4). The focus was on a set of reforms that would help to do this: a national income tax; pursuing antitrust violations; improved labor conditions; and a national currency through the Federal Reserve Act. The Progressive Era was really a start to greater state intervention being accepted by Americans at large, and made possible later appeals to state intervention in the 'New Deal' era of Franklin Delano Roosevelt.

The latter Roosevelt, as outlined in Chapter 1, inaugurated a new principle of state intervention in the economy, with the anaemic reactions to the Great Depression being taken over by massive programs of deficit spending intended to not only increase employment and recover growth, but also to protect hard-hit people from the worst effects of the depression (through the creation of the program of 'social security'). Roosevelt created numerous new federal programs and agencies that put people back to work, while at the same time promoting economic development, infrastructure modernization, and economic recovery. While there is still controversy over how successful these programs were, and a great deal of partisan fighting over their future, they did seem to gradually help the US fight its way out of depression (especially in Roosevelt's first term) (Jenkins, 2012: 204–9; Lind, 2012: 303–6; cf. Kennedy, 1999: ch. 12; Leuchtenburg, 1963), and were also eventually a victory for Roosevelt's more internationalist leanings in foreign policy and international economic policy.

World War II intervened in a crucial way: it allowed for massive state investment in industries geared towards war, solved the continuing problem of unemployment, and led to some real compromise with labor that in the long run greatly affected the balance between the state, business and labor. Additionally, due to the relative safety of the American homeland, it also meant that by the end of the war, the US was in a position to be the leading industrial power in the global economy. The war also demonstrated the unrealized potential of the economy as a backing for US geopolitical power (also see Chapters 1 and 3). Prior to the war the US was certainly recognized as a great power, with a formidable navy, but the war demonstrated the capacity of the US to mobilize its economy into a war production mode. At the start of the war, the US spent only 1.5 per cent of national income on the military (Kennedy, 1989: 429), which increased to 37.5 per cent by 1945 (White House, 2012b). As noted in the previous chapter, US productivity by the end of the war was unbelievably impressive. By the end of the war, the US was not only out of depression, but by some distance the leading economy in the world. Devastated by the war, the formerly leading industrial states needed to rebuild their productivity, with the US now accounting for some 50 per cent of global production.

World War II and the early-post-war period also extended conflict between business and labor that had been taking place since the Great Depression. The conflict in many ways concerned the future of the political economy of the US (Griffith, 1989). While there was never a fear of a more European-style social democracy, the war saw rising union militancy and potential strikes that became the norm in the early post-war period. Strikes such as that at General Motors in 1946 led to some hope in the labor movement of a move towards a more 'corporatist' state. But the reaction from the business community, encouraged by government, was to end such hopes and put legal limits on strike actions and union radicalism through the Taft-Hartley Act, signed in 1947 by the Republican-controlled Congress (Eisner, 2011: 95–8; Lichtenstein, 1989). The importance of this for understanding future state power concerns the shape it gave to the American political economy. While already an economic powerhouse, the post-war moment clarified that the future would be much like the past in terms of labor power versus corporate America.

The debates over the consequences and desirability of the New Deal and its role in the economy from the 1930s to 1960s also provided a new way of framing economic ideas in the US. While the battle between Hamilton and Jefferson was important in terms of the development of the US, after World War II the debates became more about the continued growth and expansion of US economic power, along with ways of managing crisis. The rising power of the state both domestically and internationally allowed for the possibility of an American prominence in the global economy (through international trade and the dominance of the dollar as a reserve currency), and the possibility for massive state intervention at home. While Roosevelt inaugurated the tradition of John Maynard Keynes as a form of economic interventionism (which was still devoted to capitalism, despite what present-day critics may say), the successes of the US did lead to a real backlash from traditional republican critics of deficit spending, taxes and the expansion of the state. Much of this criticism in the 1950s began to draw on Austrian-British political thinker Friedrich Hayek (e.g. Hayek, 1944), who saw a real danger to liberty in the reliance on the state. The idea of a 'big government' became anathema to republican critics from this more libertarian tradition, with a real variety of emphases. More extreme forms of libertarianism continue to prosper (seen especially in the current prominence of the work of Ayn Rand, and policy proposals concerning the abolition of the Federal Reserve and a return to the gold standard), some of which can be found in the views of the 'Tea Party' faction of the Republican Party (discussion of these various trends can be found in Cassidy, 2009; Quiggin, 2010; Wapshott, 2011).

These intellectual trends have set much of the terms for the debate over the role of the US state in the economy. 'Liberal' Democrats have taken the side of Keynes, arguing that the state can play a decisive role in dealing with economic crises (and sometimes taking this further, to an almost Hamiltonian view on the role of the state in industrial development). Conservative 'Hayekians' take the other side, mainly objecting to government regulation, taxes, and state involvement in business and the economy in any way. There are, of course, real contradictions in such positions. First, conservatives (save for more traditional economic conservatives and those with more libertarian leanings) have not been shy about proposing regulations about morality, especially in controversial areas of American politics such as gay marriage, abortion and other so-called 'wedge issues'. Second, despite the focus on a small state, there are of course a plethora of regulations and actions that are pro-business, that essentially support conservative positions on wealth distribution through tax policy, decreasing social expenditure, anti-union activity, and financial regulation (e.g. Baker, 2006; Hacker and Pierson, 2010).

Two interesting things should be noted from these trends. First, despite the overheated rhetoric at times, neither of these positions is critical of capitalism as an economic doctrine – they just vary on the terms of individual liberty within capitalism, and the kinds of regulation necessary to provide a structure for capitalism. Second, neither side has much to say about international aspects of capitalism. While traditional liberals have been keen to continue to promulgate the key tenets of liberal free trade (e.g. Krugman, 1997), politically these are continually shaped by the need of both liberals and conservatives to focus on the domestic economy. Jobs and growth are therefore often tied politically into problems with the domestic labor market and international trade. Politically, as was the case in the nineteenth century, much of the debate is connected to the regional interests of particular economic sectors, and the impact of globalization on manufacturing.

National political economy and the national interest

While economic power is usually examined in terms of its effects on international relations, it is also important to understand the particularities and peculiarities of the domestic composition of American political economy. The US domestic economy (along with the domestic economies of most of the major economic powers of the world) has long been hugely important in its own right, despite the increasing internationalization of economic life. Furthermore, foreign policy is often a contest between competing interests, not always made in a 'rational' fashion, with a predetermined national interest in mind (other than mere state survival). The internal dynamics of the American political economy, and in particular the regional character of American politics, therefore also plays into debates about foreign policy. Much of this regionalism is tied robustly to the composition of Congress, in terms of how representatives from particular regions promote that region's interest in Congress (see e.g. Fordham, 2007). However, divisions and contestation also tie in with many interesting facets of broader societal relations in the US: for example, the political culture and history of various regions, and the political economy of regions, especially in terms of divisions between economic sectors that had regional divisions. Regionalism also highlights some of the diffuseness (or pluralism) of political power in the American state: that regional interests can have the power to sway both the foreign policy process but also the overall sense of the national interest.

First, it is important to note the role of the federal government in shaping the economy. While it was noted above that the US has increasingly adopted a liberal 'laissez-faire' approach to the economy, much of this has surrounded the particular *kinds* of interventions that the government does. These interventions, despite the clear opposition between those who want less state intervention (and therefore are seemingly 'anti-regulatory') and those who want more, are always political (Hacker and Pierson, 2010: 55; cf. Polanyi, 1944). The advocates of a smaller state have also influenced the development of state–market relations that are strongly pro-business (Baker, 2006; Hacker and Pierson, 2010; cf. Eisner, 2011: ch. 7; Konings, 2009). Congress is important in two key ways:

setting rules about economic action within the economy; and through fiscal policy, seen both in setting federal income tax rates and by authorizing the budget of the federal government. The president plays a crucial role in these processes as well, trying to set and shape policy, and set the overall tone for political and economic intervention (see e.g. Bowles, 2003; McKay, 2009: ch. 18). Finally, the Federal Reserve (Fed) is a central actor in shaping the domestic economy, and also has hugely consequential international effects. The Fed is the key shaper of monetary policy, and since its creation in 1913 has been independent of direct political influence (the Board of Governors are appointed by the president for 14-year terms, but the Fed can instigate policy actions without further authorization). While the powers of the Fed have evolved over time (particularly in response to changing demands of the economy), it has the power to do a number of important actions that effect the money supply: setting interest rates, issuing bonds, injecting money into the system (e.g. through 'quantitative easing') or contracting it.

In some ways, we can say that there is a reasonably broad consensus in American society concerning the economy: there is little debate about the character of the US as a commercial and capitalist society. There has long been an interrelationship between business, elites, and the government itself, to the extent to which it is reasonably safe to say that the US state is firmly entrenched with elites who represent the business community in all sorts of ways. For example, there are numerous interest groups based around economic sectors that seek to shape and influence government policy (such as energy, agriculture, and health care). Additionally, contention can be seen in the political debates about free trade. While there is a broad, liberal consensus around the value of free trade, it is also one that tends to be tempered by the interests of particular business sectors (e.g. the agricultural sector has long been protected with subsidies). There is also often a political debate about putting American businesses and workers 'first' in times of economic hardship.

One of the most important factors in shaping US economic power is through the dynamics of 'regional sectionalism'. The US has a large and diverse geography, and its politics have long been shaped by the varieties of regional political economy that exist within the US (e.g. Bensel, 1984). These regional geographies have also historically changed in ways that have had demonstrable results both on shaping the overall 'national interest' and in the geography of political representation. It has long been noted that the US has had regional economic development with direct impact on foreign policy. For example, in the late nineteenth century there were real divisions between Northern industrialists and Southern agriculturalists, with the former looking for protection of home markets for their products, and the latter wanting greater internationalism to find foreign markets for agricultural surplus (Trubowitz, 1998: ch. 2). The inter-war period also saw divisions between internationalists and protectionists, this time between an increasingly influential group representing the financial sector who wanted to promote the internationalization of the economy (and represented in the government by the State Department), and powerful industrialists who wanted protection and a focus on domestic investment (with supporters in the Commerce Department) (Frieden, 1988).

In the post-war period, sectional conflict was suppressed to some degree by an overall consensus on foreign policy (partially by a coalition of north-eastern Republicans and Southern Democrats, who were economic beneficiaries of military spending and economic openness), the legacy of Roosevelt's internationalism, as well as domestic coalition-building (as part of the New Deal) (see Bensel, 1984: ch. 5; Trubowitz, 2012: 154–5). The 1960s and 1970s were a fractious era for US politics and economy, where the strains of the Cold War coalition started to break down. In the 1960s, the US became increasingly divided by both civil rights and the Vietnam War, which caused a fracture in the fragile Democratic Party that increasingly brought together elements of labor, 'liberals' as well as old Southern Democrats, who were against civil rights. The tensions came to a head in the 1968 election, where Southern Democrats switched to support Republican candidate Richard Nixon (and also third-party candidate, Alabama Governor George Wallace).

The 1960s and 1970s also saw a change in the economic geography of the US, with the decline of industry in the Northeast ('the rustbelt') with industry moving to the south ('the sunbelt'). The states of the 'sunbelt' (adding in Washington State as well) also became what has been described as the 'gunbelt', a broad region that had become entrenched with defense production (Markusen et al., 1991). Declining relative international competitiveness in the Northeast and increasing capital mobility within the US contributed to the changes. These areas are also competing for foreign policy influence, with the sunbelt promoting a more expansive foreign policy, and the rustbelt for more cost-consciousness (Trubowitz, 1998: ch. 4). These demographic and economic changes have also had an impact on national politics, and reflect shifts in political power, where the sunbelt has become increasingly important. The realignment of party support in the late 1960s, with Southern Democrats switching to the Republican Party, along with increased support for Republicans in the 'Mountain West' region, were a large part of this change – and are easily seen in the changing electoral map of presidential elections. 'Red' (Republican) states push for the primacy of security and power projection; while 'blue' (Democratic) states on the Pacific Coast and Northeast want less power projection and a more domestic focus, as well as a greater internationalism (Trubowitz, 2012).

American leadership and hegemony

While the evolution of domestic political economy aids our understanding of domestic contention over the national interest and foreign policy, we also need to examine the international side of American economic power. The end of World War II saw the creation of a new global economic system, or at least one centered on the Western capitalist states, with the US as the main backer. While the origins of the system were firmly in the war itself, with the US and Britain setting up the essential institutions, it came to full fruition in the early years of the Cold War. Often referred to as the Bretton Woods system, after the historic conference in 1944 at Bretton Woods, New Hampshire, it was intended as an open, institutionalized international economic system that would overcome the preferential bi-lateral trading system of the interwar years, seen as being at least partially responsible for the economic problems of the interwar period, and the war itself (see e.g. Eichengreen, 1996: ch. 4; Ikenberry, 1993; Helleiner, 1994: ch. 2). While the creation of the institutional architecture was not without debates and controversies (with the US mainly getting its way in opposition to most of the British proposals), the system that was put in place has been remarkably robust over time, even if it has gone through a number of crises, and changed in purpose. However, the Bretton Woods system needs to be seen as more than just an economic system, as it was at the heart of the post-war political order. As Mastanduno describes, 'the United States essentially made a long-term investment in the economic viability and political stability of other advanced industrial states – states that would eventually provide growing markets for U.S. exports and foreign direct investment and serve as anti-communist bulwarks in the two major theatres of the Cold War, Europe and East Asia' (Mastanduno, 2009: 129).

At its heart were two formal organizations: the International Monetary Fund (IMF) was created to deal with balance of payments problems in order to ensure economic stability; and the World Bank was created to help provide capital to countries devastated by war. Additionally, if less a part of a formal organization, the international monetary system was also bolstered by two crucial elements: the maintenance of capital controls to stop destabilizing movements of capital; and the system of 'pegged' currencies, using the dollar as the international reserve currency backed by gold held in reserve in the US (Eichengreen, 1996: ch. 4; Gilpin, 2001: ch. 9). While not formally part of Bretton Woods, the General Agreement on Tariffs and Trade (GATT), agreed in 1947, was created as an ongoing forum to reduce tariffs and avoid the protectionism that was endemic in the interwar years.

The international order was backed up by the increase in US economic power post-World War II. With the US homeland untouched by war and bolstered by wartime production, and the traditional great powers all devastated by the war, the US was in a real position of dominance. However, these gains in power were never going to be forever, especially with American policy-makers promoting an open international economy and the recovery of the countries in Europe. Indeed one of the biggest problems for the US in the early post-war years was the lack of growth in the rest of the world and the impossibility of states to have enough dollars to import goods they needed from the US. The so-called 'dollar gap' dominated American foreign policy elites in the post-war years, to an extent that is often lost in the literature on the start of the Cold War, which tends to emphasize strategic issues and geopolitics (Cardwell, 2011). The key early programs of the Truman Administration – the 1947 Greek and Turkish aid program (the announcement of the Truman Doctrine), the 1948 European Recovery Program (the 'Marshall Plan') – were not just political moves to help shore up allies that might be threatened by communism, but also ways of getting dollars to western Europe that could then be used to buy American goods.

The US plan was highly successful, if not amounting to a complete victory for the economic liberalism those US planners might have desired. In terms of successes, the fixed exchange rate policy combined with the Marshall Plan gave much stability to the post-war financial system, and spurred on the economies of Europe. On the trading side, there was much reluctance to inaugurate entirely free trade. The GATT formed a compromise system, which still allowed for protectionism in a number of key areas, most notably agriculture. The gradual move towards non-discrimination also still allowed for older preferential legacies of the interwar era to continue. The various GATT rounds conducted throughout the Cold War were meant to gradually chip away at this system, until a free trade system was ensconced.

US global economic leadership met its first major crisis in the 1960s, leading to the eventual abandonment of the Bretton Woods system by 1973. The dollar scarcity of the 1950s gave way to a dollar glut in the 1960s, which started to undermine the status of the dollar: more dollars were held outside the US than it could cover in gold. The dollar glut was caused by a number of factors: the return to convertibility of European currencies, rising industrial productivity outside the US, increasing US current account deficits, and increasing US public debt (much to do with the dual pressures of the Vietnam War and the increasing expenditure on various aspects of social security). A series of events in the 1960s – the 1967 devaluation of British Sterling, market pressures on the dollar via the 'Eurodollar' markets (the dollar glut had led to a market for dollar deposits in European banks, both to do something with the dollar surpluses and to get around US bank regulations), the over-valuing of the dollar (and subsequent pressures to devalue) – demonstrated that convertibility to gold was no longer feasible. These problems in the international monetary system were compounded by the relative decline in US industrial production (especially compared with West Germany and Japan), and the fiscal and monetary problems within the US caused by spending on the Vietnam War. The response to the long crisis was the eventual withdrawal of gold convertibility in 1971; and the Bretton Woods system was effectively over by 1973, with the end of fixed exchange rates (see generally: Eichengreen, 1996: ch. 4; Gilpin, 2001: 235–9; Kiely, 2007: 59–61; and Mastanduno, 2009).

The end of the Bretton Woods system saw the US struggling to find a new structure for the global economic order. For the first time since the interwar years, the US economy was struggling, and now showing signs of a relative decline. The oil crisis of 1973, spurred on by events in the Middle East (especially the 1973 Arab–Israeli War) and the pressures of the OPEC cartel led to huge increases in the costs of oil, which in turn created problems for US productivity. At the same time, the national economy was seeing decreased productivity, and the onset of 'stagflation', a previously unheard of economic phenomenon where the economy faces both inflation and low growth at the same time. The ending of Bretton Woods also meant that the dollar would face more severe market pressures as exchange rates floated. The problems of foreign exchange were mainly taken up by the G7: a steering committee of the leading industrial economies who agreed to maintain some solidarity in terms of fiscal and monetary policy in the hopes that that would stabilize the international financial and monetary system in the absence of a more formal regime. Finally, the 1960s were the beginnings of the internationalization of the global economy: international trade began to take up an increasing share of national output, which meant an increasing globalization of the international economy, with all of the attendant possibilities and dangers.

The advent of economic globalization in the 1970s has been crucial for American economic power (see e.g. Kiely, 2007). For one it has meant an increasing tying together of the economies of the developed (and developing) world – through the transnationalization of production and increased capital mobility – and recent crises have shown the consequences of this interconnectedness. Second, globalization has been tied up with an overall intellectual (and ideological) emphasis on 'neoliberalism', which has been seen variously as a particular set of policies of development embedded in international institutions, or an overall elite ideology of free markets, limited government, liberalization and privatization (Harvey, 2005). Third, globalization also led to major shifts in many industrial economies, especially those of smaller states and the Anglo-liberal states. The expansion of markets, opening up of trade barriers and industrial development in the periphery, meant a relative decline of industrial productivity in many states, which began a move towards the provision of services (and higher value-added production).

The early 1980s saw the US escape the problems of stagflation, but only by the imposition of harsh monetary policy that led to problems for its international allies (and questions to be asked about the impact of such policies domestically) (Eisner, 2011: 124–5). US interest rates went up, and with tight monetary policy the dollar appreciated substantially. These polices had a direct impact on problems elsewhere, including the 1982 Latin American debt crisis (see Kiely, 2007: 67–8) and the growing trade imbalances with Japan and

Germany (and ensuing adjustment issues). While this led to a (planned) recession in the US, the Reagan Administration also used the US's traditional leverage as the reserve currency as a way to avoid matching monetary discipline with fiscal discipline. The public debt rose substantially – from $914 billion in 1980 to $2.7 trillion in 1989 (Patterson, 2005: 158) – as defense spending increased in an attempt to ratchet up the Cold War rivalry with the Soviet Union. The US also pushed the burden of monetary adjustment onto its allies, through the 1985 Plaza Accord – where Japan and West Germany agreed (after much pressure from the US) to allow their own currencies to appreciate against the dollar (Gilpin, 2001: 245).

The collapse of the Soviet Union led to a real victory for global liberal capitalism. The alternatives to the US model of liberal capitalism became few and far between. While the Cold War provided both socialist and developmental alternatives to the US, the victory for liberalism led to an even firmer promotion of US economic values globally (and embedded in global economic institutions). In the main, this meant a greater consensus for the open international system that the US had promoted throughout the Cold War period. The US also continued its advocacy or pushing of its developmental model on the former communist states and the developing world. Russia, for instance, was invited to undergo a course of 'shock therapy' in order to start it on the road to a capitalist economy, involving the privatization of industry and opening up of markets with devastating consequences. Similar reforms were encouraged in the developing world – often through what had been critically dubbed the 'Washington Consensus' (though initially used by economist John Williamson in a positive way – Williamson, 2004) – especially in relation to the core Bretton Woods institutions, which had been reshaped during the 1970s and 1980s. The IMF especially had become key in promoting the American model of economic development, based on privatization and openness. In the post-Cold War era, the IMF and World Bank had also increasingly been retooled to promote governance reform as a means to development (see Kiely, 2007: 169–73). The GATT finally achieved its own formal institutional status as the World Trade Organization (WTO) in 1995.

All in all, the post-Cold War era saw both opportunities and problems for US economic power. The 'victory' for liberal capitalism certainly meant an increased potential for American hegemony, with no real alternative economic system to rival the US. Furthermore, the domestic economy received a real boost from the mid-1990s to the

2000s in terms of its overall growth, and the first budget surpluses in many years. However, the end of the Cold War also changed the broader stakes of economic power. Much of the leverage that the US gained from its allies (especially over adjustment issues in relation to current account deficits) was linked to security guarantees that the US provided. Despite the phenomenal economic growth of the US post-Cold War, it still had a decreasing share of global GDP, with economic powerhouses such as the newly unified Germany, Japan and increasingly, China, starting to rival US economic power. While it would be an overstatement to say that there was a challenge to US dominance, with the lack of a clear geopolitical rival, the increased power of other leading economies, and a more peaceful international system meant that the US increasingly had (potentially) less power to impose its will on other states (Mastanduno, 2009). Somewhat paradoxically, the victory of the US and its economic system meant there was less need to consistently rally around US interests. However, the institutional and structural power of the US has not yet unravelled. The ability of the Bush Administration post-9/11 to simultaneously increase defense spending to fund two wars and a 'Global War on Terror' and impose a major tax cut (pushing tax receipts to their lowest level in many years), meant that other states in the international system had not yet tired of the advantages that the US provided. As Mastanduno notes, 'it is hard to imagine any country other than the United States generating such massive imbalances, even in a single year much less over time, without suffering painful economic consequences' (2009: 146).

Competition, crisis and the future of US capitalism

We now have an overall portrait of US economic power: its history, its structural endurance, and the complexity of its relationship with the US state. We now return to the beginning, which is to discuss the future of US economic power. In no other area is the future of the US so challenged by various commentators than in terms of its future economic decline. The rise of Germany and China as leading exporters, and the development of other sources of economic competiveness in India and China, have all pointed to the potential limits of US economic strength. While the chapter does not dispute the relative economic decline of the US in relation to other major economies, predictions about the overall eclipsing of the US do often seem rather overstated, relying far too much on aggregate measures of national economic capacity (such as GDP), while ignoring the broader structural contours of US economic power, and the overall potential for different sites of power.

That said, since the financial crisis of 2007/08, with its origins within the US, there has been an increasing scepticism about the US as a leading power, and it is here we find the most important debates. What is key is that much of the current economic problems are part of a *domestic* crisis of US capitalism (though one with often devastating international repercussions). The financial crisis itself provides a key starting point, as it highlighted some real problems with the American economic system, as well as initially prompting ideas for change (see e.g. Crotty, 2009; Morris, 2008; Schwartz, 2009; G. Turner, 2008; Wade, 2008a, 2008b). The crisis, which was mainly caused by the securitization of so-called 'sub-prime' housing loans in the US, demonstrated on a large scale the destructive potential of boom and bust cycles within the American economy, and the over-reliance on housing finance in general (see Schwartz, 2009). It was also related to a rather destructive belief in the self-regulation of markets, and the increasingly (since the 1990s) lax regulation of the financial industry (though there was much regulation that helped to encourage the *expansion* of finance – see Konings, 2009). In particular, the 1999 repeal of key provisions of the 1933 Glass-Steagall Act, which had forced banks to separate their consumer and investment divisions, was seen as an important step in the crisis itself. A final issue is how easily the US crisis spread internationally, indicating a huge susceptibility to US economic problems.

There were a number of calls post-crisis for a return to the state in terms of intervention in economic crisis. Keynesian solutions regained prominence, both in terms of the potential for state intervention to save firms affected by the crisis (e.g. the bailing out of the auto industry), but mainly in terms of debates about the potential for deficit spending to stimulate growth and demand (e.g. Cassidy, 2009; Grunwald, 2012). In many ways, despite partisan bickering about decreasing the federal budget, the US took a much more middle road in its response to the crisis than many of its supposedly less liberal European counterparts (e.g. the UK which unleashed a severe program of austerity combined with increases in government revenue; and the collective European response to the Eurozone crisis of the 2010s). The other side of the reconsideration of a kind of hyper-liberalism has been a reassessment of the American model abroad. While this does not necessitate a move away from capitalism itself, there has been some discussion about alternative models to American capitalism (Wade, 2008b), which will be discussed further in Chapter 7.

While the financial crisis has been overcome within the US – despite lingering productivity and unemployment issues – there remain crucial challenges to US hegemonic economic power in a number of core areas. The first, and most often heatedly discussed, is the potential decline of the dollar as an international reserve currency. The importance of the dollar as part of American structural power was discussed above, and to the extent to which the dollar does decline in comparison with other currencies, it should have an impact on both US economic power and US power overall. In economic terms, it would clearly mean that consumers, the government and US firms would no longer benefit from the 'exorbitant privilege' of dollar hegemony (Eichengreen, 2011; Germain, 2009). The advantages gained in financial transactions, trade deficits, and especially in the costs of government borrowing, would all vanish.

The arguments for the decreasing power of the dollar tend to revolve around a few core issues (see Bowles and Wang, 2008; Eichengreen, 2011; Helleiner and Kirshner, 2009; Mastanduno, 2009: 149–53). First is the development of other currencies that could potentially challenge the dollar's dominance, most readily seen in the euro (though much less viable after the crises of the Eurozone starting in 2009), the renminbi, and potentially in the Special Drawing Rights (SDR) of the IMF. Second, the increasing market share of other economies means that the US is no longer indispensible for other states, with less necessity to use the dollar as a means of exchange. Third, there is also an argument surrounding the marketworthiness of the dollar, mainly concerning the twin problems of inflation and depreciation but also the real issue of the sustainability of its current account deficits. Fourth, there is also the problem that US debt brings in terms of the political leverage foreign holders of US debt. There has been some consternation over the power American rivals, especially China, have as the major holders of US Treasury Bonds. The fear here is that China could have the power to have a major impact on US economic power through the compellence effects that China's leverage might bring: threatening to de-invest in US debt, dumping its dollar holdings, or through more subtle methods (see Drezner, 2009: 11–18). Finally, the US can no longer leverage foreign borrowers through political relationships like it did in the Cold War (e.g. Germany in the 1960s, Japan in 1985). The post-Cold War threat environment is more complex, and though it seems that the US as the leading power should still have sway over its allies, the lack of clear threats means that the US does not have the same means to challenge them.

The dollar certainly is at risk, and it is clear that the dollar's role as the sole reserve currency has been a cornerstone of American structural power. However, a number of commentators have challenged the idea of decline (see Bowles and Wang, 2008; Eichengreen, 2011; Helleiner and Kirshner, 2009). Those who stress the *political* economic aspects over the purely economic tend to point to some important counter-arguments. First, even in purely economic terms the competitor currencies all have more constrained financial markets, and the US still leads. There is a continued confidence in the dollar, despite the setbacks of the 2007/08 financial crisis (seen in the relative safety of American debt, whose interest rates have remained stable); the lack of real fiscal policy and limited monetary policy in the Eurozone (and increasing instability due to the sovereign debt problems of Greece, Italy and Spain); and overall, too much state control of the renminbi (see Helleiner, 2009: 74–5).

Second, as Drezner (2009) has argued, the ability of China to use its dollar holdings to leverage US policy is much less likely than sometimes argued, and in reality would be a one-off with major consequences for both parties (cf. Kirshner, 2009: 198–9). China does indeed have massive holdings of US debt, but it needs these partially to help stabilize the value of the renminbi, and also because of its structural balance of trade with the US. It is in China's economic interest to maintain US solvency. As Drezner summarizes:

> In sum, for financial leverage to yield tangible concessions, the target state must be unable to find alternative creditors, lack the capability to inflict costs on the sanctioning country in response to coercive pressure, anticipate few conflicts with the coercing state over time, and try to maintain a fixed exchange rate regime. In looking at the current relationships between the United States and its sovereign creditors, none of these criteria is met. (2009: 20)

Overall, the use of US debt to try and leverage political outcomes is very difficult, and the US has showed little inclination to worry about such issues in the past.

Finally, while many economists point to the inevitability of the dollar's decline, the consensus seems to point more to the possibility of a basket of currencies that are used as reserve (the euro, sterling, dollar, renminbi) rather than a disappearance of the dollar (some American commentators think a more mixed set of reserves would be a good thing for the US: e.g. Bergsten, 2009). Importantly, Eichengreen (2011) has pointed to a crucial issue concerning the relationship between power and the dollar. As he notes, many commentators (especially economists) tend to look at dollar hegemony as driving US power, so its loss equates to a loss of US power. But Eichengreen contends that these views get matters backwards: dollar (currency) hegemony derives from *overall* power, not the other way around (Eichengreen, 2011: 6–7; cf. Helleiner, 2009). As Eichengreen states: 'a currency is attractive because the country issuing it is large, rich and growing. It is attractive because the country standing behind it is powerful and secure' (2009: 6). As such, the real issue may not be the overall market power of the dollar, but ways in which US economic power as a whole has become attenuated by its own internal economic problems.

Therefore, a second area of concern is the increasing US trade deficit (and current account imbalance). The US went, in the 1980s, from being a major exporter to a net importer, which became an important political issue in the years that followed. Some of the political debate has focused on the trade-off between supporting American manufacturing and the continued American reliance on cheap consumer imports, which has also been part of American prosperity over time. However, the increasing trade deficit also points to real structural issues in the global economy, which will in time lead to some sort of adjustment. In the past, the US has been able to use political leverage to make adjustment outcomes that worked in its favor, especially seen in the 1985 Plaza Accord (noted earlier). However, as Mastanduno points out, 'the erosion of leverage will not only make it difficult for the United States to dictate adjustment outcomes, it will also complicate U.S. efforts to orchestrate a soft landing or a gradual, crisis-free adjustment process' (Mastanduno, 2009: 152). Helleiner and Kirshner (2009) note that the global use of the dollar also made adjustment issues easier. This is something that is likely to change if the dollar does not retain its leading position.

A third problem is the continuing rise of public debt, which was only made worse in the recent financial crisis (see Figure 5.4). The

Figure 5.4 *US federal debt, 1980–2017*

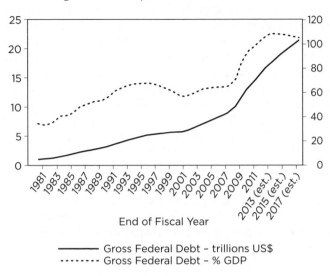

End of Fiscal Year

———— Gross Federal Debt – trillions US$
········ Gross Federal Debt – % GDP

Source: White House, Office of Management and Budget, 2012b.

1980s saw major government overspending, and turning the US from a creditor to debtor nation. While the economic boom of the 1990s (and the guidance provided by President Clinton's economic policies) led to an easing of debt with several years of balanced budgets and budget surpluses, the Bush Administration, due to the combination of large increases in military spending and massive tax cuts, led to even bigger increases in public debt. By the end of fiscal year 2011, the overall debt stood at $14.7 trillion, and 98.7 per cent of GDP (White House, 2012a). Debt does not have to be a problem if there are investors willing to pay for it, and to the extent that interest rates remain stable (as they have), the US can manage to be a debtor without too much consequence. The financial crisis demonstrated the continued global faith in American debt, with US Treasury Bonds being seen as one of the few secure investments in a time of crisis (Helleiner, 2009), and this despite the increasing problems of fiscal management in the US. However, trends projected out to 2017 continue to show over 100 per cent of debt to GDP ratios, which may not bode well for continued market confidence in US debt.

The question remains about how much debt is actually sustainable before the US itself is in a sovereign debt crisis. When combined with a number of other structural constraints, the crisis is even more pronounced. Any decline of the dollar would have a large impact on the US to engage in further deficit spending. Second, the major political parties remain deadlocked on how to solve the growing fiscal crisis in the US, with growing expenditures from entitlement programs, huge defense budgets, and inadequate income from taxation. While the parties recognize the problem, the inability to find a solution is leading to increasing instability in the markets, and the summer 2011 showdown in Congress over raising the debt ceiling (with the inevitable criticism from credit rating agencies) demonstrated the growing political problems that the US is having in dealing with debt. The so-called 'fiscal cliff' negotiations of early 2013 have enabled a tax deal to be put through Congress, but the issue of budget cuts has been deferred to the future, despite the impending automatic cuts that will come in due to the 'sequestration' of the budget that was a part of the 2011 Budget Control Act, which ended the crisis.

Conclusion

Overall, the economic power of the United States is one of its key features and power resources in international relations. The chapter charted the development of economic power over the course of American history, especially noting the ideological dimensions, the internal self-identification of the US as liberal-capitalist, as a 'commercial society'. While American economic power grew over the course of the late nineteenth and early twentieth centuries in terms of its overall power potential, it really became preponderant after World War II. Here the US combined a number of forms of power in order to clearly project its interests and values in economic terms over (and with) the rest of the democratic (or at least capitalist) world. It achieved this from its vast resources (in terms of compulsory power) but also importantly managed to include other key states in its orbit through a more consensual hegemony, which featured both an institutional dimension through the key international economic institutions in the post-World War II period, and also its structural power, found in the domination of the dollar as a reserve currency, American financial power, and its overall economic dynamism. The structural dimension also adds an interest-shaping quality, whereby other states in the international system saw the core tenets of liberal capitalism as part of their own interest.

As such, the future of American economic power is very much tied up in its continued pre-eminence in all of these types of power. As was argued, one of the key problems has been a number of crises within the American state and global capitalism, which impinge on these three forms of power in clear ways. First, the global economic crisis and continued problems with American productivity, trade deficit and levels of public debt have had an impact on compulsory power, both opening up the US to potential power differentials with competitor states, and the potential for real internal and external decline. Second, these problems have also led to potential damage to US structural power, as challengers to US dollar hegemony appear, and will further limit US power in the world (in relative terms). Inasmuch as these challenges are overcome, American economic power may well recover. But there are also two remaining issues. Institutional power has meant that the rules and norms associated with backing US hegemony are also relatively autonomous, and to the extent to which other powerful states in the global economy invest in them, they may accommodate shifts in power within the current liberal international order. To the extent to which competitors may challenge the present order, there may exist further legitimacy deficits in the international system that could lead to American decline. These issues will be revisited in Chapter 7, where they can also be brought back more clearly into relation with the other sources of power.

Chapter 6

The Power of American Values: Ideology and Identity in American Foreign Policy

At the 2008 Democratic Presidential Convention, former US president Bill Clinton pronounced that 'people the world over have always been more impressed by the power of our example than by the example of our power' (Maraniss, 2008). This statement gets to the heart of the role of values in American political life, and their connection to American power in the world. Clinton's focus on values was in many ways a rebuff to the approach of the Bush Administration, which certainly took the view that legitimacy flowed from power, whereas Clinton's view was basically the opposite: the US had to regain legitimacy in the world by reinforcing the power of its guiding values.

What is interesting about this statement is not so much that US leaders think values (and perhaps legitimation) are important for US power, but that both leaders drew different lessons from similar background premises. The Bush Administration saw American values as fundamental to its foreign policy, but one that should be tempered with actual US coercive power: that to some degree, foreign policy needs to be seen as a moral crusade (cf. Kristol and Kagan, 1996; Rice, 2008). The Clinton Administration differed only in that they saw a (somewhat) greater need to legitimate the use of power through international institutions, but one that was still focused on how American institutions and values (especially American democratic traditions) were transferable for the good of the whole world. While this may be an important difference, both draw quite strongly on a similar view of both core American values and American 'exceptionalism'.

As such it is obvious that values do matter in contextualizing US power. A core question in thinking about the role of values in

182

American power has been the extent to which such values can be considered part of a broader American ideology, and the extent to which such an ideology is just a mask for interests, or if ideology has independence from other interests. The route taken here is much towards the latter point of view. Ideology, at the very least, provides an intermediary between interests and their expression, in terms of guiding interests and legitimating action. Overall, values are important in terms of how they are expressions of commonly held cultural proclivities and beliefs, which will here be conceptualized in terms of an American ideology (especially found in American 'exceptionalism') which frames and legitimates action in the pursuit of power. In this light, there is a need to examine the role of values in US power in two broad dimensions. First in terms of the role of values within the US, as contestation and debate over what America *is*; a complex issue, folding in ideas and debates about US identity and US values. The second dimension deals with the consequences of such positions internationally: how does a distinctly American ideology impact on American power projection in the world (and more specifically in terms of foreign policy)?

In what follows, the two themes will be analysed in three steps. First, the chapter provides an overview of values and ideology in American life, situating ideological power in American foreign policy analysis. Second, the chapter moves on to a longer discussion of values in American political life, highlighting the core themes of republicanism, liberalism and laissez-faire, and how these fuse together in an ideology of exceptionalism. Finally, the chapter examines how exceptionalism has been varied in its influence on foreign policy over two hundred years, examining expansion, imperialism, internationalism, anti-communism, modernization and democratization.

Ideology in American life

A core problem in analysing the role of values in American power is not a dearth of discussion of values, but contestation over how to link values up with ideological power. Much of the discussion of 'ideas' in US foreign policy has concerned more narrow considerations of how new ideas can impact in changing or reproducing entrenched approaches to foreign policy-making (e.g. Goldstein and Keohane, 1993; cf. Ruggie, 1998; Wendt, 1999), seeing ideas as part of an overall market-place of choices. While such studies are important in their own way, we need to see ideological power in larger terms, more in line with how broad 'worldviews' can shape both interests and action. Max Weber outlined such an approach in his sociology of religion, stating that 'very frequently the "world images" created by "ideas" have, like switchmen, determined the tracks along which action has been pushed by the dynamic of interest' (Weber, 2009c: 280).

Looking at the political discourse in the US at the highest level clearly shows how prominent values as 'worldviews' actually are. While more specific 'ideas' will certainly help to change directions in foreign policy, core values and an overall American identity have been very important for thinking about the American role in the world. For example, both Republican and Democratic candidates for the presidency (and sitting presidents themselves) consistently refer to American values and traditions, especially in the discussion of foreign policy, mainly in reference to American exceptionalism. The titles of two recent books by Republican presidential candidates (one the eventual winner of the 2012 nomination) give excellent examples: Mitt Romney's *No Apology: The Case for American Greatness* (Romney, 2010), and Newt Gingrich's *A Nation Like No Other: Why American Exceptionalism Matters* (Gingrich, 2011). Such views are even in apparent in more realist policy-makers such as Condoleezza Rice, who in 2008 (while still Secretary of State) stated that 'an international order that reflects our values is the best guarantee of our enduring national interest' (Rice, 2008: 26). Recent Democratic candidates and sitting presidents have also highlighted values, but with an emphasis that is less explicit, but clearly influenced by Woodrow Wilson's expansive ideas about American democratic exceptionalism. For example, in 2009 President Obama gave a speech on national security where he stated, 'in the long run we also cannot keep this country safe unless we enlist the power of our most fundamental values. . . . the Declaration of Independence, the Constitution, the Bill of Rights – these are not simply words written into aging parchment. They are the foundation of liberty and justice in this country, and a light that shines for all who seek freedom, fairness, equality, and dignity around the world' (Obama, 2009e).

It is easy to be cynical about such statements, seeing them as a cover for various other interests, but the very fact that they continued to be deployed tells us that something important is going on. In fact, specifically 'American' values have important impacts on the ways in which elites view the US' role in the world, help to legitimate particular approaches to US foreign policy, and shape what interests actually look like (or how actors perceive interests) (Hall, 1993). We need not see values as deterministic, and in fact, the consideration of values needs to be extended to how values form a national identity, which is also influential in the broad formulation of a 'national interest'.

In order to better connect US values and ideology, a crucial starting point is Michael Hunt's classic study of ideology and US foreign policy (Hunt, 1987). Hunt argues that other scholars have misused (or ignored) ideology in looking at US foreign policy throughout history, and wants to develop a more 'culturalist' reading of US ideology and foreign policy (cf. Campbell, 1992; Hogan, 1998: ch. 1). His starting point is the examination of two key works of US foreign policy from the early Cold War period that have also been discussed in the present work: that of William Appleman Williams and of George Kennan. These two accounts are worth repeating to get a better sense of what has been at stake in such debates.

For Kennan, the problem of 'ideology' ('moralism' in his reading) was that there was too much of it in US foreign policy making and public opinion at large. For Kennan, Americans were overly influenced by a moralism in their domestic politics that was inclined to see international affairs in a legalistic fashion, much to the detriment of American interests. As he noted in his influential book *American Diplomacy*, 'the tendency to achieve our foreign policy objectives by inducing other governments to sign up to professions of high moral and legal principles appears to have a great and enduring vitality in our diplomatic practice', also 'linked, no doubt, with the pronounced American tendency to transplant legal concepts from the domestic to the international field' (Kennan, 1951: 46). Kennan thought that US foreign policy had to be expunged of moralism (and of any democratic influences) and replaced with realism in order to hone in on the real interests of the US.

At the opposite extreme, Williams saw US foreign policy as completely shaped by an overriding economic interest, and a dedication to open trade (and opening up other states to such trade) simply served as a mask for entrenched interests. Williams saw a core pattern in US foreign policy that he felt was marked very much by the 'Open Door' notes of 1899–1900 (also discussed in Chapter 1). The diplomatic initiatives towards China in the late nineteenth century – seeking to preserve China's territorial integrity and allow for open commercial competition (rather than a colonial 'spheres of influence' approach) set the stage for a broader 'open door' policy, which was always led by American economic interests. As Williams argued, the open door policy entailed 'the proposition that America's overwhelming economic power would cast the economy and the politics of the weaker, underdeveloped countries in a pro-American mold' (Williams, 1962: 57). Here ideology is all-encompassing, and merely functional, an adjunct of real material interests.

As Hunt (1987) notes, neither of these positions gets to the heart of ideology in US foreign policy. Kennan refused to see realism *itself* as an ideology, and to see a more subtle influence of American values on US foreign policy making (and assumes 'moralism' to be the result of naivety, rather than more broadly entrenched values). Williams, on the other hand, saw ideology as all-encompassing and entirely functional, a direct result of the needs of economic interests (though Hunt notes that he was over time rather looser and more generous with the concept than is often noted). These two analyses get at the heart of a problem that still exists in thinking about ideology in US foreign policy-making: that ideology (or values in a more limited sense) get in the way of interests or are just masks for 'true' interests.

Hunt argues against both of these views, seeing ideology as a 'cultural system', where values suffuse the policy-making community in a way that frames issues and policies over time. As Hunt describes, 'ideological constructs, which culture not only inspires but also sustains and constrains, serve as a fount for an instructive and reassuring sense of historical place, as an indispensable guide to an infinitely complex and otherwise bewildering present, and as a basis for moral action intended to shape a better future' (Hunt, 1987: 12). Hunt's conception has the value of moving us away from a purely functional sense of ideology, one that sets a broad context for understanding the power of values. However, we can take this further to link it to a form of power, following Mann. As Mann has written, ideological power

> cannot be totally tested by experience, and therein lies its distinctive power to persuade and dominate. But it need not be false; if it is, it is less likely to spread. People are not manipulated fools. And though ideologies always do contain legitimations of private interests and material domination, they are unlikely to attain a hold over people if they are merely this. Powerful ideologies are at least highly plausible in the conditions of the time, and they are genuinely adhered to. (Mann, 1986: 23)

If we can conceive of ideological power in American foreign policy in this way, we can see it more as a set of core values or beliefs that helps to maintain the continuity of the state and society, embedded in material interests, but also a way of viewing the world. While such views are not necessarily deterministic, they have and continue to hold a powerful grip on peoples' collective imaginations.

However, we also need a sense of the further role ideology can play domestically and internationally as a form of power. Mann attempts to do this by demonstrating how important worldviews are for both reproducing and (potentially) transforming particular social orders (Mann, 1986, 1993; cf. Bell, 2002; Bryant, 2006; Freeden, 1996; Gorski, 2006; Mannheim, 1960; Eagleton, 1991). First, there is the transformative (or transcendent) power of ideology, in terms of how it can exist as separate from and potentially pose a challenge to existing power structures. As Mann put it, 'it develops a powerful autonomous role when emergent properties of social life create the possibility of greater cooperation or exploitation that transcend the organizational reach of secular authorities' (Mann, 1986: 23). Here, we do get a stronger sense of how core ideas have travelled beyond the confines of the US. Many currently prominent globalized forms of ideological power clearly derive from the US: e.g. (neo)liberal economics; human rights discourse; consumer culture; the English language (Mann, 2001). But what is crucial in this account is the way in which such forms transcend the confines of institutionalized US power, and take on, to some extent, a life of their own. These values relate very strongly to the US, but could potentially also be used as power resources to criticize and challenge the US. While more will be said about these potentialities in Chapter 7, we can see some ways in which this is used, for example, in challenging US hypocrisy about its human rights record; or indeed through discourses that challenge the dominance of these very American ideas.

The second role of ideology is in terms of its immanent (or reproductive) power, which uses dominant ideology as a means to maintain the current social order. Much of the debate about the *domestic* function of ideological power is really about this role, about how ideology actually makes US thinking about its role in the world fairly consistent over a longer period of time. While ideology came through clearly in a 'transcendent' fashion in a few ways, it was heavily imbricated in the other forms of power, in a more immanent fashion (which was explained in greater detail in the respective chapters): first, in terms of military power in the reluctance to maintain large standing armies and focus on airpower and technology; second, with economic power, in a consistent focus on economic liberalism; and finally, with political power, a focus on the dangers of concentrations of power, which resulted in both the balancing and pluralism of the US political system.

The role of ideology in US foreign policy and power projection is strongest in reproductive terms, where particularly American values about the world influence decisions about the world itself. As Michael Hunt put it, 'ideologies are important because they constitute the framework in which policy-makers deal with specific issues and in which the attentive public understands those issues' (Hunt, 1987: 16). If we take the contention about American identity seriously, we see that it is something that filters the worldviews of policy-makers, as well as the 'attentive' general public, who follow foreign policy matters. Immanent ideological power does not have to be seen as conservative, as its reinforcement of existing power institutions means it can be utilized to change situations as well. For example, attempts to create strong international institutions as part of a liberal internationalist impulse (which clearly derives from exceptionalism) were derived from fairly traditional American values concerning power and democracy.

Before we get further into the substantive discussion of how internal and external relations have been shaped by ideological power, we also need to consider the distinction between consent (or consensus) and coercion, and how it relates to power. The distinction was already in the discussion of compulsory power versus structural (or productive) power (i.e. is power just about forcing another party to do what you want them to do, or about setting the overall conditions of what choice is, or who actors actually are?). Ideological power is very much in the realm of providing a consensus, though one that can be seen in terms of structural power, in that it sets and structures the overall interests of those that it affects (and is very much related to the idea of hegemony as formulated by Antonio Gramsci (Gramsci, 1971)). Ideological power provides a frame for policy decisions (both foreign and domestic), and frames the decision-making of foreign policy elites. It at the very least sets the limits for what is possible in foreign policy. For example, a new president is often very limited in their capacity to change a great deal of policy, as they are constrained institutionally by Congress, and in ideological terms there are also real limits to what any president would be willing to put forward as a policy option. Even the more 'radical' actions of the Obama Administration – for example pushing a policy of nuclear disarmament, a 'nuclear zero' – have always been tempered with more pragmatic nods to traditional policy goals (in this example maintaining the current strategic relationship with other nuclear powers) (Daalder and Lodal, 2008; United States Department of Defense, 2010). Additionally the American ideology impacts on the actual policies that are expressed internationally. Are they 'stamped' by American values? Are they about *universalizing* exceptionalism? Are they about legitimating American behavior? We can see how this aspect related to the issue of 'transcendent' power: to the extent to which a more autonomous baseline of American values are accepted in the world, the more legitimate American actions that have their roots in those values will be.

Liberalism, republicanism and exceptionalism

With a broad conception of the role of ideology in US power in place, we can now unpack the main components of a distinctive American ideology. For Hunt, an American ideology would consist of a number of interlocking ideas: 'they would have to be central enough to the national experience to help us account for key developments, as well as powerful enough to have performed for generations of Americans that essential function of giving order to their vision of the world and defining their place in it' (Hunt, 1987: 14). For Hunt, by the early twentieth century three elements were key: a sense of national greatness coupled to the promotion of liberty; the hierarchy of race; and the dangers of social revolution. While we won't take these elements for granted, all have played a role in thinking about an 'American creed' – a civic nationalism based on overall defense of individual rights and economic freedom – often seen as the fundamental basis for an American ideology (Foley, 2007; Lieven, 2004). While this mainly forms part of the 'exceptionalist' conception of American ideology (seen in Hunt's first element), debate and contention over both the content of the 'creed' and its expression have led to competing conceptions of the American identity and American nationalism (and have in many ways subsumed the two other aspects discussed by Hunt). While the liberal tradition (in the classical sense) is still a strong part of American ideology, it has been subject to a great deal of contention over time.

The best place to start investigating the development of an overall American ideology is with the founders of the American republic. Although there were obviously differences in opinion between figures as diverse as Thomas Paine, Thomas Jefferson, Alexander Hamilton and James Madison (to name a few) (see especially Jefferson, 1993; Madison et al., 1987; Paine, 1995), there was also a sense of commonality in the attention to both liberalism and republicanism that was necessary to imbue the new republic with both a freedom from the tyranny of old aristocratic Europe and a new system of governance that would allow the expression of individual freedoms. The new American republic would foster both individual freedom and the values of an engaged citizenry, which would be revolutionary in the sense of its own newness and historical purpose (Wood, 1991). As Bernard Bailyn notes, 'what was essentially involved in the American Revolution was not the disruption of society, with all the fear, despair, and hatred that entails, but the realization, the comprehension and fulfilment, of the inheritance of liberty and of what was taken to be America's destiny in the context of world history' (Bailyn, 1992: 19).

The linkage between core values and a core mission brings us to the discussion of American exceptionalism. While this is often presumed merely to be an expression of an American sense of superiority to the rest of the world, it has its origins in this liberal-republican sense of self emanating from the American creed: it is about how the values of America implied a mission in the world. Seymour Martin Lipset has identified five key components to American exceptionalism: (1) liberty, (2) egalitarianism, (3) individualism, (4) populism and (5) laissez-faire (Lipset, 1997: 19). As numerous scholars have noted, all of these drew from the liberalism being articulated (if not yet called that) in the late eighteenth and early nineteenth centuries (e.g. Bailyn, 1992; Kalyvas and Katznelson, 2008; Lipset, 1997; Myrdal, 1996 [1944]; Stephanson, 1995). Protestant religion (especially puritanism) also coincided with and reinforced these liberal underpinnings. Lipset (1997; cf. Stephanson, 1995), following De Tocqueville and Weber (amongst others) (Tocqueville, 2003; Weber, 2009b), notes how the 'protestant sects' clearly differed from their European counterparts, by refusing hierarchical authority (authority was mainly derived from individual congregations), and also proliferating horizontally (there was a flourishing of Christian sects rather than a dominant state religion). The strong religiosity of the United States also contributed to a real moralism (and expansionism) found in US exceptionalism that persists to this day. As Stephanson has described it, 'what unified the sacred and secular, then, was precisely the idea of "America" as a unique mission and project in time and space, a continuous process. The missionary aspect not only legitimated the enterprise but determined its whole meaning' (Stephanson, 1995: 6).

These core values have been also combined with a number of other core features that have played a variety of roles in both exceptionalism and an overall political ideology. First, these liberal underpinnings gave rise to the anti-militarist and anti-statist foundations of the US. Anti-militarism has mainly been seen in the reluctance to support standing armies in peacetime (and not a reluctance to use military power), while anti-statism has been a resistance to a strong centralized state. While both of these still feature in American politics today (though the former in a highly attenuated fashion, and the latter rather more a desire to return to the past), debates about them were core to the Constitutional Convention of 1787, as can be seen in the discussions of state power and the military found in the *Federalist* (Madison et al., 1987; cf. Friedberg, 2000), and can be seen as pervading themes in the nineteenth century.

Another core area has been the focus on economic freedom and a peculiarly American capitalism. The US is often seen as being 'exceptional' in the sense that it did not have a class-based revolution (i.e. one that was premised on economic inequalities or grievances – in fact some go as far as saying that it was not really a revolution in that sense, or was mainly a factional war – see discussions in: Mann, 1993: ch. 5; and Moore, 1966: ch. 3), and also did not develop out of a feudal society. This context allowed for a focus on equality of opportunity (if not outcome) in a way that the more rigidly class-stratified societies of Europe would not allow. As Lipset notes, 'America was able to avoid the remnants of mercantilism, statist regulations, church establishment, aristocracy, and the emphasis on social class that the postfeudal countries inherited' (Lipset, 1997: 54). There was certainly a sense that American capitalism took a very different path in the early nineteenth century from other states, and the institutional legacy was very large in terms of how the economy is viewed today (though as noted in the previous chapter, the institutional development has altered dramatically over time – the state took on a larger role in the economy at the turn of the twentieth century) (Eisner, 2011; Lind, 2012).

This is not to say that there is not contention about the economy but that save for a brief period in the early twentieth century, there has been little support for communist- or socialist-inspired class-based political movements within the US. In fact, as noted by Lipset, the main concern has been with an overall populism, a promotion of the overall needs of the people as against those of an established elite. As noted in Chapter 1 (and 4), this goes back to the populist movement inspired by the presidency of Andrew Jackson (and the Populist Party of the 1890s), but also has elements in the progressive movements at the end of the nineteenth century (Hofstadter, 1955; cf. Howe, 2007). But to start back in the early nineteenth century, we can see how individualism clearly came out in early ideas of American capitalism, which were based on individual entrepreneurial spirit and the economic exchange. Much of the debates in the late nineteenth century concerned how the rise of industrialization might destroy this earlier spirit, how industrialization was against the spirit of agriculture. In the early twentieth century, populism and progressivism came to be seen in a distrust of large corporations ('monopolies') and other types of concentrations of power. Such populism has survived to the present day, especially in a celebration of 'main street' (seen as individual entrepreneurs) against big business, as well as a continued dislike of finance ('Wall Street'). What this tells us about capitalism within American exceptionalism is a reverence for individualism and the possibility of social mobility, as against any sort of concentration of power.

Exceptionalism was also seen in the particularity of American geography. It was contended that the US was an unspoilt place that could foster a free land, separate from Europe: America really was seen as a 'new world' with fertile land, seemingly boundless, an ocean apart from Europe (McDougall, 1997: 16). Additionally, for many of the early colonists, America was seen as a 'holy land' set apart: 'the vast majority of New Englanders had learned from hard experience to be suspicious of kings and bishops, and to associate religious congregationalism with representative government' (McDougall, 1997: 17). Settlers such as the Puritan John Winthrop saw America as a 'city upon a hill', one that would serve as a beacon to others. As Lieven puts it, 'this sense of America not just as an unfulfilled dream or vision, but also as a country with a national mission, is absolutely central to the American national identity and also forms the core of the nation's faith in its own "exceptionalism"' (Lieven, 2004: 33). Additionally, the vastness of the American continent led some to see a rugged individualism develop through westward expansion, exemplified in the 'frontier thesis' in an 1893 essay of Frederick Jackson Turner (Turner, 1986).

While there is much to debate about the impact of exceptionalism on American society and foreign policy, it is clear that the devotion to individualism and the rest of the core beliefs at the heart of the American creed have done much to contribute to the overall dynamism of American society. As noted in the previous chapter on economic power, the American support of an extreme form of capitalism has without a doubt been crucial in underpinning its own power, and when combined with other important factors (such as relative size, geography and the dynamics of military power), have led to immense successes for the development of US power.

However, while exceptionalist beliefs are important for shaping elites' and more general beliefs about the world and their place within it, it must be recognized that it is also full of contradictions and contention. While American liberalism does make up a coherent political philosophy, it has historic gaps that must be recognized. Myrdal (1996 [1944]) referred to an 'American dilemma' in terms of the relationship between American ideals and the issue of race in America, Lipset (1997) referred to exceptionalism as a 'double-edged sword', and Lieven (2004) discusses the 'anti-thesis' he sees to the more inclusive civic nationalism of the American creed. These dilemmas revolve around a number of issues, but are fundamentally about the question of American identity, and how inclusive the American creed can be.

For Lieven, the 'anti-thesis' to the more inclusive civic nationalism found in the American creed is a focus on the ethno-religious roots of Americans, which often expresses itself both through a nativism and fundamentalist Protestantism. The nativism that Lieven points out has been important for US society for years. We obviously need to start with the legacy of slavery in terms of the racial politics of the early republic. Though the political economy of slavery was described in more detail in the previous chapter, slavery also played an important dynamic in framing who was to be a 'true' American: the plantation economies that relied on slavery were also part of a broader, racialized social hierarchy that saw 'blacks' as inferior (Kolchin, 1995: 192–4). Hunt's invocation of a racial element to US foreign policy ideology is a broad part of this and played an important role in westward expansion (Hunt, 1987: ch. 3; Horsman, 1986). The legacy of slavery has also had important downstream effects in the social status of African-Americans, even after the formal end of slavery. Much more could be said about these struggles in terms of policies of segregation, and the civil rights struggles that culminated in the 1964 Civil Rights Act. However, more pertinent to the point being made here is how the issue of race has framed both internal American identity (the issue of 'who is us') (e.g. Huntington, 2004), but also how these dynamics have shaped America's role in the world.

In terms of the identity of the American people, much gets put into the context of immigration and what 'types' of people are seen as upholders of American values (see King, 2000; Zolberg, 2006). Lipset (1997) notes that these are often seen as 'three waves' of immigrants to the US: the Anglo-Irish, the 'European', and the rest. Every one of these has been contentious within the US in terms of who is meant to belong. Westward expansion and 'manifest destiny' saw the destruction of populations that were seen as alien to American life (Native American populations were never going to be assimilated – those who weren't killed deliberately or by disease (the vast majority), were resettled in places that were out of the way, to devastating effect) (Stephanson, 1995: 24–6; cf. Limerick, 1987). From the issue of slavery in the nineteenth century, through racial quotas in migration in the early twentieth century, to contemporary debates about 'illegal immigrants' and the changing demographics of the US, nativism has been a profound part of the ideology of the US. That said, it is something that has changed over time, but it certainly compromises the liberal civic nationalism of exceptionalism. In international terms, there are clearly ways in which American self-perceptions and views on race have affected its role in the world, especially clear in the Cold War, an era where civil rights struggles at home were contrasted with the end of colonialism abroad, and especially the role of the US in promoting anti-colonialism and the end of formal imperialism (see Borstelmann, 2001).

These dynamics have all led to real tensions in the US today. Lieven (2004) speaks of a more reactionary nationalism, that is evocative of nationalist movements of the pre-World War I period, which is counter-posed with a more civic (and potentially inclusive) 'patriotism', and we can see how both strands vie for domination in terms of steering American politics and foreign relations. While the core of the American exceptionalist ideology can be found in the

American creed – its devotion to individual liberty and economic laissez-faire – the areas of real contestation (and countering ideologies within US domestic politics) surround the scope of these ideas, and especially their relationship to state power. Should the US promote these ideas abroad in an aggressive or assertive fashion? Should the exceptional liberalism of the US be exported? These tensions can lead to a real questioning of the universality of American exceptionalism, with potential problems for this particularly American ideology in American power projection.

Exceptionalist nationalism and American power

We can get a better sense of the link between ideology and power by looking at the relationship between American exceptionalism as a core ideology, and how it has influenced American foreign policy practices over time. Present views on the importance of values in US foreign policy tend to see them in two broad ways. The first is in terms of the negative role of US 'exceptionalism', seeing it as a very arrogant and sometimes crusading role that the US takes on, often in a paternalistic fashion (or worse – often related to Lieven's idea of the 'anti-thesis' of the American creed, discussed above). The second sense is in terms of how specifically American values can actually be moves to legitimate US foreign policy abroad: to the extent to which the US remains consistent in its self-beliefs and practices, it can convince other states and populations that they essentially desire the same things. Exceptionalism does not have a fixed set of foreign policy prescriptions, and as such we can put forward a rough sketch of the interaction between the idea(l) of America and how this has affected its projection of power. We will look at a number of core choices: the foreign policy dilemmas of the early republic; the westward expansion of the nineteenth century; the imperialism of the late nineteenth century; the liberal internationalism of the early twentieth century; the modernizing ideology and anti-communism of the Cold War period; and how the American ideology affects American power and foreign policy today.

The foreign policy choices of the early leaders of the US were constrained (and helped) by its material circumstances. A loosely affiliated collection of now ex-colonies, which had recently separated from one of the leading European great powers (with the most powerful navy in the world), put the US in a precarious position. With its very particular ideas about its ideological place in the world, as a revolutionary, anti-monarchical, republican state dedicated to individual liberty, the US had two radical choices that could potentially follow: a 'new diplomacy' rejecting balance of power, power politics and intrigue in favor of peace, idealism and moral persuasion (a kind of Kantian liberal internationalism); or a revolutionary diplomacy committing the nation to a campaign against monarchy and imperialism. That neither was chosen was quite important, and the US followed a pragmatic foreign policy that would protect exceptionalism at home (McDougall, 1997: 20–21). However, it should be stressed that despite the American Revolution being 'conservative' (Moore, 1966), it was still seen as revolutionary by the powers of Europe, and the American Revolution did serve as a reference point for numerous anti-colonial movements in the nineteenth century (and referenced by Lenin, Ho Chi Minh, and Gandhi, amongst others, in the twentieth) (Perkins, 1993: 48). As Perkins further notes, when American diplomats discarded the tradition of wearing formal 'court dress' and wore suits instead, and were chastised by officials in Berlin for looking like 'undertakers', one American diplomat responded: 'we could not be more appropriately dressed than we are, at European courts, where what we represent is the burial of the monarchy' (Perkins, 1993: 48).

Exceptionalism at home proved important, as the early ideas about America also influenced its continental policy. While it was certainly limited in its broader geopolitical ambitions (in terms of its interaction with Europe), there was a consistent theme throughout the early part of the nineteenth century of expanding the American experiment across the continent. The case of Thomas Jefferson is telling in this regard. His presidency was dedicated to renewing the civic virtues of the republic, which he saw mainly as associated with yeoman farmers: individuals engaging in the commercial utilization of nature. While pragmatic in his foreign policy towards Europe, he saw the necessity of the expansion of the republic in order for both the expansion of liberty and of commerce itself (Herring, 2009: 101–14; cf. Stephanson, 1995). The 'empire of liberty' would extend the American experiment across the US, first achieved through commerce (Jefferson's 1803 Louisiana Purchase), and later on, militarily (with the Spanish over Florida, with Mexico over Texas and the Mexican territories in present-day Arizona, New Mexico and California), and through diplomacy (the Oregon territory). Such expansionism (though not uncontested) was directly linked to ideas about what the US was and what it should be, that uneasily fit into the narrative of isolationism that we have of US foreign policy in the past: the idea of expansion being part of the 'manifest destiny' of the US was prominent in the mid-nineteenth century, and belies any sense that the US was not expansionist (Stephanson, 1995). Such an expansion also linked up with ideas about who would be part of the American experiment, as racial exclusion became prominent in westward expansion, especially of indigenous populations, directly shunted from American territories, as well as Spanish settler populations in the conquered Mexican territories (Hunt, 1987: ch. 3; Stephanson, 1995: ch. 2).

With continued expansion the focus of exceptionalism became more inward-looking through the conflict over slavery, as a contest between a more liberal vision of the US and the Southern slave-holding states. Expansion to the west made the issue of slavery even more prominent in terms of whether or not the new territories would be slave-holding. The Civil War that lasted between 1861 and 1865 was due to a host of broad issues concerning the relationship between slavery and the virtues of a republic, of states' rights, but also over clashing forces of political economy: the political economy of Southern slavery was against the freedom of individual famers (the 'free soil' movement) and laborers, economic sectionalism and potentially, different modes of capitalism (see e.g. Ashworth, 1995; Foner, 1995; McPherson, 1990; Moore, 1966: ch. 3). While much more could be said about the tensions that brought out the Civil War, and the tensions that remained in its wake, the war essentially 'solved' the problems for American exceptionalism, which now was much more coherent across the whole of the United States and became an American nationalism.

The end of the nineteenth century saw the US as a rising economic power, one that was more respected by the European great powers, and one that was in very different circumstances from the small state of 1783. With continental expansion complete, and in a global geopolitical context where the scramble for colonies had begun (combined with social Darwinist views on race), debate began about the need for the US to partake in such activities as well. While the western portion of the US was assimilated as part of the 'empire of liberty', the debate about the world outside the US concerned foreign policy and the politics of empire, and therefore the desire of some leading American policy-makers and thinkers to become part of the scramble for empire became controversial (Stephanson, 1995: ch. 3). Here the problem consistently became the tension between the US as an anti-colonial state, and the perceived need to expand in colonial terms, especially in competition with leading European states (Herring, 2009: ch. 8). While the US never became as embroiled with settler colonialism as the European imperial powers did, the more that it expanded abroad, the more these tensions came to the fore, which was seen in the events surrounding the Spanish-American War (1898). American exceptionalism seemed to provide the guide to policies, but also created huge contradictions in American actions, as in Theodore Roosevelt's 'corollary' to the Monroe Doctrine, creating a more paternalistic role for the US, which meant that it could decide when regimes were not acting in the interests of their people, and act accordingly. Interventions in Cuba, Haiti, the Dominican Republic, Mexico all lived up to this principle. As Walker describes, 'before 1890, America's core values were held up to others as qualities worth of emulation. Thereafter the United States actively engaged the world to protect its economic interests and enhance its security. The question quickly became how best to preserve order abroad so that others would have an opportunity to make American values their own' (Walker, 2009: 58).

Moving forward to the twentieth century brings us some real insights into how exceptionalism relates to more present-day dichotomies and dilemmas. President Woodrow Wilson (1913–21) is often seen as a real shift in how exceptionalism might be promoted in the world. Wilson predicated American entry into World War I on the acceptance of his '14 Points', which included the right to self-determination, the end of secret diplomacy, open trade, and the development of international governance (Knock, 1995). Though it is certainly right to credit Wilson with this turn to internationalized liberalism, we can also see how it is based on tendencies relating to American exceptionalism (Mead, 2002: ch. 5). The narrative of exceptional liberalism had always been important to the American understanding of the world, and Wilson's ideas about international relations were merely a way of transposing this onto the world. While the US had never shied away from abrogating the sovereignty of those in the way of its interests (especially in the Americas) or the use of secret diplomacy, and while Wilson's own prejudices regarding race did not fit well with the claims to self-determination, the US was always meant to be an example to the world but now was in a position to help the world become more like itself.

Thus the 1919 Paris Peace Conference (setting the terms of peace for the end of World War I) was meant to establish American principles as founding ideas for a new international order. The emphasis on self-determination of the 'pieces' of empire (seen in the re-establishment of sovereignty for numerous states that had been part of both the Ottoman and Austro-Hungarian empires) and the focus on the establishment of an international organization for dealing with international conflict were very true to American exceptionalism. That such ideas were not accepted at the time is partly to do with their radicalism: it is not that many states or peoples did not agree, but the US and others did not have the power to transform the world of geopolitics, nor, ironically, the US Congress. Congress rejected the Versailles Treaty as an abrogation of US sovereignty (and also as a slight to Wilson himself, who was seen to have overreached his presidential power and had not been deferential enough to the Senate), a tension between the US backing for a world order based on its values and a desire not to be constrained by such an order.

Liberal internationalism's full moment would have to wait for the end of World War II, when the competition between major ideologies – fascism, communism, and capitalist-democracy – would reach a denouement of sorts. While communism remained a competing ideological worldview, and crucially shaped the dynamics of the international order, the success of liberal internationalism in the American sphere of influence (especially western Europe and Japan) showed a renewed acceptance of some aspects of the American model – especially the institutionalization of liberalism on an international level (Ikenberry, 2001: ch. 6). The United Nations was set up to deal with the problems of international politics and conflict management. A liberal economic order, based on the importance of free trade and economic openness, was attempted through the Bretton Woods institutions, not only to move away from preferential trading systems, but also to ensconce the American ideal of a (potentially) global liberal-capitalist order. To be sure, these institutions were created in the interests of the US. But what is of concern here is how ideological power shaped the acceptance of these values. If these broadly American values were anathema to numerous powerful states in the post-World War I period, there was broader acceptance of them in 1945 – partially due to the material dominance of the US (in many ways a final acceptance of the American approach to the global economy, as set out in the 'Model Treaty' and in the 'Open Door' notes). As such, the projection of liberal values became important in two key ways during the Cold War: first, to keep allies on side and reproduce the liberal order that they established; and second, as a battleground between ideologies of development.

In terms of the first, the institutionalization of liberalism was crucial. Here the work of John Ikenberry (2001; 2011) is very help-ful in examining the ways in which order-building worked in the post-war period. Ikenberry notes the way American predominance (and liberal order) was maintained through institutional relation-ships that set limits to US power. All of the international institutions mentioned above were imbued with core US values, but because they were institutionalized, it meant that their acceptance by other states was more consensual, on the basis that while the US would back up the system, all could gain without fear of the US acting entirely against them. The institutionalization of US hegemony really did become the grand bargain of the post-war world.

The second issue can be seen in terms of the rival development strategies of the US and the Soviet Union. Historians have come to pay much more attention to how US policies of 'modernization' became a 'weapon' of the Cold War (e.g. Ekbladh, 2011; Gilman, 2003; M. Latham, 2010; cf. Bromley, 2008: ch. 1). Modernization theories had become popular in the post-war period, theorizing the development paths of states to industrial democracies; for example, as argued by Walt Rostow in his book *The Stages of Economic Growth: A Non-Communist Manifesto* originally published in 1960 (Rostow, 1990). American ideas about modernization drawn from the academy and experiences with big modernization projects of the New Deal (like the Tennessee Valley Authority) led policy-makers to attempt to implement these policies abroad, especially in developing states where the potential influence of a rival model – socialist devel-opment – would challenge US hegemony in the Cold War, and poten-tially the overall balance of power. As Ekbladh describes it, 'as world war gave way to cold war, development ideas were mobilized as a means to security and extend an American-dominated liberal order' (Ekbladh, 2011: 8).

While the push for modernization rather slowed down (and potentially died) in the 1970s, the ideas were revived in a somewhat different fashion as part of the so-called 'Washington Consensus' of the 1980s and beyond. Here, American principles of economic development were pushed into the core international development agencies – chiefly the World Bank and IMF – and loans and other forms of aid became predicated on 'conditionality', that if accepted a series of reforms would have to be implemented to liberalize the economy, including privatization and the opening up of trade (see Kiely, 2007: 69–73). While this can be seen as a purely economic form of power, we can also see ways in which it is folded into exceptionalism: to the extent to which states want to be part of the American-led order, they have to submit to liberal-capitalist ideals. While structured as a choice, there are obviously real penalties for failing to conform. However, we should be careful to note that to the extent to which such reforms 'work' (in the narrow sense of states becoming more viable, or even just brought into the liberal system), it does help to reproduce and expand the liberal order itself.

The end of the Cold War did nothing to stop these trends, and in fact the discussions of the 'end of history' and the 'New World Order' came directly out of the liberal internationalism of the Cold War. And while liberal internationalism always had a challenger in a more traditional realpolitik approach to international relations, the US always retained some sort of balance between morals (ideals) and realpolitik (and realism). Indeed it would probably be fairer to say that the US has always charted a pragmatic course through international affairs, one that became more difficult as the US gained power. The post-Cold War moment was one that was, as such, fraught with problems. While much of the debates were already discussed in substance in Chapter 1, it is worth revisiting them, putting values at the forefront.

The immediate post-war period saw a kind of vindication for US-promoted liberal internationalism. The first major foreign policy action of the new era was the 1991 Gulf War, which was seen very much as a foundation for the new order (see Clark, 2001). As President Bush emphasized in his 1990 speech outlining the 'new world order', the rule of law was meant to be at the center, and the Gulf War provided an opportunity for further dedication to the institutions and processes of global governance through the UN system. While the US was the dominant partner in the military action that followed, the decision was very clearly made in the UN Security Council, the rationale was made following a clear principle of international law (that non-intervention is sacrosanct, and Iraq violated it by invading Kuwait), and the aims were meant to fulfil the injustice that was seen as being done (restoration of the 'status quo ante' – i.e. giving Kuwait back its sovereignty).

The Clinton Administration never had such a clear-cut case upon which to impose American ideological power. The various interventionary wars that were undertaken in the name of liberal humanitarian values – in Somalia, Haiti, Kosovo, and the former Yugoslavia – did not fit for a variety of reasons (for an overview see DiPrizio, 2002; cf. Wheeler, 2000). While it was clear that there were violations of the international liberal values that the US wanted to protect and promote, the interventions themselves seemingly violated the non-intervention principle in an attempt to forge a new norm of humanitarian intervention. Additionally, the seemingly limitless aims of the interventions, which often went beyond stopping violence to restoring political order, made for imprecise missions that militaries – even those as powerful as the US – had trouble carrying out or completing.

While there were critics – both inside and outside the US – of the first Gulf War, it is hard to question that it fitted within the contemporary boundaries of legitimate action in the international order. However, the moves towards humanitarian intervention were increasingly criticized from two angles (discounting the important debate over whether or not they worked). First was in terms of increasing opposition to the 'imperial' behavior of the US. While it would be difficult to say straightforwardly that US interventions were only about securing US power, the fact that they tended to be one-sided, often not entirely effective in rebuilding order, and furthermore partial in terms of the places that were worthy of intervention (e.g. why in the former Yugoslavia and not Rwanda?) meant that hypocrisy became an increasing criticism (e.g. Chandler, 2005; Foley, 2010; Johnstone, 2002). If we put American ideological power in broader structural terms, we can also see how such interventions were ways of demonstrating the effectiveness of American values (to the extent to which various interventions were successful in upholding the values the US espoused).

A second criticism came from traditional realists and newly resurgent 'neo-conservatives'. Both started from the point that the US must be clear about its interests and pursue them more purposefully – and that the Clinton approach to intervention was problematic, especially moving away from a clear focus on the 'real', objective threats to American interests: great power relations focused on China and Russia (e.g. Krauthammer, 1990/91; Mandelbaum, 1996). While the realists drew on a typical sense of scepticism about moralizing in international affairs (not dissimilar to Kennan's older critique), neo-conservatives brought a new twist to these debates. Instead of just asking for a clarity of interests, the neo-conservative critics also demanded a more aggressively exceptionalist approach to international affairs, aimed no less at shifting the international order ever more decisively towards the US.

A good example can be found in a provocative article in *Foreign Affairs* written by William Kristol and Robert Kagan (1996), entitled 'Toward a Neo-Reaganite Foreign Policy'. In the article, Kristol and Kagan put forward a vision of a 'benevolent hegemony' based on both US interests, and its own moral vision and purpose of and in the world. It is important to see this as a critique both of liberalism and realism as approaches to foreign policy, and is centered on a re-establishment of republican virtues as values guiding the US, both at home and abroad (Williams, 2005; cf. Drolet, 2011). The 'Project for the New American Century' (Kagan and Kristol were co-founders) put forward such views very strongly, and included amongst their members a number of key foreign policy thinkers who would also play a role in the Bush Administration. While Bush and the key leaders of his foreign policy team (Powell, Rumsfeld, Rice) were not neo-conservatives (e.g. Rice, 2000), the role of neo-conservative ideas in framing the approach to US foreign policy became very clear after the 9/11 attacks (see e.g. Daalder and Lindsay, 2005; Kaplan, 2008; Mann, 2004). Here we see a real importance of values in framing and influencing a particular vision of foreign policy, but also in affecting the way in which American visions of international relations were legitimated and de-legitimated.

The neo-conservative view was that legitimacy stemmed from the US itself: it did not need to legitimate its actions through international institutions or anything else. Such views can be seen, for example, in Under-Secretary of State John Bolton's approach to the International Criminal Court: as the George W. Bush Administration's key figure in the debate, Bolton heavily criticized the proposed treaty, partially on the grounds that it was part of a 'desire to assert the primacy of international institutions over nation-states' (cited in Halper and Clarke, 2004: 122). While the initial build-up to the Iraq War went through the UNSC in an attempt to shore up legitimacy and support, when this route did not work, the US just went on its own, building up a 'coalition of the willing' to support its invasion. Additionally, while the war itself was predicated on security concerns, the neo-conservative vision went much further, seeing Iraq not just in terms of narrow security concerns to do with its potential possession of Weapons of Mass Destruction (WMD), but to see a shift in Iraqi governance to a democracy that would be amenable to American influence (or just a friendly state) combined with the potential strength of Iraq as a regional power, which would mean a transformed Middle East. The neo-conservative vision was one that saw not only US legitimacy and moral power emanating from within (consistent with exceptionalism), but also a need to transform other states to reflect the American image (e.g. Halper and Clarke, 2004; Smith, 2007).

The Iraq and Afghanistan wars are still prominent factors in American ideological power. While the invasion of Afghanistan was reasonably well legitimated (note this is not the same as saying everyone agrees, but it went along fairly consistently with principles of international law that are internationally accepted), the Iraq War was hugely contested, and a source of problems for the US both in terms of geopolitics and in dealing with Iraqi state-building (e.g. Finnemore, 2009; Reus-Smit, 2004; Tucker and Hendrickson, 2004). This is also not to say that the core of liberal internationalism was overturned, just that the US, as one of its leading exponents, having turned away from it, was becoming more detached from the institutions that in effect it co-created.

One of the ways in which a counter-reaction to the neo-conservative approaches to international relations was developed was through a 'soft power' approach to US foreign relations. Originally coined by Joseph Nye (e.g. Nye, 2002; 2011), the idea of soft power was specifically to advocate policies that did not rely on coercion, but the power to get other states and actors to become attracted to the US through its core values. Nye and others who utilized the concept were specifically concerned with the accumulating legitimacy deficit that the US was building in international relations, and saw through the concept of soft power a way of rebuilding legitimacy (e.g. Nye, 2003). There is an obvious overlap with the concept of ideological power, in that 'soft power' is meant to appeal to values, 'getting others to want what you want' (Nye, 2002: 9); however, it is meant to be an active policy, and not just an analytic device for understanding the operations of power (see Nye, 2011). As Mann has pointed out, it does not really exist outside 'hard' power, and can only be seen in the context of more extensive US material power (and especially American hegemony). As Mann states, 'I doubt whether Britain in the nineteenth century or the United States today could command other states merely by offering attractive values or policies' (M. Mann, 2012: 20). It is of interest in this light that Nye has rearticulated soft power as part of 'smart power', a way of mixing coercion with soft power as a more effective way of shaping US foreign policy goals (which has been influential within the Obama Administration) (Nye, 2011).

President Obama was elected in 2008 in part due to a real dissatisfaction with the Bush years, and one important area where he was meant to achieve a shift was in terms of foreign relations. This also brings us back to the beginning of the chapter, with President Clinton's ringing endorsement of Obama at the 2008 nominating convention, drawing precisely on the exceptionalist narrative, but utilizing it in a way more consistent with Nye's soft power approach. When Obama came to power, one of his key concerns was to recover US reputation from the problematic foreign policy of the Bush Administration. While it was not clear if this would just be a move back to liberal internationalism, it was clear that the international legitimacy deficit was at the heart of his rethink. Key officials taken on for State Department roles and other national security roles reflected the push towards institutions and international law (e.g. Anne-Marie Slaughter as Policy Planning Director; Harold Koh as legal advisor; Susan Rice as Ambassador to the UN; Samantha Power on the NSC Staff). President Obama's 2009 Cairo speech on the role of the US in the world specifically reflected a move towards reconciliation (and re-legitimation), pointing to the promotion of peace and shared values (Obama, 2009d).

Part of the re-legitimation was done through a repudiation of past policies – especially that of the Iraq War – but it was also done by a rearticulation of exceptionalism. Obama's foreign policy speeches of 2009 attempted to link the US with restraint, while still seeing it as a force for good in the world. Exceptionalism was also seen in a new light, with Obama's (and his close circle of foreign policy advisors) view that the US would have to make do with having less power in the world relative to rising (or 'risen') states, and would need to rethink its direct commitments. While still supportive of democracy and other liberal principles important to the American ideal, they were also tempered with claims that went against 'imposing' political systems on other states. In many ways, Obama's position was about recognizing the limits of American power, a realism tempered with idealism. This was made abundantly clear in his Nobel Peace Prize acceptance speech, in December 2009, making an impassioned case for the limited use of force in the 'Just War' tradition (Obama, 2009a). What was interesting about the speech was that it attempted to justify the use of force on humanitarian grounds, while not neglecting security: the policy context of the speech was the impending troop surge in Afghanistan.

While often characterized as an idealist (both by opponents and supporters), Obama's first year in office indicated a more 'realistic' foreign policy, that would shy away from over-commitment and expansionism, lessening American responsibilities, but not the support of American values internationally. The role of these two factors were probably at their clearest in a speech given at West Point a week prior to the Nobel speech, an Address specifically about Afghanistan. Here he stated quite bluntly that 'as President, I refuse to set goals that go beyond our responsibility, our means, or our interests' (Obama, 2009c). However, later in the speech, he also notes the support given for broad-based American values: 'And we must make it clear to every man, woman and child around the world who lives under the dark cloud of tyranny that America will speak on behalf of their human rights, and tend to the light of freedom and justice and opportunity and respect for the dignity of all peoples. That is who we are' (Obama, 2009c). The Obama Administration took the ideology of the past and reshaped it to new purpose. However, as the first Administration went on, it became characterized by slightly contradictory strands. Secretary of State Hillary Clinton was less impressed by the idea of the limitations of the US, and went to stress in several addresses at the end of 2010 the importance of sustained American leadership, and the importance of American values in this context (e.g. Clinton, 2010). President Obama himself, while still stressing the limits of power, was becoming more turned around to the idea of promoting democracy and other liberal values. The 2011 Arab Spring became a real test for all of these ideas (e.g. Obama, 2011).

The discussion demonstrates a number of important arguments concerning US ideological power and international power projection. First, the US has been extremely successful in embedding liberal principles in international relations. Values concerning self-determination, liberty, human rights, but also to do with freedom of opportunity and trade have been well ensconced internationally, and even more so after the end of the Cold War. However, it is important to see these values as being embedded in international institutions, so that, consistent with institutional power, these help the US to pursue its specific interests through them while also taking on a life of their own. Second, to the extent to which the US pursues foreign policies that are consistent with the values supported in those institutions (including following their rules), it is easier to pursue its interests in international relations, as they are then seen as broadly legitimate. When it does not, as was the case with the 2003 Iraq War – though the international legality is murky, there was no clear UNSC decision, and attacking Iraq therefore was an aggressive action that also broke the non-interference principle – it can incur legitimacy deficits that make it harder to pursue other actions. Third, as the power of American liberalism has concerned how other people have adopted and drawn on those ideas in their own politics and international relations, there is a sense that a number of aspects of American ideological power projection have become autonomous from the US itself. Finally, the American ideology, as projected into the world, is intimately related to hegemonic power inasmuch as the ideology itself can shape consensus and interests: that is, it forms an overarching form of power that protects American interests by getting other actors to accept them as well.

Conclusion: the future of ideological power

The chapter has argued that values as ideological power form an essential aspect of US power, reproducing the internal identity of the US, giving scope to the legitimate bounds of foreign policy actions, and concerns how the specific 'ideology' of exceptionalism translates into policies in the world. I have argued that American exceptionalism – in all its varied forms and evolutions – has been the key ideological framing for the expansion or projection of American power internationally. However, it has been suggested that such ideologies do not give guidance for specific policies, but give an overall shape of how and what the US should be, why its values might be desirable for others in the world, and how it might expand them to the rest of the world. To the extent to which the US exports its core values it can use them as a way of shaping legitimate action in world politics, which gives substantial weight to the kinds of foreign policies it wants to implement.

Much of the ideological power of the US since World War II has been in the promotion of a specific idea of liberal international order that by the end of the Cold War was broadly accepted. This is not to say that it inaugurated the internal transformation of all states, but that the US was fairly convincing that the ideas behind liberal international order were good for everyone, and as Ikenberry (2001) has argued, also promoted a normative and institutional framework that would restrain the US from using coercive power, or abusing its power. However, the basis of legitimacy requires some degree of restraint, and part of the problem in the 2000s was that repeated breaking of rules began to endanger the legitimacy of US foreign policy actions, on the terms of the very rules it created.

The chapter also argued that ideological power is highly diffused, and so while the specifics of exceptionalism remain tightly linked to American identity and the American state, in other ways, many of the American ideological tenets have diffused throughout the international system in ways that are not necessarily controllable by the US state. There are potentials for ideological power to become transcendent in some sense, when it is mobilized by other actors for new purposes; and also as an opposition to US liberal values, especially seen in global anti-Americanism (which will be expanded upon in Chapter 7).

Responses to American Power

The final chapter considers global responses to American power, in terms of both direct challenges and the ways in which American power has been broadly incorporated into the international system. The chapter does this by revisiting the 'types' of power discussed in Chapter 2 (and utilized throughout), and argues further that responses (or 'resistance') need to be contextualized within the context of these different types of power, in order to see better the forms resistance can possibly take, and whether it is actually occurring. The intention is not to look exclusively at *direct* counter-pressures to American power (although these will be examined), but also to look at ways that American power has been structurally opposed, incorporated and adapted by other actors within the international system.

Much of the debate on the future of American power has currently centered on rising power from other competitor states, focused especially on the rise of China, traditional geopolitical competitors (Russia), but also to greater or lesser degrees on other developing economies (such as Brazil and India), and also more traditional economic competitors (Europe, Japan) (e.g. Brzezinski, 2012; Kaplan, 2011; Kupchan, 2012; Layne, 2006, 2009; Zakaria, 2009; cf. US National Intelligence Council, 2008). These are not always necessarily discussed in terms of military or security threats, but mainly in terms of the threat they pose to continued American preponderance in the international system. What is interesting about the debates is that they tend to look at the comparative potential power indicators between the US and other peer competitors. Dominant in the academic and policy discourse on American decline, the emphasis on relative potential power focuses most intently on economic power, which for even the most staunch realists (who examine aggregate military power as the key to understanding interstate relations) is core to the background of American power. This results in much attention on the linkages between economic and military power, and discussion of the potential for 'balance' and conflict.

While a number of these arguments will be surveyed, the usefulness of the approach taken here is that it can divide up the various claims into more analytically distinct criteria. The chapter will do this by reflecting back on the four international categories of power discussed in Chapter 2. While it is clear that the various challenges to American power are not necessarily discrete, analytically disentangling them will permit greater clarity of understanding, and a richer take on what the future of American power can be, also premised on the deeper historical and institutional background that formed the bulk of the argument. As noted above, it is important that we also conceptualize different ways of understanding responses or 'resistance'. Some of these will be more direct, in terms of competitors vying for different policy goals (much more the 'first' dimension of power). Here it is very important to understand the current limits of American power, as often any decision that does not go the way that the US wants is seen as evidence of decline: i.e. it cannot 'impose' its interests. But, as a number of commentators have pointed out (Brooks and Wohlforth, 2008; Ikenberry, 2011; Kagan, 2012), this not only sets a mythical idea of what American power has been in the past, but it also sets an impossible benchmark, that even the US as a 'unipole' can hardly expect to achieve. However, this is not to say that there are not real challenges to US power, and the chapter will set 'relative decline' in a broader context of the ability of the US to shape the legitimacy of the international system.

It is also clear that the key institutions of international relations – UNSC, NATO, WTO, the Bretton Woods organizations – are fundamental ways of mobilizing American interests, and have long existed as part of an American-backed international system. However, looking at institutional power, we can also see ways in which the interests of institutions can become relatively autonomous from those of its members, and we might see more subtle shifts over time, if other strong members can invoke rules, decisions, or other ways of taking certain items 'off the agenda', or even altering the constitution of institutions themselves. Similarly, the structural organization of American power in the world has been stressed throughout the book as being paramount in understanding American power in the past, present and future. Therefore, we will also look at more structural changes, which are less about the immediate goals of policy-makers, and more about how the international system is gradually or suddenly reshaped by shifting power differentials. As outlined in previous chapters, the US has a real dominance in many ways in the various aspects of power, very much held together by an ideological hegemony. It is clear that, other than an imminent internal collapse of the United States, a real shift in global sources of power would require the rise of other ways of organizing power through the international order, or direct opposition to American policies or power as a whole.

The chapter that follows begins with a discussion of different ways of conceptualizing 'resistance', which relies on the discussion of typology of power utilized in the book. It then examines each 'type' of power in turn, to look at ways in which we can see resistance to US power in the world, and attempt to add depth to the analysis of the future of American power. It starts with 'direct' resistance, focusing on balance of power arguments, but also highlighting the potential clash of interests found in economic peer competitors, and, through the threat and potential of asymmetric violence, to counter American military power. Second, the chapter examines challenges to institutional power from various ways of channelling resistance through already existing institutions, or by abandoning or overturning them. Finally, the chapter looks at resistance to structural power, which is mainly seen through attempts to counter American ideological power, either through anti-Americanism or through alternative schemes or visions for international order.

Conceptualizing resistance to US power

As a starting point, we need to conceptualize ways in which other states and actors in the international system might oppose, resist or otherwise form credible opposition to US power. As a starting point, it is useful to revisit the power debates elaborated in Chapter 2. First, it needs to be pointed out that different forms of power will have different strengths and weaknesses, and thus will have different forms of opposition that will be more or less effective. Second, in asking the question about resistance, we also have to assume that in many cases there is little resistance, as US power is seen as a good thing. Steven Lukes (2005) has noted how sociologist Charles Tilly's account of resistance can be helpful for a better understanding of power. Tilly asked the questions that 'if ordinary domination so consistently hurts the well-defined interests of subordinate groups, why do subordinates comply? Why don't they rebel continuously, or at least resist all along the way?' (1991: 594). He gave seven possible answers to this question:

1. The premise is incorrect: subordinates are actually rebelling continuously, but in covert ways.
2. Subordinates actually get something in return for their subordination, something that is sufficient to make them acquiesce most of the time.
3. Through the pursuit of other valued ends such as esteem or identity, subordinates become implicated in systems that exploit or oppress them. (In some versions, no. 3 becomes identical to no. 2.)
4. As a result of mystification, repression, or the sheer unavailability of alternative ideological frames, subordinates remain unaware of their true interests.
5. Force and inertia hold subordinates in place.
6. Resistance and rebellion are costly; most subordinates lack the necessary means.
7. All of the above. (Tilly, 1991: 594).

While Lukes notes that answer no. 7 is clearly the correct one, these different types of arguments also get to the core of how difficult it is to discuss resistance to US power. As much of the present discourse involves direct competition or direct resistance to American power, what can be forgotten is more subtle ways that power is resisted, co-opted, or merely reproduced. We can also see ways in which each of these ideas relates to particular forms of power.

First, one of the most direct ways we think of international resistance is in terms of direct military resistance, either in balancing behaviors (e.g. strengthening internal military spending, or alliance formation) or the threat or use of force. Although this kind of direct resistance to US hegemony is seldom discussed in purely military terms, it is sometimes seen as the inevitable result of great power conflict, and especially in terms of US relations with a 'rising' China (e.g. Mearsheimer, 2010). Looking at Tilly's list, we can see a variety of ways in which such resistance is challenged. First and foremost, such direct coercive resistance is extremely costly, in terms of political, economic and potential human costs; additionally, as was seen in Chapters 4 and 5, there are no real challengers to US military power in terms of spending (though China may be a 'potential' peer competitor in this regard). Additionally, we would want to expand this out to look at non-state and sub-state resistance (in terms of terrorism and insurgency, which have been especially important in the past twenty years) (Brooks and Wohlforth note the importance of these as challenges to US hegemony – 2008: 209–10). Furthermore, we can also see that many state elites still see the benefits of US hegemony in terms of coercive power – that is, the ability to provide broad security guarantees – and, to the extent to which the US can still make such guarantees, it will still be powerful.

A second area where we can see challenges is the international institutional power of the US. As has been noted repeatedly, one of the real advantages in institutionalizing power is the sense of legitimacy it incurs by linking the hegemon into established rules that it is expected to follow as well (which distinguishes hegemony from more coercive empire – see Ikenberry, 2011; M. Mann, 2012). Additionally, it is important to note that point 2 above sets a crucial context for institutionalization: inasmuch as we see that there might be some desire to resist, that other states, elites and even domestic populations do get something in return for the structural power of the US, and in this sense the relative decline debate surrounds the decreased ability of the US to provide such goods (see e.g. Ikenberry, 2011). However, the caveat is that the rules themselves can also be potential areas where challenges from weaker states and potential peer competitors can arise. We can see this in a few different ways. First, it may be in terms of the more subtle 'everyday' resistance discussed by Tilly (and also see Scott, 1985), in that there may not be 'direct' conflict with the dominating power (both because such strategies are inherently risky, and because they may appear revisionist and illegitimate in their own right), but ways in which dominant institutions are challenged through everyday practices. Of particular relevance in this regard is what Schweller and Pu (2011) have referred to as 'rightful resistance', where challengers partially accept the rules of the hegemon, but from within find ways of increasing their own power, and potentially de-legitimizing the hegemonic power as well. In this way, we might also see ways in which actors attempt to use the rules against the hegemonic power in order to challenge its legitimacy. Finally, other actors can try to reshape institutions so they are more inclusive of other interests.

A third way we can see resistance is in terms of more direct challenges to the legitimacy of structural power. These can range from attempts to de-legitimate actions through everyday politics to more direct attempts to set up alternative systems of rules and norms. While the former can be done at less cost, the latter is more substantially difficult, but may be plausible in times of decline. While it has been argued that the US should only be seen in *relative* decline, these are moments when potential competitors may attempt to shift the rules of the game. The following sections will deal with each of these issues in turn.

Compulsory power: the balance of power, US coercive power and economic challengers

Much of the debate over the future of American power is in the realm of compulsory power: it is about how the relative decline of American economic power related to how the US can achieve its interests in the world. It concerns the direct application of 'power over' other states in the international system. As has been argued throughout, overemphasis on this level of power tends to obscure other important dynamics, and also has a real tendency to inflate certain power resources in terms of what they are able accomplish. With the future of compulsory power, the former is most clearly seen in debates about economic decline and its impact on American power, while the latter is most clearly seen in the debates about military power. Basically, those who see economic power distributions changing tend to overlook structural power (and to some degree institutional power), while those who note the preponderance of military power overlook the real limitations in terms of what military power can achieve in the contemporary world. As such, trying to discuss 'challenges' and 'resistance' in this area is heavily mitigated by the limits of the compulsory approach.

As was argued in Chapter 4, US military power is still an area where the US is preponderant. It still is the biggest spender on the military by some distance, and has qualitative advantages to its forces that most states cannot compete with (IISS, 2011). However, as was suggested, the main problem with US military power is in terms of what this power can be expected to do. In the wake of rather demoralizing experiences for the military in Iraq and Afghanistan, the power of the military to achieve particular outcomes is in some ways in doubt. While much of these issues relate to the perceived purpose of the military (e.g. is it for national defense, or more broad foreign policy goals?), it also may be the start of considering where challenges to American preponderance may emerge. There appear to be two main areas to consider. The first is the traditional conception, often discussed in terms of the 'balance of power'. In its simplest form, the idea is that other great powers will eventually balance American military power through some combination of alliances and domestic military spending. It also links to the rise of economic challengers to US interests, inasmuch as such challengers increase their own ability to achieve interests at the expense of US interests, but also to how economic peer competitors can have the potential to challenge the US militarily (through increased military spending), and also potentially upset the ability of the US to provide security guarantees to allied states regionally. The second are the techniques that have developed to counter American military power in more practical ways, mainly through the practices of insurgency.

The balance of power and future competitors

We need to start with how we can conceive of geopolitical resistance to US power. Conventionally this is seen in the concept of the 'balance of power', which, in broad terms, merely accounts for the overall distribution of power in the international system. However, the concept is often given a further dynamic, which involves the *reactions* of other states to the (potential) dominance of one state. The idea is that states will tend to resist the domination of the international system by one great power, and form an 'anti-hegemonial' coalition, potentially augmented by increasing their own spending on defense. Such power-balancing is conventionally seen, for example, in past coalitions of resistance against the domination of Europe by Napoleon in the early nineteenth century, and by the alliances against Germany in both world wars (e.g. Craig and George, 1995).

However, the balance of power is also a concept fraught with difficulty, both conceptually and empirically. To start with the conceptual problems, there are numerous different (and often incompatible) ways in which the concept has been used, which compounds the problems of using it to read into the international power dynamics of the present international system, and also the evidence for such behavior, both past and present (Haas, 1953; Nexon, 2009). While there are a number of ways we might categorize these different views, core for understanding the relevance of balancing to American power are three differing views. First is the view that the international system is structurally disposed to balancing, in that there is a built-in mechanism towards an equal distribution of power. This is the argument most equated with neo-realist thinking on the issue, that states tend to 'balance' rather than 'bandwagon' (to join up with the rising power) (Mearsheimer, 2001; Waltz, 1979; cf. Little, 2007). Here there are mechanisms at work in the international system that ensure no state can become preponderant – usually that the potential transformation of the status quo convinces (or necessitates) other states to 'externally balance' through the creation of alliances and/or 'internally balance' through increased defense spending. Major problems have been noted with this theory, both from within the realist tradition (Schweller, 1994) and beyond (Nexon, 2009), both for conceptual reasons, and, increasingly, from the lack of overall historical evidence (e.g. Kaufman et al., 2007; Schroeder, 1994; Wohlforth et al., 2007). While the neo-realist version is fairly rigid in proposing a structural mechanism, a slightly weaker version merely posits that states *tend* to balance (when the conditions are right). Finally, there is a more normative injunction that state leaders should try and balance when there are potentially dominating states.

The differences between these views are important as they link up rather strongly with ideas about the future of American power in terms of rising powers. In practice the debate about power-balancing runs into a number of problems. First is the conceptual issue about who is balancing whom. There is a sense that the balancing is of the US, but as Brooks and Wohlforth (2008) point out, in the more narrow versions of neo-realist theory, balancing behavior only encompasses balancing against rising and revisionist states. The US has already 'risen' (and gained preponderance and unipolarity through the fall of the Soviet Union), and is a fairly rigidly 'status quo' oriented actor. As the debate about potential challengers usually concerns challenges to established US power, the issues to do with balancing US power seem rather confused. However, we may be on safer ground looking at the debate from another angle, which is from the concerns of hegemonic stability. As pointed out in Chapter 2, here the leading state in the international order – the hegemon – backs up the international order through its particular powers, and is at risk when its power declines (e.g. Gilpin, 1981). At this stage great power war is ever more likely as challenges to the present order see weakness in the current hegemonic power. While there may be more truth in this argument, it also hinges on important debates about what is being challenged in the case of rivals to American power, and usually also centers on the need for leading states to take risks in order to preserve their power (e.g. the 'imperial overstretch' thesis of Kennedy). Much of the problems here concern how we conceptualize the unipolarity of the present system. The US continues to have enormous freedom of action in the international system, and the costs of maintaining its hegemony – due to relative power imbalances in the system – are not anywhere near those of previous hegemons (see the comparison between Britain and the US in Chapter 2: 71–2). Wars such as those in Iraq and Afghanistan – while costly in many ways – were 'wars of choice', and not necessitated by threats to American hegemony. While these might be poor choices that could lead to real problems for American power (much as future poor choices might), the US has mainly been able to absorb much of the material cost of the wars (if not the costs of international legitimacy).

The overall tenor of the debate is more in line with the Kennedy thesis as outlined in the Introduction – that what will rise will fall – and as there appears to be a rather uncontested sense that US economic power is in relative decline, therefore challengers will rise to balance the US geopolitically (and economic power is here also important in terms of delineating power differentials). The debates over the rise of China fit this scheme quite well (e.g. Friedberg, 2005; Glaser, 2011; Kupchan, 2012). Where some writers are categorical in the coming clash the US will have with China – often seen in military terms (potentially over the status of Taiwan, or in support of regional allies) – there seems to be less consensus on why this must be the case. Some of it is drawn from a sense that US decline means there will be direct challenges for power. So in reality these do not draw on the debate about balancing at all, but in a more general sense that conflict between great powers (aspiring or otherwise) is inevitable as ambitions grow, and interests clash.

However, as a number of authors critical of this view have pointed out, there are just as many factors pointing towards a more peaceful rise of China. First, China is not really challenging US interests in a direct way (Jisi, 2011; Fravel, 2008; cf. Nathan and Scobell, 2012), and in a number of ways China is just as dependent on the international order backed up by the US – in terms of the international political status quo through the UN, and through international economic institutions – for its rise to power (Glaser, 2011; Ikenberry, 2008). As Ikenberry has argued, China's road to power has been through these organizations and sources, and as such a clash is really rather over-determined. However, Ikenberry is right to point out that the lack of direct opposition to the US is determined by the willingness of China to continue in this fashion, or whether it will seek a more transformational, revisionist route (cf. Schweller and Pu, 2011). We should also add that Ikenberry's account is reliant on the importance of institutional power, and there is a real sense that to the extent to which China and other rising economic powers challenge the US through these institutions, American influence may wane.

There is also the important issue of China–US interdependence. While critics rightly point out that China has leverage over the US in being one of the major foreign holders of US Treasury Bonds, there is also real reciprocity in the fact that China is heavily reliant on American consumption of consumer goods to fuel its own economic growth: China remains heavily reliant on US markets, and US consumers are in thrall to cheap consumer goods that China provides (see Drezner, 2009; Kirshner, 2008; cf. Cappaccio and Kruger, 2012). These interdependencies are further embedded in the power of the dollar as a reserve currency, something that China does not seem in a hurry to overcome. The renminbi is not in a similar position (and remains inconvertible on the capital account due to Chinese controls on capital), and China still relies on its large dollar reserves as a way of keeping the value of the renminbi (artificially) low. As noted in Chapter 5, it is not necessarily easy for China to use its debt holdings in a coercive fashion, as it could only really be a one-off action, and would also have real consequences for the Chinese economy. China has shown that its economy might be slowing down and may even shift focus to domestic spending which might have a gradual transformation in China–US economic relations. But perhaps even more importantly is the way in which China benefits from the core institutions of US economic hegemony – particularly the architecture of global economic governance. While it is not to say that there is no potential conflict, it potentially points much more towards a rising state that sees its rise as part of the existing order, rather than in opposition to it (Ikenberry, 2008).

The debates about China also rather over-predict military conflict based on these balance-of-power-style arguments. China does not have real capacity to challenge the US militarily at home, but there are of course potential clashes over who can dominate or have hegemony in particular areas (see Glaser, 2011). Although, as Mann (2011) has pointed out, real Chinese aggression would likely be met with greater US power as its increasingly ambivalent regional allies would recommit to the US in the face of regional aggression from

China (cf. Schweller and Pu, 2011). The US has some problems with both the efficacy of force abroad and how regional challenges may affect its overall purpose (and how it is channelled through allies), but overall it faces no real rivals in this area (Posen, 2003).

However, some IR scholars have tried to keep the balancing idea alive in the face of little direct balancing – in the form of alliances or internal balancing – through the concept of 'soft' balancing (Pape, 2005b; Paul, 2005). Here balancing is done through more minute challenges to US decision-making – such as protests over the US's belligerence towards Iraq, or through regional partnerships such as that between Russia and China in the Shanghai Cooperation Organisation. Though this debate has ceded some interesting points, Brooks and Wohlforth's (2005; 2008) critique of it is thoroughly convincing. Their basic argument is that none of this behavior amounts to real balancing, which is seen to entail real commitments and real sacrifices and real risks. However, Schweller and Pu (2011) have added to the soft-balancing debate by looking at how contention can erode legitimacy over time, which is quite an important factor to consider, but one that takes us away from the focus on military and coercive power, and towards politics and ideology – this is likely where the soft-balancing debate makes a better contribution.

To re-focus on the issue of military power also requires looking at the present context of military power, which for some sixty years has not been concentrated on great power war. That is not to say that such a war will not happen again, but two aspects here are important for thinking about the real lack of 'pushback' in more direct coercive terms. First, the failure of militarism in World War II (or better put, the failure of purely militarist regimes) actually took military dominance off the agenda as a key motor of social change (Mann, 2011). Gone were anything like the bellicose interwar debates that were found in both Germany and Japan, that saw great wars as uniting the nation and fulfilling social promise (Berghahn, 1984). Though this is not to forget the huge impact of World War II on US power – and of course the militarized geopolitics of the Cold War – but great power war as a solution to particular social conflict, economic problems or as an ideal in its own right was rather destroyed by World War II.

Second, the invention of nuclear weapons dramatically shifted the calculations by great powers over war (Brodie, 1959; Jervis, 1989; Mandelbaum, 1981). Even during the Cold War when great power rivalries were at their highest, the Soviet Union and the United States refrained from direct military competition, preferring instead to deal with geopolitics through surrogates and proxies (and covert action). The continued salience of nuclear weapons in this regard puts a damper on the potential of enhanced geopolitical competition due to the catastrophic potential of such weapons (Glaser, 2011). As such, it is not so surprising that the US still puts a great deal of weight on nuclear strategy, even when non-proliferation and (less enthusiastically) 'global zero' are stated policy goals. The contradictions contained in the 2010 Nuclear Posture Review only highlight these realities: where the US tries to hold itself up to standards that it will aim to reduce its own arsenal (and President Obama's earlier claims to endorse the 'global zero' disarmament project), but to continue to maintain a strategic deterrent (with perceived nuclear rivals in mind), and also expand out the conditions where they can be used (Obama, 2009b; United States Department of Defense, 2010). The intense debate surrounding the Bush Administration's nuclear policy was even more contentious, with some scholars claiming that Bush was aiming for a kind of nuclear preponderance, which would have negative consequences for the current regime of deterrence (Lieber and Press, 2006; cf. Lieber and Press, 2009).

We can also see ideas about balance in terms of shifts in the economic distribution of power. As military power is based on economic power as well as the ability to extract labor (both productive and through military 'man'-power), economic growth and population dynamics also play a role in thinking about shifts in power and potential redistribution of balance (e.g. Kupchan, 2012: ch. 4). As such, it is not surprising that the debate about American power is highly pronounced in terms of economic power. While there are often discussions of direct challenges to economic power (mainly by rising economies), the debate really seems to be about relative decline and what it means for the American-led global economy. Again, as with the issues with military power, it is fraught with problems about how we conceive power in terms of outcomes. Here it is useful to recount some earlier examples of predicted American decline in economic power. The debate about the rise of Japan in the 1980s was based on some similar ideas about how the economic power of the US might be challenged, and also provides lessons about these kinds of claims. Japan was held up as a new model of economic growth, one based on the particularities of Japanese capitalism, and one that was bound to overtake US industry, with suitably negative consequences for the US. Apocalyptic tomes and articles were written to that effect. The result? Japan ended up in a recession that it was mired in for almost twenty years (Kiely, 2007: 196–7; Krugman, 1997). While the causes of this are debated, it does provide a salutary lesson for the difficulties of predicting decline, but also in terms of how we look at economic power in a capitalist international system.

For example, to look at China again, it is clear that China's growth figures remain impressive, and certainly do demonstrate a clear relative overall decline of American economic power. US policy-makers themselves see China as potentially threatening even in an economic sense, and have been especially vigorous in challenging the policies of the Chinese state surrounding perceived currency-manipulation and other issues to do with trade (such as intellectual property). That the Chinese economy is set to overtake the US economy in size in approximately 10–30 years is often seen to have grave problems for American leadership. However, we need to take a step back from the figures to look at a number of core areas. First, it is unclear whether or not China will be able to retain these levels of growth without facing numerous internal economic problems. That much growth has been reliant on maintaining large trade surpluses (especially with the US) also means that reliance on external demand may become problematic in the future. China's GDP/capita figures also show that economic prosperity is nowhere near that of the US, and recent trends have pointed to growing inequalities within China. That China's political structure makes it fairly straightforward to shift resources and priorities quite quickly means that these problems might be fixed; however, there is still a sense that we need to be cautious about how economic power operates in this context. Additionally, with future problems associated with population, there is surely an impending demographic crisis with an aging population as well.

For a somewhat different example, the European economies still account for some of the most dynamic and productive economies in the world. While the UK, France and Germany might not have a comparable size to the Chinese economy, they are still important players with vast and differing economic resources. That does not even consider the continued power of some of the other European states, such as the Nordic states, which also have real variety amongst them. But to focus on the key players gives us some insights into the European approach to American economic power. The UK remains important in the world economy, mainly due to the financial power of the City of London, which rivals New York in terms of the power of finance. The UK retains other important advantages in certain industries, but has obviously declined a great deal in many of these areas. However, as a staunch supporter of the US and American-led capitalism, there is little sense of the UK as a challenger to the current order. France is often seen as an outlier in Western Europe in terms of its lack of overall support for American policies. French leaders have on numerous occasions challenged the American 'hyperpower' (to use former French foreign minister Hubert Védrine's phrase), and have explicitly focused on the predatory form of American capitalism as a key problem. Despite these differences, there is little sense that France challenges American economic power in any focused sense (outside rhetoric), or by promoting an alternative model of state capitalism. Germany perhaps can be seen as the biggest challenge to the US, as the one European state that actually exceeds the US in global markets in terms of industrial outputs and international exports. The EU itself is often seen as a potential counter-balance to American economic power, precisely because, combined, its economy is a rival to the US, and also, through European institutions, does have the ability to act as one (though recently beset with internal economic problems). However, despite all of these issues, it is fairly clear that none of these states, separately or together, is interested in directly challenging US economic power, and in fact all derive considerable benefits from remaining within the US-led international economic order. While numerous European states provide different 'varieties of capitalism' that could potentially provide a sense of a different model to American-style capitalism, none of these is necessarily anathema to American hegemony.

Overall, while it is clear that the other states are catching up with the US, and that some of its structural internal weaknesses can be preyed upon by rivals and competitors (there will be further discussion of these internal problems in the Conclusion), this overlooks the importance of the maintenance of the core international institutional manifestations of US power (which also go beyond the US) and the continued importance of US structural power. If these latter two remain fairly solid, then US economic power may decline somewhat in relation to other states, but also retains a legitimacy and legacy that is not presently at risk, but may transform over time to accommodate rivals.

Insurgency, terrorism and asymmetric warfare

Although there has been much contestation over power-balancing and the relative decline of the US, much of the real issues with American compulsory power has come from the challenges of so-called 'asymmetric' violence. These concerns have mainly come in two forms. The first has been the ability of terrorist organizations with limited resources and capacities to incur major destruction on US homeland and military targets abroad. The second concerns the increasingly effective resistance to American military power abroad, something that connects with issues about the efficacy of military force discussed in Chapter 4.

The end of the Cold War did lead to a search for different kinds of threats, with the decline of great power conflict. If the real concerns of US geopolitics were no longer exclusively the great powers, what would they be? Although, as we saw previously, various forms of liberal internationalism took precedence, the threat of international (and domestic) terrorism had been a looming problem. The issue existed in two different dimensions. One, in the wake of the attacks of the American embassy in Lebanon in 1983 (and also the earlier Iranian hostage crisis), were attacks on US military forces and diplomats and consular services abroad. On the other hand was the potential for domestic attacks on the US homeland. A series of incidents in the 1990s started to raise both of these concerns. In particular, the attacks on US embassies in Kenya and Tanzania in 1998, the attempted bombing of the World Trade Center in 1993, and the Oklahoma City bombing in 1995 – all showed the potential of terrorists to inflict damage on the US.

It is still questionable how effective in the long term terrorist strategies could be, but it was clear that terrorism could have an important impact on perceptions of US power (of course not ignoring the direct impact on people injured and killed in such attacks). Each of the incidents already mentioned was used in various ways to demonstrate the inability of the US to project power, or that there existed support for violent acts against the US, both domestically and abroad. Terrorist attacks are in many ways meant to demonstrate the ability of groups and individuals to inflict mass casualties against civilian populations, as a means of discrediting the state itself, through the spectacle of violence and insecurity. While the Clinton Administration attempted to deal with such issues – targeting domestic survivalist groups, investigating and attacking sources of international terrorism, particularly Al-Qaeda and its leader Osama bin Laden – the responses (especially internationally) did not have the effect of ending such threats, and many of the attempts (such as cruise missile attacks on Afghanistan and Sudan) were seen as blunt instruments that led to much collateral damage, and further support for actions against the US.

The attacks on the World Trade Center on 11 September 2001 (9/11), killing some 3,000 people, raised the stakes of terrorism as a national security issue, and also intensified debates about the causes of anti-American terrorism. While much of the discussion within the US tried to de-legitimate those that sought to see what goals the terrorists and their sympathizers had (especially those who would be unlikely to directly support or carry out terrorist acts, but thought the US 'had it coming'), the motivations are important for understanding terrorism as a form of political contestation (Barkawi, 2004; cf. Pape, 2005a; Tilly, 2004). If we see terrorism just as irrational hatred, then it does not get us very far in understanding causes (and one presumes potential policy responses). But not attempting to legitimate such actions (nor to entirely imbue the actions of 9/11 in terms of rational political goals – the plotters and the leadership are rife with contradictions), we can see various ways in which the narrative of grievance played a role in the kinds of sympathies that were played out – especially in seeing terrorism as a 'weapon of the weak' in a broad sense (for different perspectives, see: Burke, 2003; Esposito, 2003; Kepel, 2006; Wright, 2006).

However, the policy response became much more vigorous than that of the Clinton years, and actually took forward a number of ideas from that Administration – especially in regards to domestic enforcement and homeland security. The creation of the Department of Homeland Security in 2002, combining 22 government departments dealing with issues to do with domestic security, was an important policy initiative that was seen as a way to get domestic agencies dealing with terrorism and issues to do with the protection of the homeland to share information and work more effectively together (Mabee, 2012). The intelligence agencies were also seen as culpable for the various 'firewalls' that had been created between the organizations, and led to a lack of information sharing between agencies (e.g. Wright, 2006). On the international front, a vigorous 'global War on Terror' was inaugurated, that had elements of police actions, Special Forces hunting down Al-Qaeda leadership, and the folding into a broader narrative of security problems and order-building in the Middle East, that culminated in both the Afghanistan and Iraq wars. The counter-terrorism polices of the Bush Administration have been carried on with renewed vigour by the Obama Administration (Singh, 2012).

While there is much to be critical in these policies – especially in terms of their broad impacts on the societies involved, the massive overreach in terms of policy (both domestic and international), the levels of destruction, the continuing problems with the effects of American policies in countries at the forefront of anti-terrorism (e.g. Pakistan) – the counter-terrorism campaign did have successes over time, but ones that were hard fought through the de-legitimation of Al Qaeda's techniques, and especially after a series of other bombings (in London, Madrid, Bali). In the end, the influence of these groups is much more limited, to splinter organizations in the margins, mainly in Yemen (Arabian Peninsula) and Somalia and in North Africa. Mostly they are thriving in areas where there is state collapse, and other potential political problems, some of which has been exacerbated and heightened by the Arab Spring of 2011–12. For example, the September 11 attack on the American embassy in Benghazi, Libya in 2012 (which resulted in the death of the American ambassador and three other members of the diplomatic mission), as well as the ongoing problems of terrorism and separatism in Algeria (with spill-over effects into Mali) and Syria have been prominent recent examples. However, while global terrorism was certainly an important challenge to US power post-9/11, it is one that has had an increasingly marginal effect on American power, but with some really problematic effects on the discourse of security within the US (e.g. Jackson, 2011) and lingering policy problems (Singh, 2012: ch. 4; Indyk et al., 2012: ch. 3).

What has been even more remarkable has been the questioning of the capability of the American armed forces, through their inability to impose outcomes that were seen as desirable in Iraq and Afghanistan. In the former, the initial invasion, which relied on a clash of conventional forces, was a real success in military terms. However, it was the 'second' war that became more about state-building that was increasingly intractable in both Iraq and Afghanistan (Packer, 2007; Ricks, 2006, 2010). What is important here is to show the difficult space within which the use of military power operates. While military force is seen as entirely legitimate in defending the homeland from invasion, there are much bigger problems when forces are used for other kinds of purposes internationally. The legitimacy of both wars aside, the insurgencies that developed in both states, and the complex politics of ethnicity and religious affiliation that came out of the destruction of state authority meant dealing with a much more complicated environment. It also (once again) demonstrated the ease with which insurgents can disrupt even the strongest conventional forces, when dealing with the politics of national sovereignty and self-determination (amongst other issues) (see e.g. Arreguín-Toft, 2005; Mack, 1975; Merom, 2003). Though there can be debates about operational practice, in terms of how an effective counter-insurgency campaign can be waged (and there clearly were influential debates about this with a more human-centered COIN taking priority in the years after 2007) (Kilcullen, 2009; Nagl, 2005; Ricks, 2010), much of this has to do with the complex politics of nationalism as well. Insurgents find it quite easy to de-legitimate outside military forces, even if it is initially seen as a good thing – e.g. ending Saddam Hussein's rule in Iraq, overthrowing the Taliban in Afghanistan. This de-legitimation happens through a number of processes that all work together: the inability of outsiders to provide adequate security, narratives of occupation and imperialism, the initial optimism of change overthrown by political realities of division and sectarianism. Insurgents are able to exploit all of these things, even as they add to the problems by accentuating them as well.

Both forms of asymmetry have highlighted the real potential problems with American military power, which connect to broader issues with the character of war today. While such things could be put in the context of American decline, the best way of demonstrating their power is that they point to the real limits of American coercive power (and other 'superior' powers have had similar experiences in the past), outside any sense of decline. As with the debates about geopolitical competition, much revolves around the issues of legitimacy and the goals of the actors involved.

Institutional power: mobilizing bias and interest

While the debates around a kind of 'hard' and 'measurable' power are made more problematic if we start to question tangible possibilities of resistance, we need to add in ways in which international institutions may provide another set of challenges for US power. While it has been highlighted previously (especially in Chapters 2 and 5) that the architecture of international governance has been predominantly led and guided by the US, and thus clearly linked to American power and interests, what is important about institutional power is that it de-links power from its creators, by embedding power within institutions themselves. International organizations, of course, get power to do things from their members, and 'mobilize bias' in the sense that those who create them and set the rules codify particular kinds of behaviors and actions that are possible in these organizations.

This kind of arrangement can be seen in Ikenberry's (2011) account of institutions as means of conducting 'hegemonic bargains' with other states: that the US will provide global public goods through international institutions, that will further its own interests, but will also embed its actions in institutions with defined rules and norms, that will restrain the powers of the US (cf. Lake, 1999; 2011). To the extent to which other states in the international system take up this bargain, and join up to international institutions regulating the international system, they thereby accrue its benefits. But what is important about this system is that it provides a way for the US to 'set the agenda' through institutions, but also allows other states to potentially use the rules against the US as well. As institutional power is still reliant on broader measures of compulsory power – especially economic and military (otherwise the US could not make any 'bargains' concerning the provision of global public goods) – if there is a relative decline in these measures, there is a possibility that institutions themselves will decline. But by allowing in other members, this also leads to the possibility of other members using the rules to further their own interests (which might conflict with the US), powerful states trying to change the rules, or changes in the constitution of the organization.

There are really three options. First that American relative decline makes it impossible for the US to fulfil the kinds of bargains made through international institutions, and thus those institutions become massively degraded, and eventually lose their legitimacy (and become either substantively hollow, or are abandoned entirely). Here the world might fracture into more regionally oriented blocs, with their own institutions and norms. Second, institutions could still be broadly accepted in terms of the rules and norms that are inherent in them, but either become more 'multilateral' and based on their acceptance by a number of other leading states, or another state takes over their leadership (which can be seen as a kind of 'managed' decline). Finally, it is possible that another leading state or group of states will set up alternative global institutions. The following will examine these propositions by looking at two core sets of institutions: the United Nations Security Council (as a proxy for global security governance) and the Bretton Woods institutions (World Bank and IMF) and WTO as representing global institutions of economic governance.

As a founding member of the United Nations and a permanent member of the UNSC, the United States is still well ensconced within the institution. In fact the character of the rules of the UNSC have given it a real stability over time, in that due to the ability of permanent members to essentially have a veto over decisions it means that in the main the leading powers have been able to get what they want in terms of stopping contentious actions. While there has been controversy over the development of principles surrounding 'humanitarian intervention' and the 'responsibility to protect' (in terms of how these violate principles of non-intervention), the real challenge in the UNSC in recent years has not been about the rules, but about the make-up of the permanent members. Some see it as rather antiquated, representing as it does the victorious powers after World War II (and in some ways representing ideas of an older multipolar European system), and the debate has come to be about how it might better represent the world as a whole. Discussion about adding regional members – e.g. from South America, Asia or Africa (Brazil, India and South Africa have been contenders here) – or other leading economic powers (e.g. Germany, Japan, India again) have all be mooted. As such, overall there has not been much of a desire to overturn the UNSC, but rather expand and reform it (for different views, see Brooks and Wohlforth, 2009; Kupchan, 2012: ch. 7; Weiss, 2003, 2011).

The key global economic institutions continue to be robust as well, though here there is more contention and attempts to reform and provide alternative models (see e.g. Drezner, 2007; Wade, 2011; Woods, 2010). The main problems with these institutions – and especially with the Bretton Woods institutions – is in terms of representation. In the World Bank and IMF, votes are distributed by contribution, so there has been much contention about the overwhelming dominance of the United States and Europe. There have been some moves – by the US – to change voting quotas in the IMF (Drezner, 2007: 42). China's admission to the WTO in 2001 certainly concerned bringing China into the institutional order. With the WTO, there have been attempts to reform aspects of its rules to make a better deal for the developing world (particularly seen in the creation of a bloc of developing countries within the WTO – sometimes known as the G20). In fact here we do have more contention over the rules of the game, that are sometimes challenged fundamentally, but are also disputed in terms of their overall 'fairness' – they are seen as transparently being in favor of established developed states (for example, in the protection of agriculture and patents), and here there have been attempts to try to negotiate between these groupings of states (particularly as part of the Doha Development Round). Similarly, the G8 as a kind of steering committee for monetary and fiscal policy has also been challenged by the development of an alternative G-20 of major economies (different from the G20 bloc within the WTO), which includes China and India. In recognition of the changing distribution of power, the US has also invited China to attend G7 meetings (Drezner, 2007: 42). In the wake of the 2007/08 financial crisis there have also been increasing suggestions for reforms on an international level – but this has not come to much, particularly in terms of a real shift away from previous institutional arrangements, other than the potential for stronger regulation at the national level (see Germain, 2009).

Overall, the result here does see some challenge from the relative decline of the US: the decline is really relative in the sense that it is the developing world which is rising, and the US is staying about the same. Due to this we see some challenges from within international institutions, but ones for the most part that continue to want to have the same rules, but to have them more fairly applied (on China, see: Johnston, 2008). As Drezner points out, 'global institutions cease to be appropriate when the allocation of decision-making authority in them no longer corresponds to the distribution of power – and that is precisely the situation today' (Drezner, 2007: 39).

Structural power: challenging American hegemony

The previous chapters have tried to stress the importance of both structural power and institutional power as a way of understanding American power. This is not to say that these other forms have to take causal priority, it is rather that without them, the other forms are too limiting for us to understand the general dynamics of American power, or the potential future challenges. Looking at structural power is in many ways key, as it has been highlighted a number of times that structural power has been the strongest way that the US maintains its position in the world. The structural strength comes from a broader sense of setting the terms of what other states want and where they are situated in the international system. This is clear even with something more robustly material as American economic power, which even as dollar hegemony provides real advantages to the US (and others to some degree – perhaps politically), it goes along with a broader sense of the desirability of an open international economy, thus also relying on American ideological power resources. In that regard, it is here we start to find the crux of the matter in terms of the future of American power, which is the challenges to this structural strength.

But how can we see resistance in this sense? Resistance mainly seems to come in two main forms: direct material challenges, and challenges to legitimacy. The first concerns direct challenges to the material bases of American hegemonic power. Though hegemony is built on ideas around consensus, it still needs a material base to give consensus real weight. In the case of American hegemonic power, much of this comes from its extensive networks of military power and from its more diffuse authority over the global economy. While in terms of military power the main forms of opposition would be in terms of the kind of challenges seen with coercive power (and also, potentially, moves that reclaim sovereignty over military power – such as rejecting bases, status of forces agreements, etc.). With economic power, however, the diffuseness of authority stems from both how much of that authority is embedded in international institutions and also how it relies on the transnationalism of capitalism itself, a social force that is not entirely controllable by the US.

A key example can be found in the future of the dollar as an international reserve currency. While dollar hegemony is based on material power, it does rely on other states accepting it as in their interest. Structural economic power counts for a lot of how the US maintains its international economic position. While, of course, the dynamism of the domestic economy also backs this up, structural power is what makes it so difficult to dislodge the US (and indeed, as argued in Chapter 5, the biggest challenge the US faces is in many ways an internal one). It also demonstrates how measures of economic power need to go beyond just looking at quantitative measures of output or GDP to show how power operates. The interlinked character of global capitalism makes it difficult to see economic power just in national terms. While reliant on international processes, states are constantly at the mercies of forces that may turn economic booms into depressions and crises. While US economic power may still overcome its myriad internal challenges, despite relative decline, it is also clear that other states and actors in the international system have interests and potential goals that conflict with those of the US, and these challengers have some potential to either work through existing power structures and institutions to their advantage, or to provide direct opposition to the US. When we move away from conceiving of the material just in terms of power potentials or distributions, we can see that much of this overlaps with consideration of general de-legitimation of US interests.

The second core area is direct challenges on American legitimacy, or the consensus holding together its structural power. As has been suggested, American ideological power is something that helps reproduce American legitimacy in the world, and is rather under-appreciated as a source of power (though with some links to the idea of 'soft power' as discussed in Chapter 6). There are two core ways which we can look at opposition to American ideology in the world. First, there is the direct opposition of populations (sometime supported by governments) to 'Americanism', broadly speaking, found in 'anti-Americanism'. Though anti-Americanism is in many ways a problematic concept, the growing literature on it also points to some important ways in which it undercuts American legitimacy and potential for action in the world – and the extent to which it is serious, to a decline in American ideological power internationally. The strength of global anti-Americanism, which often stems from attempts to reject American values, may point to weaknesses in the ability of the US to convince people and other states that its interests are the same as the rest of the world – though there may be disjunctures between the acceptance of such values by elites and general populations (see Ikenberry and Kupchan, 1990).

A second challenge to legitimacy is through the already mentioned 'de-legitimation' strategies of other states, which attempt to challenge American authority in the decisions it makes. Such challenges do not have to necessitate putting forward alternative frameworks of legitimation, but can merely attempt to undermine the overall sense of authority the US has internationally. However, such de-legitimation can be more powerful with the related potential of other leading states to challenge American ideological power through alternative frameworks of international political order, which may also be potentially seen as alternative frameworks of international legitimacy. These are challenges to the basis of US legitimacy itself, by putting forward rival visions of international order, with different legitimating principles. This is in essence what was in place during the Cold War period, so it is not impossible, especially inasmuch as American relative decline becomes more firmly entrenched.

Global anti-Americanism and American legitimacy

The study of the phenomenon of anti-Americanism increased as an adjunct to broader worries about the 'dislike' of the US internationally, mainly in the context of 'War on Terror' and the wars in Afghanistan and Iraq. While the popular discourse looked at issues like 'why do they hate us' (and the response of President Bush: 'they hate us because of our freedoms'), the academic literature searched for a broader set of means to explaining a perceived rise in anti-Americanism internationally (Farber, 2007; Hollander, 2004; Katzenstein and Keohane, 2007a; Markovits, 2007). It also further tried to connect global anti-Americanism with the result of specific policies of the Bush Administration. Prior to the Iraq War, views of the US were mainly positive, except in a few key areas: North Africa, the Middle East and Pakistan (see Katzenstein and Keohane, 2007c; cf. Pew Global Attitudes Project, 2010). However, the history of anti-Americanism can be seen to have a longer historical lineage. The eighteenth century and the American Revolution inaugurated anti-Americanism, as the very idea of the US challenged the established European elite (see Kennedy, 2007; cf. Ceaser, 2004). Post-World War II, anti-Americanism was less of a problem in the European context, as American troops were greeted as liberators in Europe during (and after) World War II. But views have fluctuated since, especially with a much more internationalist foreign policy during the Cold War period. American interventionism has especially complicated the role of American ideological power in Latin America and the Middle East (Lynch, 2007; Radu, 2004), where views of US policy went through dramatic shifts as the US government was involved in regime change (often covertly) in a variety of instances. Such attitudes have lingered in the post-Cold War environment, and remain today. However, the overall analysis obscures the real differences in the intensity of feeling for anti-Americanism, and what it means in terms of action. Such attitudes often reflect a degree of dislike or distrust of the US (and not Americans themselves), but still provide recognition of the possibilities of America itself.

Part of the problem in the concept is indicating what exactly anti-Americanism means. Is it an opposition to American ideological power? Or just a general dislike of 'Americanism'? It is also important to see the differences in how anti-Americanism is used by elites: elites may still subscribe to the American-led order (especially if they are already quite secure in their positions of power/authority), but use domestic anti-Americanism as a means to retain some connection with a home society. The academic literature has tended to divide anti-Americanism into two core categories, which are helpful for understanding the phenomenon and its relationship to resistance (Katzenstein and Keohane, 2007c). The first is described as *bias* based on what America *is*, in terms of values and bias against the American system itself. Such views are much more prevalent in conservative circles in Europe, and link much more back to the early anti-Americanism of the eighteenth and nineteenth centuries. The second category is *opinion*, conceived in terms of what America *does*, relating mainly to the actual foreign policy (and policy more generally) actions of the US and direct opinions of these actions.

Though possibly overlapping and therefore not entirely separable, the distinction between bias and opinion is useful for engaging the importance of global anti-Americanism for American power in the world (especially ideological power). We can see this in terms of challenges to American power on two levels: on domestic politics in the US, and on the US approach to international politics (see Katzenstein and Keohane, 2007b). In terms of domestic politics, interpretations of the sources of anti-Americanism are important for thinking about potential policy initiatives to stem anti-Americanism. As Katzenstein and Keohane (2007b) note, in the US the left broadly sees anti-Americanism as a consequence of specific policies, while the right see it in terms of bias, and therefore the solutions are very different: the left want to change policies, while the right think it should just be ignored. In foreign policy, the problems of global anti-Americanism have become recognized in the Obama Administration: as was noted in previous chapters, the early focus of Obama on reconciliation – especially seen in his Cairo speech in 2009 – was an attempt to shift global opinion by a change of tone and a change in policy itself. However, this approach has also been criticized by the right as an 'apology tour', that weakens US power (see Singh, 2012: ch. 3).

Alternative visions of international order

The other area of potential challenge in terms of legitimacy would be putting forward an alternative model that would challenge directly the rules of the game established by the US. They would, of course, have to be backed up by substantial material power as well, or else the drive for order would not be very convincing. We have seen that the Cold War already provided an example of what this might look like: the Soviet Union and the United States actually comprising competing systems of international order (Halliday, 1993; cf. Saull, 2007), with different guiding rules and institutions (and legitimation strategies), can be very helpful for understanding that international system. There were also challenges to order from within, such as the non-aligned movement and the New International Economic Order of the 1970s. The latter two were not quite as powerful in setting up an alternative counter-hegemonic movement, but were certainly important in pushing for alternative visions of world order.

Gat (2007), for example, sees the potential for a rise of new authoritarian 'second world' powers, mainly seen in Russia and China. These powers might provide major spoilers to a liberal order. And there is certainly a sense, at least with the latter, of a state capitalist model that China represents as being a potential challenger as a developmental model to other states (Kupchan, 2012: ch. 5). Whether this is actually a challenge to international order is really another question. The liberal order has managed to accommodate a variety of states, which, while mainly democratic, not all subscribe to the economic liberalism of the US (or the Anglo-liberal economies more generally) (e.g. Hall and Soskice, 2001; L. Weiss, 1998). The states of Northern Europe, for example, have long subscribed to a more corporatist model of political economy, which sits uneasily in some ways with the liberal American model (Hilson, 2008). Can a liberal international order also manage to accommodate states such as China?

There is a further question of whether or not China has or is interested in promoting a Chinese version of international order. Kupchan (2012) predicts that the world is headed for 'multiple versions of modernity', which would be in tension with one another. However, the issue is whether a rising state or peer competitor would see an interest in actively promoting such an order. While it was noted in the previous section that most states are content with a fair share of the current institutional framework, is there a real push for 'spoiling' the current system? As Schweller and Pu point out:

While the consensus opinion is that U.S. power is eroding, the legitimacy of the United States' international order and authority to rule have not, to this point, been seriously undermined. Any challenger that seeks to restore global balance-of-power dynamics, therefore, must put forward an alternative idea of order that appeals to other powerful states. Delegitimizing U.S. unipolarity and proposing a viable new order are prerequisite exercises for traditional balancing behavior to commence. (Schweller and Pu, 2011: 72)

It will likely be some time before we can come to any conclusions about the potential for a 'new' international order.

Conclusion

There exist a real variety of ways in which states and other actors may challenge American hegemony, especially in the context of relative American economic decline, and due to the numerous internal challenges the US faces, as indicated in the previous chapters. While there is broad acceptance that the international order is becoming evened out, and the US will face challenges to its leadership as numerous peer competitors come to the fore, there additionally needs to be greater attention to what this might mean for American power. While there have been a number of critics who see an inevitable decline for American hegemony (and potential destabilization for the international system), these often overestimate the nature of the challenges, and underestimate international and structural power that the US maintains. The US continues to shape the international system through structural and institutional power, but relative decline may provide opportunities for other actors to mount challenges to American legitimacy, first through institutions and later, potentially, through new visions of international order. However, at present, these challenges seem rather unlikely, as there have been few alternative schemes put forward that have been convincing, and the more likely outcome in the medium term would be a more multipolar system. In the short term, it appears that the greatest challenge to American power does not emanate from the international system as a whole, but instead from a variety of internal problems – especially economic and political – that will be the source of further discussion in the Conclusion.

Conclusion: The Second American Century and Beyond

The conclusion will attempt to synthesize and summarize the points made in the preceding chapters, in order to develop a more sustained theoretical overview of American power. While we can use the model developed in the book to think about the future, the main aim was not to make predictions, but rather to better chart the conditions by which American power may decline, remain robust, or potentially rise further. While it seems a banal historical truth that great powers 'rise and fall', we do need to get a better sense of why this is the case, the kinds of power resources states rely upon, and how we can see combinations of variables leading to relative or more severe decline. Part of the focus of the book was also to chart dimensions of power that are qualitatively American, so we are not just discussing American *power*, but *American* power. The main point made in this regard relates to the novel manner in which American core values were institutionalized in international relations, providing an important context for legitimacy in the international system. While such legitimacy has not gone uncontested, many of those core values have been embedded in international institutions to the extent that when the US does not live up to them, it is criticized for hypocrisy.

There is a real value in attempting to synthesize the conceptualization and historicization of American power, in order to get a clearer sense of where the US stands now. In what follows I intend to do three core things. First, I will rearticulate the conceptual framework of power put forward, in terms of the typology offered in the Introduction, and the use of Mann's four-fold model of power resources. Second, I will go on to explain how these were used in the book to provide a sense of how power works in the contemporary international system, and the particularities of American power. Finally, I will reflect on how both of these things come together in an argument about the future of American power in the international system. As should be clear, the key focus of my argument has been a continued stress on the importance of attending to both institutional and structural power as a means to getting a better hold on the present state of American power resources in the international system.

The concept of power revisited

Chapter 2 developed a typology of power derived mainly from Barnett and Duvall's framework, with the addition of Mann's (ideological, economic, military and political) (IEMP) model for understanding power. While these frameworks have some real overlaps, they also have different purposes, and therefore do not quite mesh together. Barnett and Duvall (2005) wanted to develop a typology of power that went beyond the power debates and typologies of International Relations theories that utilize the concept of power, in order to get a better sense of the different ways in which power is theorized and might be operationalized to examine international relations. They settled on a four-fold typology – compulsory, institutional, structural and productive – each of which highlights something different about power. While each is embedded in a specific background theory of power, they provide useful (and cumulative) ways in which we might see power in operation, which are not by necessity mutually exclusive.

Mann's framework adds something important to this: by showing more discrete 'ideal types' of power focused in the *social* (in terms of acting in concert through organizations) operation of ideological, economic, military, and political power, we can illustrate that the typology offered above appears to work differently within these different strands of power. Ideological power, being highly diffused and lacking authoritative relations (for the most part), fits more squarely in the realm of institutional and structural power (with some real potential to shape identities). Economic power, which shares some of these affinities, is also at its most powerful in arranging economic relations over a large scale, often embedded in specific institutions, but also highly structured and even hegemonic in its relationships with states and societies. Military power is the most bluntly coercive, and therefore in its more specific manifestations of coercive potential it is easily slotted into the 'compulsory' category. However, as noted in Chapter 4, it still contains other international power relations, especially in the way in which it institutionalizes and projects its military power through alliances and basing agreements. Finally, political power seems an important combination of the different types of power – coercive at its heart and through its direct relations of authority, but in terms of the 'infrastructural power' of the state it can also work in ways that are more hegemonic, shaping interests within the state itself .

What this has added to the discussion of American power is two-fold. First, using Barnett and Duvall's typology draws our attention away from only looking at power in terms of a contest of interests, which tends to be settled by the actor with greater material power. For the US, as the leading power in the international system, merely focusing on this aspect not only overstates the amount of power the US has in shaping outcomes that are in its interest, but also glosses over the other ways in which US power is maintained. Both of these areas are where the debates about American power often lie, and the sense in which the US is seen as being 'in decline' relates to it not getting its way, or by relative decline of material power measures. However, by adding in the analysis of both institutional and structural power (leaving aside for the present discussion the issue of constitution and identity formation), we get a richer sense of American power, how it is maintained, and what is (potentially) its future. While these emphases are quite common in the critical literature on international political economy, they are not as often brought out in literature focusing on other realms, especially the military and the ideological.

This is where Mann's four sources of power are exceedingly help-ful. While Mann has been criticized for not giving enough priority to one source of power as the prime causal motor of history (especially from those who see economic power as the source of all change – often arguing that Mann is too focused on military power; e.g. Brenner, 2006), I would argue that it is more the case that he sees different sources being pre-eminent at different times. It is very clear that in Volumes 2 and 3 of his 'sources' (Mann, 1993; M. Mann, 2012), the economic power of capitalism has been at the core of change, but it has interacted in important ways with militarism and geopolitics, as well as with competing political forms of empire and the nation-state. As such, what we can gain for the analysis of American power is a richer sense of the dynamics of power: how the US relies on different forms of power, how those different forms interact, and how they may be the sources of friction and problems in the future. The second contribution we get from Mann (and historical sociology more generally) is attentiveness to the past and the cumulative building of power relations over time. The present

United States is very much a product of its past, not just through the 'mythical' attention to origins that are part and parcel of contemporary American politics. The past is also important in terms of the ways in which the experiences and development of the American state historically have not only set in place the domestic contours of the state over political, economic and military life, but also shaped the ways in which it has acted internationally, gradually but dramatically leading to the preponderance of American power that we see today.

The particularities of the US state and US power

What remains is to look at the sources in more substantive detail: first to summarize the core argument made in Chapters 1–6, and second to detail how all of the types of power combine, which was only hinted at in Chapter 7. However, we must remember that all of the sources of power manifest themselves in both domestic and international ways, thereby muddying the easy bracketing of those as two distinct realms. Additionally, the different types of power also overlap and combine in specific ways, which goes some way towards examining the specific character of the American state.

Political power is at the heart of American power, and was discussed in detail in three of the chapters. Chapters 1 and 2 examined the development, expansion and conceptualization of American state power, in both its internal and external dimensions. The core argument was that the peculiarities of the American state and approach to power came out of a particular philosophy of American politics and government that also led to important state-building dynamics over the course of the nineteenth and twentieth centuries. Furthermore, it has been hard to distinguish an exclusively inward-looking development of state power, as the American state has always looked beyond its borders: first in terms of westward expansion and the expansion of capital; second in terms of 'imperial' relations or formal political control; and finally through the development of a global geopolitics in the early Cold War. The creation of the 'national security state' in the early post-World War II period was given particular emphasis, as that moment of state-building had crucial consequences for the Cold War period, and for the expansion of American power after the Cold War. Chapter 2 framed the expansion of American power more thoroughly in its international sphere, demonstrating the ways in which we can conceptualize US power in the world. Both institutionalism and a variety of approaches to structural power were emphasized as being crucial to understanding US power projection.

Chapter 3 turned inwards, providing an overview of the power of the American state, but also looking more thoroughly at the power and politics of foreign policy-making, in an attempt to clearly articulate the pluralism of the American state. The relationship between Congress and the executive branch was emphasized – particularly the rise of executive power over the course of the twentieth century in formulating foreign relations (and power projection). There was also much attention paid to the other sources of power in the American system, particularly looking at institutional power within the executive bureaucracy, and the power of organized interests, seen most clearly in the synergy between business and those in political power.

The clear outcome of these analyses has been to show the continued tension in the American system between a particular form of openness and a concentration of power in the state. While the US remains a federal system with much allowance for organized interests (and one that has been ever expanding in recent years, especially in terms of economic interests), it also has a very powerful executive in terms of the prerogatives of foreign policy-making, and a Congress that is very deferential to presidential power, combined with a fairly narrow realm of debate about how the US can and should act in the world. Its political power internationally has mainly (at least since the post-war period) expressed itself in terms of the formal institutions it has backed (such as the United Nations, Bretton Woods organizations, and the World Trade Organization), embedding core values in these institutions as a means to get other states on board. At the same time, these core values – especially those of liberal capitalism – have crucially extended the reach of American structural power. While numerous critics refer to this as an 'empire', conceiving it in terms of hegemony seems much more consistent with the type of power wielded; i.e. that power was employed through economic openness, which structured the interests of those actors which took part in the system. That is to say that the extension of American political power has mainly been informal, mainly (but not exclusively) non-coercive, but with a real shaping of interests according to its core values.

However, as with most hegemons, American power is backed up with a substantial degree of military power. As has been noted throughout, military power has been used in all sorts of cases to impose American interests abroad. These uses of force have sometimes been regarded as legitimate (e.g. World War II; the 1991 Gulf War), often less so (e.g. interventions in Latin America and the Middle East). The military interventions of the Cold War showed the dynamics of geopolitics and hegemony, and that the motivations for the use of force were often wildly contradictory. Probably the two most contentious interventions, both internally and externally, since World War II have been the wars against Vietnam and Iraq. Both of these can be seen in one sense as 'imperial' wars, to the extent to which they are about furthering American control over sovereign states. However, neither are straightforwardly grabs for resources or territory in the sense of nineteenth-century imperialism. In the case of Vietnam, there was certainly an element of imposing a form of hegemony, but this was also wrapped up in the broader politics of anti-communism, the impact of this on the geopolitics of the Cold War, and the divergent thinking of civilian and military leadership within the US. While interests in oil were certainly part of the war on Iraq in 2003, they should not be seen in the straightforward sense of the US merely taking direct control of them. As has been pointed out by a number of scholars, it is clear that the US would be better able to secure oil in the way it always has: by dominating global markets. That the oil situation in Iraq ten years after the invasion has not switched in the US's favor shows the problems with such an assumption (both analytically and in policy terms). The Iraq War was again tied up with a variety of positions, including an expansive sense of national security interests, a proselytizing for liberalism and democracy, and the attempt to bring Iraq into a more open system for the supply of oil.

Chapter 4 demonstrated two key points. First, a key claim (also articulated in Chapter 1) has concerned the development of the dominance of military and strategic issues in the internal politics of the US in the early Cold War period. The dynamics that developed in this era of rising defense budgets and militarized geopolitics have dominated the civil–military divide ever since. The second argument is that the blunt power of military coercion is not as useful as it may seem, as it is not fungible into other power resources. While military force is certainly the form of power most easily tied into compulsory power, its ends seem rather limited in the contemporary world. These two things point to a real dilemma for American power. As the US is preponderant in military power, and the domestic discourse of national security and militarism precludes decreasing defense budgets or rethinking the role of military power, military force is still seen as an easy solution to international problems. While there are increasing critical voices (and even with the Department of Defense there is clearly a growing sense that the budget cannot remain at current levels), the constraints of domestic politics – the continual push for military action against various 'problem areas' (e.g. Syria, Iran) – makes it difficult to challenge the discourse of militarism, and highlights how it may both be destructive to US power in the world (and those on its receiving end) and a real force of de-legitimation of American power globally.

Chapter 5 took aim at a core area of alleged American decline: its economic power. While the case was made that it is clear that a number of states and regions are 'catching up' with the US, the numbers can be misread. The key question is the extent to which institutional power and structural power are being challenged, and here, despite some talk of a push for a new international reserve currency which would be a challenge to US economic might, there seems to be little prospect of change in the short run. The core components here are two-fold. First, institutional power remains reasonably robust through the core institutions of global governance of the world economy: the IMF, World Bank, World Trade Organization, and the G7(8). While the creation of a more robust G20 does indicate some moves towards a more 'multipolar' economic system, there are no real systemic challenges to the core institutions, and the key challengers have all been co-opted in various ways. However, that is not to say that shifts might not happen over time in this area, as noted in Chapter 7. Second, US hegemony in the world economy still seems reasonably robust, if partially faltering. There are real future challenges to dollar hegemony, which would be the key material aspect of US power that would pose problems, as cheap lending and essentially unlimited spending would be constrained if other reserve currencies gained parity or overtook the dollar. While this is likely inevitable, other factors show that there is still a robust acceptance of the core American values of an open liberal economy, despite the differences in how particular states run their economies. So, regardless of China's 'state capitalism', or the more social democratic states of Northern Europe, they still buy into the core logic of the American-led global economy. However, it was argued in Chapters 6 and 7 that there is a potential for these institutions and values to be utilized against the US as well. As institutional power is embedded in the institutions themselves, the extent to which other actors start to share power or provide more leadership of those institutions they can possibly use to their advantage. There is also the issue of the transcendence of many of the economic (and political values) the US puts forward: they can be co-opted by other actors and states in the international system and used in ways that might be adverse to American interests.

However, the key problems with US economic power are internal. The discourse of libertarian 'small state' government, which is anti-tax and pro-market, has strong roots in the American past. But it is at odds in many ways with the realities of the size of state spending, the fact that most people do not want current programs cut, and the lack of sufficient revenue streams. While the core ideology of libertarian Republicans may well be more consistent with the founders (though Hamiltonian federalists may disagree!), with debt levels reaching 100 per cent of GDP, this will be a continuing issue in the future, which will almost certainly have an impact on the structural power of the US if borrowing becomes more difficult.

Chapter 6 proved a pivotal chapter. While the importance of more material power found in the economic and military realms is of course at the base of US power and power projection, it has been argued throughout that it is of crucial importance how such power is legitimated, both internationally and domestically. The American ideology, found at its strongest in an overall 'American creed' associated with American exceptionalism, plays an essential role in this regard, both reproducing the limits of the American polity and society at home and playing an integral role in legitimating international action, but also constituting the very identity of the US itself. As such, this power resource plays a crucial role in backing up American power in the world, especially if seen in terms of hegemony. However, ideology has also played a central role in the institutionalization of American power in the world. The core international organizations have been profoundly influenced by American designs and principles, and in many ways these embedded values – at the more abstract level – have been part and parcel of those organizations. Values such as liberalism (seen in human rights discourses), laissez-faire, commitment to a market society, and democracy have all played an important role internationally. This is not to say that the US is disinterested in these organizations: in fact I have argued the opposite. The embedding of core American values ensures that the US can get mainly what it wants from them.

However, there is also potential for those values to be used against the US if it violates them, and potential for institutional transformation over time, especially if the US declines in material power.

The future of American power: domestic crisis?

With the overview of the argument complete, we can conclude with some final thoughts on the future of American power, starting with the most problematic aspect: the crisis of the American domestic economy and polity. Although the book has told a story of a continued rise of power, one where the dynamism of the American state has been in good measure a reason for the rise in American power, there are signs that it is reaching its limit. The political system has been in much focus in this regard. A core issue has been the continued polarization of American politics. Recent commentators have increasingly bemoaned the lack of bi-partisanship, and the sheer obstructionism in the law-making process. An important factor has been the ideological push behind an anti-government agenda (drawing on past manifestations of anti-statism). Much of this has found a focus in the 'Tea Party' faction in the Republican Party, libertarian tendencies within republicanism, and the Libertarian Party itself.

A further issue lies in the continued problems with gerrymandering and re-districting in congressional politics. State governments have the power to set congressional districts within the state, and re-districting often occurs after the decennial census, when changes in population can lead to a reapportioning of the Electoral College and the number of House seats per state, which are based on population. The changes are then put in place by state governments, which usually means re-districting in a way that will enhance the incumbency of whichever party is in power in that state. While this is obviously something that can be of benefit to either party, it has increasingly been seen as responsible for skewing representation in Congress. There may be some way out of this problem, if a non-partisan solution can be found. However, the issue of gerrymandering has also increasingly being linked to a bunching of similar voters in geographic areas, so the uniformity of some districts is actually being affected by the population shifts themselves rather than by changing electoral boundaries.

However, perhaps the biggest obstacle is dealing with the fiscal problems of the state: a combination of increased government spending (for both military and non-discretionary spending) and tax cuts inaugurated by the Bush Administration. Defense spending is certainly an important issue in this context. Though the US did cut defense spending in the early years after the Cold War (while still amounting to 4 per cent of GDP), the wars in Iraq and Afghanistan helped to greatly increase overall spending. Defense budgets over the period post-2003 have routinely been at levels above $700 billion. The potential of a 'fiscal cliff' in January 2013 meant that the Department of Defense has needed to plan for potentially large spending cuts. There has been increasing talk of how costs may be lowered, and whether or not the US spends too much on defense (and whether it could use the money it spends more efficiently). Secretary of Defense Robert Gates in his first term of office for the Bush Administration did try and cut back on some of the spending, and get to the source of some of the most egregious waste. There have also been some recent studies that have noted ways in which defense could be cut while still maintain the military at necessary levels.

Though defense spending is an important part of the debate, a further issue surrounds the future of entitlement programs (Social Security and Medicare). As we have seen previously, since their inauguration in the 1960s, entitlement spending has taken up an increasingly large portion of the federal budget, and one that will not slow down, both due to rising health costs and demographic shifts. These have led to a substantive federal debt, which is getting close to being 100 per cent of US GDP. As countries in the EU have been facing a sovereign debt crisis, which seems to be the next phase of the current crisis in the global economy, here the US federal debt becomes more worrying. However, as has been noted, US debt is still seen as a secure investment, despite its high levels. This is likely a result of the continued power of the US – or the continued perception of power by other actors in the international system. The confidence that the US will still be able to pay its debt is reflected in the rather low interest rates that US Treasury bonds still pay.

Two recent examples can be especially highlighted as examples of the deadlock in government being faced over fiscal matters. First, the increasing problems that Congress has had in passing the 'debt ceiling' (Congress has to formally approve any spending over a previously agreed limit) have become a major political issue within the US, but also a cause of concern internationally. Previously the debt ceiling has barely been an issue, as it is basically just approving spending that Congress has already approved in authorizing the federal budget. However, the crisis over the debt ceiling in the summer of 2011 almost led to a breakdown of government, and although a new ceiling was eventually approved, it showed both the problem of the lack of compromise and the impact of these fiscal matters on global markets, with one ratings agency downgrading US debt. Republicans also continue to use these moments as means to get leverage over non-discretionary entitlement spending.

A second (and related) example can be seen in the more recent crisis over the so-called 'fiscal cliff' that the US faced in January 2013. As a means of dealing with the debt (and as part of the Budget Control Act of 2011 that ended the debt ceiling crisis), President Obama created a bi-partisan 'supercommittee' to tackle the problem. However, the committee found no bi-partisan solution, and part of the mandate was an automatic trigger for $1.6 trillion in spending cuts to come in light of no recommendation being made, including cuts to defense and non-discretionary spending. These potential cuts not only represent the years of lack of any consensus between the parties or willingness to compromise over matters to do with spending or revenue enhancement, but will also will have a big impact on the economy overall. The real question at the moment is whether or not Congress can deal with them: while they were able to make a deal on taxes, and it looks as if spending cuts will remain in place, while complex debates over the budget for fiscal year 2014 begin.

Overall, these domestic economic and political issues give a real sense of the lack of desire of the US state to pay its way. The current fiscal crisis of the state (not confined to the US) that has been the result of massive overspending by the federal government (at least since the 1980s) has led to a real problem with paying for things Americans want, and the question of how the state will be funded. The problems associated with economic influence over the polity itself also leads to problems with imposing larger tax burdens, which has now become anathema to the Republican Party, and has made it difficult to discern how to move forward. While this does draw on past ideological commitments, it is also the case that tax burdens on wealthy individuals were much higher in the 'golden years' of American capitalism, in the 1950s and 60s.

The future of American power: a 'post-American world'?

As has been noted throughout the book, while the US has been a leading state in the international system since the post-World War II period, it is not as if this leadership was not 'challenged' at various stages. From the Soviet Union and an alternative system in the Cold War period to the various structural issues that threatened US preponderance, there was never a stable sense of American superiority. For example, in the economic realm, the problems of the dollar glut in the late 1960s led to a challenge to US structural power, eventually leading to the end of the Bretton Woods system (though this turned out to be a boon for the US, in that it was released from the strictures of gold convertibility, but still received the benefits of having the dollar as a reserve currency). With military power, the US defeat in Vietnam showed a real decrease in American power (especially in international legitimacy, but also in terms of the perceived effectiveness of its own military power). The end of the Cold War was a reinvigorating moment in many ways: the US was certainly preponderant, aided by an economic boom, and unchallenged in any serious fashion. But the 2000s have changed this. As has hopefully been demonstrated, it would be fanciful to say that the US is in terminal decline, but it is clear that its global leadership is much more fragile. Part of this is due to the 'rise' of other states economically (and the impact that has had on their own wealth and clout, and the expansion of influence through institutional power), but also do to the lack of fungibility of military power, the paradox of an international political system with one dominant power (it is not as easy to coerce allies without a compelling threat to oppose), and finally, the inherent fragility of an economic system so dominated by financial power. All of these factors play a role in the potential power problematics of the US in the future. In what follows I point to some key areas and issues that will play a role in the American future.

The first key issue is the future of the dollar, one of the most discussed problems for the future of American power. As it has been discussed in detail in Chapters 5 and 7, it does not need to be repeated in too much detail. However, it should be stressed that dollar hegemony is an important facet of American power. But it seems that we should be careful in terms of how we read the problem of the dollar. Many who point to just economic factors note that a crisis of confidence in the dollar itself, or US debt, would lead to competitors and decline. However, as Eichengreen (2011) has pointed out, this misreads the situation: dollar hegemony arises *from* American power, it is not the *source* of American power. That is to say that the confidence arises from the continued belief and (potentially) acceptance of American power, rather than the other way around. The real sign of the continuation of US power even after the financial crisis that it itself produced was that the safest investment was still seen in US Treasury bonds. As such, much of the future of the dollar is first in terms of reproducing and enhancing American power, and to the extent to which there is confidence in its power, it will retain its strength.

Second, the rise of China has been noted throughout as a key concern for US power internationally, and it is indeed one that analysts and US policy-makers take very seriously. However, we need to be critical in terms of how we look at potential 'peer competitors' to the US, and what role they play in the international system. As noted in the previous chapter, most of the peer competitors happily work within the bounds of the current international order, and there is little sense that it is either in their interest or ability to challenge the system more fundamentally. China is a perfect example of this. China's mixed model state (a state capitalism) has been so successful because of its adaptation to US multilateralism, not despite it. It is heavily embedded in the system, and withdrawal from it – either in some fundamental challenge to the US, or some more gradual retreat – would likely do immense damage to its own economy. That is not to say that this would never happen, but certainly it limits it as a more immediate-term possibility. As China is by far the strongest (in a traditional sense of great power rival: i.e. militarily and economically), the other states that are put into this category tend to be broadly similar in terms of their 'challenge' to US power.

Third, there is a continuing series of 'trouble spots' for American power in the world, primarily in the Middle East and Asia. The contention here is that these are less troublesome than they seem in a larger perspective. They are, of course, crucially important areas and issues in international relations, but in reality play a more marginal role in the future of American power, except in terms of the potential contingencies that might be produced and their relationship to international legitimacy. In this area the most crucial appear to be the challenge of Iran in the Middle East, Pakistan in Asia, the residue of issues to do with Arab Spring (especially in North Africa), and the security situation in East Asia.

Finally, nuclear proliferation is also a key area, though more broad than any one region (despite the core focus on Iran, as noted above). President Obama came to power with a commitment to disarmament, as outlined in his speech in Prague in 2009. The 'New

START' with Russia in 2010, agreeing to large reductions in both nuclear arsenals, provided a beginning to this process. However, the commitment is also riddled with contradictions, in that the Nuclear Posture Review from 2010 reiterated that commitment to disarmament, but one also tempered with a very traditional approach to strategic forces, and one that also put forward new rationales for attempting to deter states which are not signatories to the NPT, and also to deter other forms of WMD with nuclear weapons. The potential expansion of 'legitimate' targets of deterrence does not seem in the spirit of attempts to disarm, and may have future impacts on the ability to pursue non-proliferation globally. Some more commitment to a more robust international regime dealing with proliferation, a reduction of both force levels and the centrality of the weapons within US strategic planning is likely necessary, to try and re-focus efforts surrounding both proliferation and the potential for nuclear disarmament.

Conclusion

All of this begs the question of the future of American power. If the structural and institutional aspects of American power remain robust (though possibly more fragile at the moment than previously), and the main concerns of the US are domestic, what are the prospects for another American century? While much depends on contingent events that are unpredictable, there is also the sense that there is much work to do at home in the US, especially in terms of the way the political system is affecting the possibilities of effective foreign policy. While it is right that political parties do not agree, and have differing agendas based on their own constituencies, the politics of anti-government (or anti-state) forces within the US is beginning to hinder the ability to deal with real structural problems facing the US. While these might wash out in the short term (it may not matter whether or not Congress can agree on issues to do with debt if the US economy starts growing again), it does seem that political gridlock may have detrimental effects on American power in terms of the confidence the world (and the market) has in the stability of American politics, especially in terms of dealing with pressing fiscal problems that do have effects on the world as a whole.

However, much of the stress in the account given has been about overall structural constraints and opportunities that the US has faced over several hundred years of history. Robert Kagan (2012) has rightly stressed in his recent work that a focus on the difficulties of the present for the US underestimate the difficulties of the past: the Cold War, where American power was consolidated, was also fraught with crises, and even in times of almost absolute strength, the US could not always get what it wanted. In these broader terms, the future of American power is very much linked with American ideas about the international system, and whether or not the lingering liberal internationalism of the post-World War II period is still desirable and legitimate in today's international system. While the argument presented shows that in many ways it does still seem robust, there may well be challenges here in the future. The American response to such challenges will likely be a crucial part of securing future power. While there are numerous challenges in the international sphere – from allies, from unstable regions and regimes, from nuclear proliferation, from the environment, from global economic forces – none of these is so great that it seriously undermines the freedom for action of the US. It is still able to maintain its hegemony without seriously overstretching its resources. Its ability to rebalance its public expenditure and therefore not only secure its future internally, but also increase the confidence of markets, is thus an essential part of maintaining hegemony.

References

Allison, Graham and Philip Zelikow (1999), *Essence of Decision: Explaining the Cuban Missile Crisis*, 2nd edn, Harlow: Longman.

Anderson, David L. (2005), *The Vietnam War*, Basingstoke: Palgrave Macmillan.

Arendt, Hannah (1970), *On Violence*, New York: Harvest.

Arreguín-Toft, Ivan (2005), *How the Weak Win Wars: A Theory of Asymmetric Conflict*, Cambridge: Cambridge University Press.

Ashworth, John (1995), *Slavery, Capitalism and Politics in the Antebellum Republic, Volume 1: Commerce and Compromise, 1820–1850*, Cambridge: Cambridge University Press.

Axlerod, Robert, and Robert Keohane (1993), 'Achieving Cooperation under Anarchy: Strategies and Institutions', in David A. Baldwin (ed.), *Neorealism and Neoliberalism: The Contemporary Debate*, New York: Columbia University Press.

Bacevich, Andrew J. (2002), *American Empire: The Realities and Consequences of US Diplomacy*, Cambridge, MA: Harvard University Press.

Bacevich, Andrew J. (2006), *The New American Militarism*, New York: Oxford University Press.

Bacevich, Andrew J. (2009), *The Limits of Power: The End of American Exceptionalism*, New York: Henry Holt.

Bachrach, Peter and Morton S. Baratz (1962), 'Two Faces of Power', *American Political Science Review*, Vol. 56, No. 4: 947–52.

Bailey, Beth L. (2009), *America's Army: Making the All-Volunteer Force*, Cambridge, MA: Harvard University Press.

Bailyn, Bernard (1992), *The Ideological Origins of the American Revolution*, enlarged edn, Cambridge, MA: Harvard University Press.

Baker, Dean (2006), *The Conservative Nanny State: How the Wealthy Use the Government to Stay Rich and Get Richer*, Washington, DC: Center for Economic and Policy Research.

Baker, James A. and Warren Christopher (2008), 'Put War Powers Back Where They Belong', *New York Times*, July 8.

Balakrishnan, Gopal (2005), 'States of War', *New Left Review*, No. 36 (Sept–Dec): 5–32.

Barkawi, Tarak (2004), 'On the Pedagogy of "Small Wars"', *International Affairs*, Vol. 80, No. 1 (2004): 19–38.

Barkawi, Tarak and Mark Laffey (1999), 'The Imperial Peace: Democracy, Force and Globalization,' *European Journal of International Relations*, Vol. 5, No. 4: 403–34.

Barnett, Michael and Raymond Duvall (2005), 'Power in International Politics', *International Organization*, Vol. 59, No. 1: 39–75.

Baum, Matthew A. and Philip B.K. Potter (2008), 'The Relationships between Mass Media, Public Opinion, and Foreign Policy: Toward a Theoretical Synthesis', *Annual Review of Political Science*, Vol. 11: 39–65.

Beckley, Michael (2011/12), 'China's Century? Why America's Edge will Endure', *International Security*, Vol. 36, No. 3: 41–78.

Beetham, David (1996), *Bureaucracy*, 2nd edn, Milton Keynes: Open University Press.

Bell, Duncan S.A. (2002), 'Anarchy, Power and Death: Contemporary Political Realism as Ideology', *Journal of Political Ideologies*, Vol. 7, No. 2: 221–39.

Bemis, Samuel Flagg (1937), *A Diplomatic History of the United States*, London: Jonathan Cape.

Bemis, Samuel Flagg (1949), *John Quincy Adams and the Foundation of American Foreign Policy*, New York: Alfred A. Knopf.

Bensel, Richard Franklin (1984), *Sectionalism and American Political Development, 1880–1980*, Madison: University of Wisconsin Press.

Bensel, Richard Franklin (1990), *Yankee Leviathan: The Origins of Central State Authority in America, 1859–1877*, Cambridge: Cambridge University Press.

Berenskoetter, Felix and Michael J. Williams (eds) (2007), *Power in World Politics*, Abingdon: Routledge.

Berghahn, Volker R. (1984), *Militarism: The History of an International Debate*, Cambridge: Cambridge University Press.

Bergsten, C. Fred (2009), 'The Dollar and the Deficits: How Washington can Prevent the Next Crisis', *Foreign Affairs*, Vol. 88, No. 6: 20–38.

Berrigan, Frida and William D. Hartung (2005), *U.S. Weapons at War 2005: Promoting Freedom or Fueling Conflict? U.S. Military Aid and Arms Transfers Since September 11*, New York: World Policy Institute.

Berry, Jeffrey M. (1989), *The Interest Group Society*, New York: Harper-Collins.

Biddle, Tami Davis (2002), *Rhetoric and Reality in Air Warfare: The Evolution of British and American Ideas about Strategic Bombing, 1914–1945*, Princeton, NJ: Princeton University Press.

Block, Fred (1980), 'Economic Instability and Military Strength: The Paradoxes of the 1950 Rearmament Decision', *Politics and Society*, Vol. 10, No. 1: 35–58.

Borstelmann, Thomas (2001), *The Cold War and the Color Line: American Race Relations in the Global Arena*, Cambridge, MA: Harvard University Press.

Bourdieu, Pierre (1991), *Language and Symbolic Power*, Cambridge: Polity.

Bowles, Nigel (2003), 'Economic Policy', in Robert Singh (ed), *Governing America: The Politics of a Divided Democracy*, Oxford: Oxford University Press.

Bowles, Paul and Baotai Wang (2008), 'The Rocky Road Ahead: China, the U.S. and the Future of the Dollar', *Review of International Political Economy*, Vol. 15, No. 3: 335–53.

Brands, Hal (2010), *Latin America's Cold War*, London: Harvard University Press.

Brenner, Philip, Patrick J. Haney, and Walter Vanderbush (2002), 'The Confluence of Domestic and International Interests: U.S. Policy Toward Cuba, 1998–2001', *International Studies Perspectives*, Vol. 3, No. 2: 192–208.

Brenner, Robert (2006), 'From Theory to History: "The European Dynamic" or Feudalism to Capitalism?', in John A. Hall and Ralph Schroeder (eds), *An Anatomy of Power: The Social Theory of Michael Mann*, Cambridge: Cambridge University Press.

Brinkley, Alan, Nelson Polsby and Kathleen Sullivan (1997), *New Federalist Papers: Essays in Defense of the Constitution*, New York: Twentieth Century Fund.

Brodie, Bernard (ed.) (1946), *The Absolute Weapon: Atomic Power and World Order*, New York: Harcourt, Brace & Company.

Brodie, Bernard (1959), *Strategy in the Missile Age*, Princeton, NJ: Princeton University Press.

Bromley, Simon (2008), *American Power and the Prospects for International Order*, Cambridge: Polity.

Brooks, Stephen G. and William C. Wohlforth (2002), 'American Primacy in Perspective', *Foreign Affairs*, Vol. 81, No. 4: 20–33.

Brooks, Stephen G. and William C. Wohlforth (2005), 'Hard Times for Soft Balancing', *International Security*, Vol. 30, No. 1: 72–108.

Brooks, Stephen G. and William C. Wohlforth (2008), *World Out of Balance: International Relations and the Challenge of American Primacy*, Princeton, NJ: Princeton University Press.

Brooks, Stephen G. and William C. Wohlforth (2009), 'Reshaping World Order: How Washington Should Reform International Institutions, *Foreign Affairs*, Vol. 88, No. 2: 49–63.

Bryant, Joseph (2006), 'Grand, yet Grounded: Ontology, Theory, and Method in Michael Mann's Historical Sociology', in John A. Hall and Ralph Schroeder (eds), *An Anatomy of Power: The Social Theory of Michael Mann*, Cambridge: Cambridge University Press.

Brzezinski, Zbigniew (2012), *Strategic Vision: America and the Crisis of Global Power*, New York: Basic Books.

Burk, James (2007), 'The Changing Moral Contract for Military Service', in Andrew J. Bacevich (ed.), *The Long War: A New History of U.S. National Security Policy Since World War II*, New York: Columbia University Press.

Burke, Jason (2003), *Al-Qaeda: Casting a Shadow of Terror*, London: I.B. Tauris.

Bush, George H.W. (1991), 'Address Before a Joint Session of the Congress on the Persian Gulf Crisis and the Federal Budget Deficit, September 11, 1990', in George H. W. Bush, *Public Papers of the Presidents 1990, Vol. 2*, Washington, DC: GPO.

Callanan, James (2009), *Covert Action in the Cold War: US Policy, Intelligence and CIA Operations*, London: I.B. Tauris.

Callinicos, Alex (2003), *The New Mandarins of American Power*, Cambridge: Polity.

Campbell, David (1992), *Writing Security: United States Foreign Policy and the Politics of Identity*, Minneapolis: University of Minnesota Press.

Cappaccio, Tony and Daniel Kruger (2012), 'China's U.S. Debt Holdings Aren't Threat, Pentagon Says' *Bloomberg.com*, September 10, http://www.bloomberg.com/news/2012-09-11/china-s-u-s-debt-hold-ings-aren-t-threat-pentagon-says.html

Cardwell, Curt (2011), *NSC 68 and the Political Economy of the Early Cold War*, Cambridge: Cambridge University Press.

Cassidy, John (2009), *How Markets Fail: The Logic of Economic Calamities*, London: Penguin.

Ceaser, James (2004), 'The Philosophical Origins of Anti-Americanism in Europe', in Paul Hollander (ed), *Understanding Anti-Americanism*, Chicago: Ivan R. Dee.

Chandler, David (2005), *From Kosovo to Kabul and Beyond: Human Rights and International Intervention*, new edn, London: Pluto.

Clapp, Priscilla, Morton Halperin, and Arnold Kanter (2007), *Bureaucratic Politics And Foreign Policy*, 2nd edn, Washington, DC: Brookings Institution Press.

Clark, Ian (2001), *The Post-Cold War Order: The Spoils of Peace*, Oxford: Oxford University Press.

Clinton, Hillary (2010), 'Remarks on United States Foreign Policy', Council on Foreign Relations, 8 September.

Clinton, Hillary (2011), 'America's Pacific Century', *Foreign Policy* No. 189: 56–63.

Coll, Steve (2005), *Ghost Wars: The Secret History of the CIA, Afghanistan and Bin Laden*, London: Penguin.

Congressional Research Service, Library of Congress (2001), *Treaties and Other International Agreements: The Role of the United States Senate: A Study Prepared for the Committee on Foreign Relations, United States Senate*, Washington, DC: GPO.

Connolly, William E. (1993), *The Terms of Political Discourse*, 3rd edn, Oxford: Blackwell.

Cox, Michael (2001), 'Whatever Happened to American Decline? International Relations and the New United States Hegemony', *New Political Economy*, Vol. 6, No. 3: 311–40.

Cox, Michael (2004), 'From the Cold War to the War on Terror', in John Baylis and Steve Smith (eds), *The Globalization of World Politics*, Oxford: Oxford University Press.

Cox, Michael (2007), 'Is the United States in Decline, Again?' *International Affairs*, Vol. 83, No. 4: 643–53.

Cox, Robert W. (1987), *Production, Power, and World Order: Social Forces in the Making of History*, New York: Columbia University Press.

Cox, Robert W. (1996), 'Social Forces, States and World Orders: Beyond International Relations Theory', in Robert W. Cox and Timothy J. Sinclair, *Approaches to World Order*, Cambridge: Cambridge University Press.

Craig, Gordon A. and Alexander L. George (1995), *Force and Statecraft: Diplomatic Problems of Our Time*, 3rd edn, Oxford: Oxford University Press.

Crockatt, Richard (1996), *The Fifty Years War: The United States and the Soviet Union in World Politics 1941–1991*, London: Routledge.

Crotty, James (2009), 'Structural Causes of the Global Financial Crisis: A Critical Assessment of the "New Financial Architecture"', *Cambridge Journal of Economics*, Vol. 33: 563–80.

Cumings, Bruce (1990), *The Origins of the Korean War, Vol.2, The Roaring of the Cataract, 1947–1950*, Princeton, NJ: Princeton University Press.

Cumings, Bruce (2011), *The Korean War: A History*, New York: Modern Library.

Daalder, Ivo H. and James M. Lindsay (2005), *America Unbound: The Bush Revolution in Foreign Policy*, updated edn, John Wiley & Sons.

Daalder, Ivo H. and Jan Lodal (2008), 'The Logic of Zero: Toward a World Without Nuclear Weapons', *Foreign Affairs*, Vol. 87, No. 6: 80–95.

Daalder, Ivo H. and I. M. Destler (2009), *In the Shadow of the Oval Office*, New York: Simon and Schuster.

Dahl, Robert (1957), 'The Concept of Power', *Behavioral Science*, Vol. 2, No. 3: 201–15.

Dalby, Simon (1997), 'Contesting an Essential Concept: Reading the Dilemmas in Contemporary Security Discourse', in Keith Krause and Michael C. Williams (eds), *Critical Security Studies: Concepts and Cases*, London: UCL Press.

Dallek, Robert (1979) *Franklin D. Roosevelt and American Foreign Policy, 1932-1945*, New York: Oxford University Press.

Davis, Mike (1982), 'Nuclear Imperialism and Extended Deterrence', in *Exterminism and Cold War*, edn New Left Review, London: Verso.

Desch, Michael C. (1999), *Civilian Control of the Military*, Baltimore: Johns Hopkins University Press.

Desch, Michael C. (2007), 'Bush and the Generals', *Foreign Affairs*, Vol. 86, No. 3: 97–108.

Destler, I. M. (1981), 'National Security II: The Rise of the Assistant (1961–1981)', in Hugh Heclo and Lester M. Salamon (eds), *The Illusion of Presidential Government*, Boulder, CO: Westview Press.

Deudney, Daniel and G. John Ikenberry (1999), 'The Nature and Sources of Liberal International Order', *Review of International Studies*, Vol. 25, No. 2: 179–96.

Digeser, Peter (1992), 'The Fourth Face of Power', *Journal of Politics*, Vol. 54, No. 4: 977–1007.

DiPrizio, Robert C. (2002), *Armed Humanitarians: U.S. Interventions from Northern Iraq to Kosovo*, Baltimore, MD: Johns Hopkins University Press.

Doyle, Michael (1997), *Ways of War and Peace*, New York: Norton.

Drezner, Daniel W. (2007), 'The New New World Order', *Foreign Affairs*, Vol. 86, No. 2: 34–46.

Drezner, Daniel W. (2009), 'Bad Debts: Assessing China's Financial Influence in Great Power Politics', *International Security*, Vol. 34, No. 2: 7–45.

Drolet, Jean-François (2011), *American Neoconservatism: The Politics and Culture of a Reactionary Idealism*, London: Hurst.

Dumbrell, John (1997), *The Making of US Foreign Policy*, 2nd edn, Manchester: Manchester University Press.

Dumbrell, John (2002), 'Was There a Clinton Doctrine? President Clinton's Foreign Policy Reconsidered', *Diplomacy and Statecraft*, Vol. 13, No. 2: 43–56.

Eagleton, Terry (1991), *Ideology: An Introduction*, London: Verso.

Earle, Edward Meade (1986), 'Adam Smith, Alexander Hamilton, Friedrich List: The Economic Foundations of Military Power', in Peter Paret (ed.), *Makers of Modern Strategy: From Machiavelli to the Nuclear Age*, Princeton, NJ: Princeton University Press.

Edsall, Thomas B. and Molly Moore (2004), 'Pro-Israel Lobby has Strong Voice', *The Washington Post*, September 5, A10.

Eichengreen, Barry (1996), *Globalizing Capital*, Princeton, NJ: Princeton University Press.

Eichengreen, Barry (2011), *Exorbitant Privilege: The Rise and Fall of the Dollar*, Oxford: Oxford University Press.

Eisenhower, Dwight D. (1961), 'Farewell Address to the American People', *Public Papers of the Presidents of the United States: Dwight D. Eisenhower, January 1 1960 to January 20, 1961*, Washington, DC: GPO.

Eisner, Marc Allen (2011), *The American Political Economy: Institutional Evolution of Market and State*, London: Routledge.

Ekbladh, David (2011), *The Great American Mission: Modernization and the Construction of an American World Order*, Princeton, NJ: Princeton University Press.

Esposito, John L. (2003), *Unholy War: Terror in the Name of Islam*, Oxford: Oxford University Press.

Evans, Peter B., Dietrich Rueschemeyer, and Theda Skocpol (eds) (1985), *Bringing the State Back In*, Cambridge: Cambridge University Press.

Farber, David (ed.) (2007), *What they Think of US: International Perceptions of the United States since 9/11*, Princeton, NJ: Princeton University Press.

Ferguson, Niall (2004), *Colossus*, London: Allen Lane.

Ferguson, Niall (2003), 'Hegemony or Empire?', *Foreign Affairs*, Vol. 82, No. 5: 154–61.

Finnemore, Martha (2009), 'Legitimacy, Hypocrisy, and the Social Structure of Unipolarity: Why Being a Unipole Isn't All It's Cracked Up to Be', *World Politics*, Vol. 61, No. 1: 58–85.

Fisher, Louis (2004), *Presidential War Power*, 2nd rev. edn, Lawrence, KS: University Press of Kansas.

Foley, Conor (2010), *The Thin Blue Line: How Humanitarianism Went to War*, London: Verso.

Foley, Michael (2007), *American Credo: The Place of Ideas in US Politics*, Oxford: Oxford University Press.

Foner, Eric (1988), *Reconstruction: America's Unfinished Revolution, 1863–1877*, New York: Harper & Row.

Foner, Eric (1995), *Free Soil, Free Labor, Free Men: The Ideology of the Republican Party before the Civil War*, rev. edn, Oxford: Oxford University Press.

Fordham, Benjamin O. (2007), 'Paying for Global Power: Costs and Benefits of Postwar U.S. Military Spending', in Andrew J. Bacevich (ed.), *The Long War*, New York: Columbia University Press.

Fortune (2011), 'Fortune 500', Fortune Magazine, URL: http://money.cnn.com/magazines/fortune/global500/2011/index.html

Foucault, Michel (1980), *Power/Knowledge: Selected Interviews and Other Writings, 1972–1977*, New York: Pantheon Books.

Foucault, Michel (2002), *Power: The Essential Works of Michel Foucault 1954–1984, Vol. 3*, London: Penguin.

Fravel, M. Taylor (2008), 'China's Search for Military Power', *The Washington Quarterly*, Vol. 34, No. 3: 125–41.

Freeden, Michael (1996), *Ideologies and Political Theory: A Conceptual Approach*, Oxford: Clarendon Press.

Freedman, Lawrence (2003), *The Evolution of Nuclear Strategy*, 3rd edn, London: Palgrave.

Friedberg, Aaron (2005), 'The Future of U.S.-China Relations: Is Conflict Inevitable?', *International Security*, Vol. 30, No. 2: 7–45.

Friedberg, Aaron L. (2000), *In the Shadow of the Garrison State: America's Antistatism and its Cold War Grand Strategy*, Princeton, NJ: Princeton University Press.

Frieden, Jeffry A. (1988), 'Sectoral Conflict and U.S. Foreign Economic Policy: 1914–1940', *International Organization*, Vol. 42, No. 1: 59–90.

Fukuyama, Francis (1992), *The End of History and the Last Man*, Harmondsworth: Penguin.

Gaddis, John Lewis (1987a) 'The Insecurities of Victory: The United States and the Perception of Soviet Threat after World War II', in *The Long Peace*, Oxford: Oxford University Press.

Gaddis, John Lewis (1987b) 'The Long Peace: Elements of Stability in the Postwar International System', in *The Long Peace*, Oxford: Oxford University Press.

Gaddis, John Lewis (1997), *We Now Know: Rethinking Cold War History*, Oxford: Oxford University Press.

Gaddis, John Lewis (2004), *Surprise, Security and the American Experience*, Cambridge, MA: Harvard University Press.

Gaddis, John Lewis (2005), *Strategies of Containment*, rev edn, Oxford: Oxford University Press.

Gat, Azar (2007), 'The Return of Authoritarian Great Powers', *Foreign Affairs*, Vol. 86, No. 4: 59–69.

Germain, Randall (2009), 'Financial Order and World Politics: Crisis, Change and Continuity', *International Affairs*, Vol. 85, No. 4: 669–87.

Gerston, Larry (2007), *American Federalism: A Concise Introduction*, New York: Sharpe.

Giddens, Anthony (1987), *The Nation-State and Violence*, Berkeley: University of California Press.

Gilbert, Felix (1970), *To the Farewell Address: Ideas of Early American Foreign Policy*, Princeton, NJ: Princeton University Press.

Gill, Stephen (2003), *Power and Resistance in the New World Order*, Basingstoke: Palgrave Macmillan.

Gilman, Nils (2003), *Mandarins of the Future: Modernization Theory in Cold War America*, Baltimore, MD: Johns Hopkins University Press.

Gilpin, Robert (1981), *War and Change in World Politics*, Cambridge: Cambridge University Press.

Gilpin, Robert (2001), *Global Political Economy*, Princeton, NJ: Princeton University Press.

Gingrich, Newt (2011), *A Nation Like No Other: Why American Exceptionalism Matters*, Washington, DC: Regnery Publishing.

Glaser, Charles (2011), 'Will China's Rise Lead to War?', *Foreign Affairs*, Vol. 90, No. 2: 80–91.

Goel, Ran (2004), 'A Bargain Born of Paradox: The Oil Industry's Role in American and Domestic Foreign Policy', *New Political Economy*, Vol. 9, No. 4: 467–92.

Goldsmith, Jack (2007), *The Terror Presidency: Law and Judgement inside the Bush Administration*, New York: Norton.

Goldstein, Judith and Robert O. Keohane (1993) 'Ideas and Foreign Policy: An Analytic Framework', in Judith Goldstein and Robert O. Keohane (eds), (1993) *Ideas and Foreign Policy: Beliefs, Institutions and Political Change*, Ithaca, NY: Cornell University Press.

Gorski, Philip S. (2006), 'Mann's Theory of Ideological Power: Sources, Applications and Elaborations', in John A. Hall and Ralph Schroeder (eds), *An Anatomy of Power: The Social Theory of Michael Mann*, Cambridge: Cambridge University Press.

Gould, Lewis L. (2003), *The Modern American Presidency*, Lawrence, KS: University Press of Kansas.

Gramsci, Antonio (1971), *Selections from the Prison Notebooks*, trans. and ed. Quintin Hoare and Geoffrey Nowell-Smith, London: Lawrence & Wishart.

Gregory, Shaun (1996), *Nuclear Command and Control in NATO: Nuclear Weapons Operations and the Strategy of Flexible Response*, Basingstoke: Macmillan.

Griffith, Robert (1989), 'Forging America's Postwar Order: Domestic Politics and Political Economy in the Age of Truman', in Michael J. Lacey (ed.), *The Truman Presidency*, Cambridge: Cambridge University Press.

Grimmett, Richard A. (2008), 'The War Powers Resolution: After Thirty-Four Years', Congressional Research Service Report RL32267, US Congressional Research Service.

Grimmett, Richard A. (2010), 'Instances of Use of United States Armed Forces Abroad, 1798-2010', Congressional Research Service Report R41677, US Congressional Research Service.

Grodzins, Morton (1966), *The American System*, Chicago: Rand McNally.

Grunwald, Michael (2012), *The New New Deal: The Hidden Story of Change in the Obama Era*, New York: Simon & Schuster.

Guzzini, Stefano (1993), 'Structural Power: The Limits of Neorealist Power Analysis', *International Organization*, Vol. 47, No. 3: 443–78.

Guzzini, Stefano (2005), 'The Concept of Power: A Constructivist Analysis', *Millennium*, Vol.33, No.3: 495–521.

Haas, Ernst B. (1953), 'The Balance of Power: Prescription, Concept, or Propaganda', *World Politics*, Vol. 5, No. 4: 442–77.

Hacker, Jacob S. and Paul Pierson (2010), *Winner-Take-All Politics*, New York: Simon & Schuster.

Halberstam, David (2007), *The Coldest Winter: America and the Korean War*, New York: Hyperion.

Hall, John A. (1993), 'Ideas and the Social Sciences', in Judith Goldstein and Robert O. Keohane (eds), *Ideas and Foreign Policy: Beliefs, Institutions and Political Change*, Ithaca, NY: Cornell University Press.

Hall, Peter A. and David Soskice (eds) (2001), *Varieties of Capitalism: The Institutional Foundations of Comparative Advantage*, Oxford: Oxford University Press.

Halliday, Fred (1986), *The Making of the Second Cold War*, 2nd edn, London: Verso.

Halliday, Fred (1993), 'The Cold War as Inter-Systemic Conflict: Initial Theses', in Mike Bowker and Robin Brown (eds), *From Cold War to Collapse: Theory and World Politics in the 1980s*, Cambridge: Cambridge University Press.

Hallin, Daniel (1986). *The 'Uncensored War': The Media and Vietnam*, New York: Oxford University Press.

Halper, Stefan and Jonathan Clarke (2004), *America Alone: The Neoconservatives and the Global Order*, Cambridge: Cambridge University Press.

Hammond, Paul Y. (1977), *Organizing for Defense: The American Military Establishment in the Twentieth Century*, Westport, CT: Greenwood Publishing.

Haney, Patrick J. and Walt Vanderbush (1999), 'The Role of Ethnic Interest Groups in U.S. Foreign Policy: The Case of the Cuban American Foundation', *International Studies Quarterly*, Vol. 43, No. 2: 341–61.

Harbutt, Fraser J. (2002), *The Cold War Era*, Oxford: Blackwell.

Hardt, Michael and Antonio Negri (2000), *Empire*, Cambridge, MA: Harvard University Press.

Hartz, Louis, (1991), *The Liberal Tradition in America*, new edn, San Diego: Harcourt Brace Jovanovich.

Harvey, David (2003), *The New Imperialism*, Oxford: Oxford University Press.

Harvey, David (2005), *A Brief History of Neoliberalism*, Oxford: Oxford University Press.

Hayek, Friedrich von (1944), *The Road to Serfdom*, London: Routledge and Kegan Paul.

Hayward, Clarissa Rile (2000), *De-Facing Power*, Cambridge: Cambridge University Press.

Heale, M. J. (1990), *American Anti-Communism: Combating the Enemy Within, 1830-1970*, Baltimore, MD: Johns Hopkins University Press.

Helleiner, Eric (1994), *States and the Reemergence of Global Finance: From Bretton Woods to the 1990s*, Ithaca, NY: Cornell University Press.

Helleiner, Eric (2009), 'Enduring Top Currency, Fragile Negotiated Currency: Politics and the Dollar's International Role', in Eric Helleiner and Jonathan Kirshner (eds), *The Future of the Dollar*, Ithaca, NY: Cornell University Press.

Helleiner, Eric and Jonathan Kirshner (2009), 'The Future of the Dollar: Whither the Key Currency?' in Eric Helleiner and Jonathan Kirshner (eds), *The Future of the Dollar*, Ithaca, NY: Cornell University Press.

Herman, Edward S., and Noam Chomsky (1994), *Manufacturing Consent: The Political Economy of the Mass Media*, London: Vintage.

Herring, Eric and Piers Robinson (2003), 'Too Polemical or Too Critical? Chomsky on the Study of the News Media and US Foreign Policy', *Review of International Studies*, Vol. 29, No. 4: 553–68.

Herring, George C. (1996), *America's Longest War: The United States and Vietnam, 1950–1975*, London: McGraw-Hill.

Herring, George C. (2009), *From Colony to Superpower: U.S. Foreign Relations since 1776*, Oxford: Oxford University Press.

Hertzberg, Hendrik (2004), 'Front Man: The Moral Decline of the American Ruling Class', in *Politics: Arguments and Observations 1966–2004*, London: Penguin.

Hilson, Mary (2008), *The Nordic Model: Scandinavia Since 1945*, London: Reaktion Books.

Hindess, Barry (1996), *Discourses of Power: From Hobbes to Foucault*, Oxford: Blackwell.

Hofstadter, Richard (1955), *The Age of Reform: From Bryan to F.D.R.*, New York: Alfred A. Knopf.

Hofstadter, Richard (1996 [1964]), 'Cuba, the Philippines, and Manifest Destiny', in *The Paranoid Style in American Politics and Other Essays*, Cambridge, MA: Harvard University Press.

Hogan, Michael J. (1998), *A Cross of Iron: Harry S. Truman and the Origins of the National Security State 1945–1954*, Cambridge: Cambridge University Press.

Hogan, Michael J. (ed.) (1992), *The End of the Cold War: Its Meaning and Implications*, Cambridge: Cambridge University Press.

Hollander, Paul (ed.) (2004), *Understanding Anti-Americanism*, Chicago: Ivan R. Dee.

Horsman, Reginald (1986), *Race and Manifest Destiny: The Origins of American Racial Anglo-Saxonism*, New edn, Cambridge, MA: Harvard University Press.

Howe, Daniel Walker (2007), *What Hath God Wrought: The Transformation of America, 1815–1848*, Oxford: Oxford University Press.

Howell, William G. and Jon C. Pevehouse (2005), 'Presidents, Congress, and the Use of Force', *International Organization*, Vol. 59, No. 1: 209–32.

Howell, William G. and Jon C. Pevehouse (2007), 'When Congress Stops Wars: Partisan Politics and Presidential Power', *Foreign Affairs*, Vol. 86, No. 5: 95–107.

Hunt, Michael H. (1987), *Ideology in US Foreign Policy*, New Haven, CT: Yale University Press.

Hunt, Michael H. (2007), *The American Ascendancy*, Chapel Hill: University of North Carolina Press.

Huntington, Samuel P. (1957), *The Soldier and the State*, Cambridge, MA: Belknap Press.

Huntington, Samuel P. (1993), 'The Clash of Civilizations?', *Foreign Affairs*, Vol. 72, No. 3: 22–49.

Huntington, Samuel P. (2004), *Who are We?: The Challenges to America's National Identity*, New York: Simon & Schuster.

Hurd, Ian (1999), 'Authority and Legitimacy in International Politics', *International Organization*, Vol. 53, No. 2: 379–408.

Hurd, Ian (2003), 'Too Legit to Quit', *Foreign Affairs*, Vol. 82, No. 4: 204–5.

Ikenberry, G. John (1993), 'Creating Yesterday's New World Order: Keynesian "New Thinking" and the Anglo-American Postwar Settlement', in Judith Goldstein and Robert O. Keohane (eds), *Ideas and Foreign Policy: Beliefs, Institutions and Political Change*, Ithaca, NY: Cornell University Press.

Ikenberry, G. John (2001), *After Victory: Institutions, Strategic Restraint, and the Rebuilding of Order after Major Wars*, Princeton, NJ: Princeton University Press.

Ikenberry, G. John (2008), 'The Rise of China and the Future of the West: Can the Liberal System Survive?' *Foreign Affairs*, Vol. 87, No. 1: 23–37.

Ikenberry, G. John (2011), *Liberal Leviathan: The Origins, Crisis and Transformation of the American World Order*, Princeton, NJ: Princeton University Press.

Ikenberry, G. John and Charles Kupchan (1990), 'Socialization and Hegemonic Power', *International Organization*, Vol. 44, No. 3: 283–315.

Ikenberry, G. John and Anne-Marie Slaughter (2006), *Forging a World of Liberty under Law: U.S. National Security in the 21st Century*, Princeton, NJ: Princeton Project on National Security.

Indyk, Martin S., Kenneth G. Lieberthal and Michael E. O'Hanlon (2012), *Bending History: Barack Obama's Foreign Policy*, Washington, DC: Brookings Institution Press.

International Institute for Strategic Studies (IISS) (2011), *The Military Balance 2011*, London: Routledge.

Issac, Jeffery C. (1987), 'Beyond the Three Faces of Power: A Realist Critique', *Polity*, Vol. 20, No. 1: 4–31.

Isaacson, Walter (1999), 'Madeline's War', *Time Magazine*, March 9.

Jackson, Richard (2011), 'Culture, Identity and Hegemony: Continuity and (the Lack of) Change in US Counterterrorism Policy from Bush to Obama', *International Politics*, Vol. 48, Nos. 2/3: 390–411.

Jacobs, Lawrence R. and Benjamin I. Page (2005), 'Who Influences U.S. Foreign Policy?', *American Political Science Review*, Vol. 99, No. 1: 107–23.

Jefferson, Thomas (1993 [1781]), 'Notes on the State of Virginia', in *The Life and Selected Writings of Thomas Jefferson*, New York: Modern Library.

Jenkins, Philip (2012), *A History of the United States*, 4th edn, Basingstoke: Palgrave Macmillan.

Jentleson, Bruce (2003), 'Tough Love Multilateralism', *Washington Quarterly*, Vol. 27, No. 1: 7–24.

Jervis, Robert (1989), *The Meaning of the Nuclear Revolution*, Ithaca, NY: Cornell University Press.

Jessop, Bob (2008), *State Power: A Strategic-Relational Approach*, Cambridge: Polity.

Jisi, Wang (2011), 'China's Search for a Grand Strategy', *Foreign Affairs*, Vol. 90, No. 2: 68–79.

Johnson, Chalmers (2004), *The Sorrows of Empire: Militarism, Secrecy and the End of the Republic*, New York: Verso.

Johnson, Robert David (2005), *Congress and the Cold War*, Cambridge: Cambridge University Press.

Johnston, Alastair Iain (2008), *Social States: China in International Institutions, 1980–2000*, Princeton, NJ: Princeton University Press.

Johnstone, Diana (2002), *Fools' Crusade: Yugoslavia, NATO and Western Delusions*, London: Pluto.

Kagan, Robert (2004), *Paradise and Power: America versus Europe in the New World Order*, London: Atlantic.

Kagan, Robert (2006), *Dangerous Nation*, New York: Knopf.

Kagan, Robert (2012), 'Not Fade Away: Against the Myth of American Decline', *The New Republic*, January 11, Accessed at: http://www.tnr.com/article/politics/magazine/99521/america-world-power-declinism#.

Kalyvas, Andreas, and Ira Katznelson (2008), *Liberal Beginnings: Making a Republic for the Moderns*, Cambridge: Cambridge University Press.

Kaplan, Fred (2008), *Daydream Believers*, Hoboken, NJ: John Wiley & Sons.

Kaplan, Robert D. (2011), *Monsoon: The Indian Ocean and the Future of American Power*, New York: Random House.

Katzenstein, Peter J. and Robert O. Keohane (eds) (2007a), *Anti-Amercianisms in World Politics*, Ithaca, NY: Cornell University Press.

Katzenstein, Peter J. and Robert O. Keohane (2007b), 'The Political Consequences of Anti-Americanism', in Peter J. Katzenstein, and Robert O. Keohane (eds), *Anti-Americanisms in World Politics*, Ithaca, NY: Cornell University Press.

Katzenstein, Peter J. and Robert O. Keohane (2007c), 'Varieties of Anti-Americanism: A Framework for Analysis', in Peter J. Katzenstein, and Robert O. Keohane (eds), *Anti-Americanisms in World Politics*, Ithaca, NY: Cornell University Press.

Katznelson, Ira and Martin Shefter (eds) (2002), *Shaped by War and Trade: International Influences on American Political Development*, Princeton, NJ: Princeton University Press.

Kaufman, Stuart J., Richard Little and William C. Wohlforth (eds) (2007), *The Balance of Power in World History*, Basingstoke: Palgrave Macmillan.

Kennan, George F. (1946), 'Moscow Embassy Telegram #551: "The Long Telegram"' in Thomas H. Etzold and John Lewis Gadis (eds) (1978), *Containment: Documents on American Policy and Strategy, 1945–1950*, New York: Columbia University Press.

Kennan, George F. (1947) 'The Sources of Soviet Conduct', *Foreign Affairs*, Vol. 25 (July): 566–82.

Kennan, George F. (1951), *American Diplomacy 1900–1950*, Chicago: University of Chicago Press.

Kennedy, David M. (1999), *Freedom from Fear: The American People in Depression and War 1929–1945*, Oxford: Oxford University Press.

Kennedy, David M. (2007), 'Imagining America: The Promise and Peril of Boundlessness', in Peter J. Katzenstein, and Robert O. Keohane (eds), *Anti-Amercianisms in World Politics*, Ithaca, NY: Cornell University Press.

Kennedy, Paul (1989), *The Rise and Fall of the Great Powers: Economic Change and Military Conflict from 1500–2000*, London: Fontana Press.

Kepel, Gilles (2006), *Jihad: The Trail of Political Islam*, new edn, London: I.B. Tauris.

Keohane, Robert O. (1984), *After Hegemony: Cooperation and Discord in the World Political Economy*, Princeton, NJ: Princeton University Press.

Kiely, Ray (2006), 'United States Hegemony and Globalisation: What Role for Theories of Imperialism?', *Cambridge Review of International Affairs*, Vol. 19, No. 2: 205–21.

Kiely, Ray (2007), *The New Political Economy of Development: Globalization, Imperialism, Hegemony*, Basingstoke: Palgrave Macmillan.

Kiely, Ray (2010), *Rethinking Imperialism*, Basingstoke: Palgrave Macmillan.

Kilcullen, David (2009), *The Accidental Guerrilla*, London: Hurst.

King, Desmond (2000), *Making Americans: Immigration, Race, and the Origins of the Diverse Democracy*, Cambridge, MA: Harvard University Press.

King, Desmond and Marc Stears (2011), 'How the U.S. State Works: A Theory of Standardization', *Perspectives on Politics*, Vol. 9, No. 3: 505–18.

Kinzer, Stephen (2007), *Overthrow: America's Century of Regime Change from Hawaii to Iraq*, New York: Times Books.

Kirshner, Jonathan (2008), 'Dollar Primacy and American Power: What's at Stake', *Review of International Political Economy*, Vol. 15, No. 3: 418–38.

Kirshner, Jonathan (2009), 'After the (Relative) Fall: Dollar Diminution and the Consequences for American Power', in Eric Helleiner and Jonathan Kirshner (eds), *The Future of the Dollar*, Ithaca, NY: Cornell University Press.

Kissinger, Henry (1979), *White House Years*, Boston, MA: Little, Brown.

Klein, Ezra (2013), 'Let's Talk: Is it Time to Reform the Filibuster?', *The New Yorker*, January 28: 24–9.

Knecht, Thomas and M. Stephen Weatherford (2006), 'Public Opinion and Foreign Policy: The Stages of Presidential Decision Making', *International Studies Quarterly*, Vol. 50, No. 3: 705–27.

Knock, Thomas J. (1995), *To End All Wars: Woodrow Wilson and the Quest for a New World Order*, Princeton, NJ: Princeton University Press.

Koh, Harold Hongju (1990), *The National Security Constitution: Sharing Power after the Iran-Contra Affair*, New Haven, CT: Yale University Press.

Koistinen, Paul A.C. (2004), *Arsenal of World War II: The Political Economy of American Warfare, 1940–1945*, Lawrence, KS: University Press of Kansas.

Kolchin, Peter (1995), *American Slavery, 1619–1877*, Harmondsworth: Penguin.

Konings, Martijn (2009), 'The Construction of US Financial Power', *Review of International Studies*, Vol. 35, No. 1: 69–94.

Kovach, Bill (1996), 'Do the News Media make Foreign Policy?', *Foreign Policy*, No. 102: 169–80.

Krasner, Stephen D. (1976), 'State Power and the Structure of International Trade', *World Politics*, Vol. 28, No 3: 317–47.

Krasner, Stephen (1983), 'Structural Causes and Regime Consequences: Regimes as Intervening Variables', in Stephen Krasner (ed.), *International Regimes*, Ithaca, NY: Cornell University Press.

Krauthammer, Charles (1990/1), 'The Unipolar Moment', *Foreign Affairs*, Vol. 70, No. 1: 23–34.

Kristol, William and Robert Kagan (1996), 'Toward a Neo-Reaganite Foreign Policy', *Foreign Affairs*, Vol. 75, No. 4: 18–32.

Krugman, Paul (1997), *Pop Internationalism*, Cambridge, MA: MIT Press.

Krugman, Paul (2008), *The Return of Depression Economics*, Harmondsworth: Penguin.

Krutz, Glen S. and Jeffrey S. Peake (2009), *Treaty Politics and the Rise of Executive Agreements: International Commitments in a System of Shared Powers*, Ann Arbor: University of Michigan Press.

Kull, Steven, Clay Ramsay and Evan Lewis (2003), 'Misperceptions, the Media, and the Iraq War', *Political Science Quarterly*, Vol. 118, No. 4: 569–98.

Kupchan, Charles A. (2012), *No One's World: The West, the Rising Rest, and the Coming Global Turn*, Oxford: Oxford University Press.

LaFeber, Walter (1995), *The Cambridge History of American Foreign Relations: Vol. 2, The American Search for Opportunity, 1865–1913*, Cambridge: Cambridge University Press.

Lake, David A. (1999), *Entangling Relations: American Foreign Policy in Its Century*, Princeton, NJ: Princeton University Press.

Lake, David A. (2011), *Hierarchy in International Relations*, Ithaca, NY: Cornell University Press.

Latham, Andrew (1999), 'Re-imagining Warfare: The 'Revolution in Military Affairs', in Craig Snyder (ed.), *Contemporary Security and Strategy*, London: Macmillan.

Latham, Michael E. (2010), *The Right Kind of Revolution: Modernization, Development, and U.S. Foreign Policy from the Cold War to the Present*, Ithaca, NY: Cornell University Press.

Layne, Christopher (2006), 'The Unipolar Illusion Revisited: The Coming End of the United States' Unipolar Moment', *International Security*, Vol. 31, No. 2: 7–41.

Layne, Christopher (2009), 'The Waning of U.S. Hegemony – Myth or Reality?: A Review Essay', *International Security*, Vol. 34, No. 1: 147–72.

Lebow, Richard Ned and Robert E. Kelly (2001), 'Thucydides and Hegemony: Athens and the United States', *Review of International Studies*, Vol. 27, No. 4: 593–610.

Ledbetter, James (2011), *Unwarranted Influence: Dwight D. Eisenhower and the Military Industrial Complex*, New Haven, CT: Yale University Press.

Leffler, Melvyn P. (1992), *A Preponderance of Power: National Security, the Truman Administration, and the Cold War*, Stanford, CA: Stanford University Press.

Leffler, Melvyn P. (1994), 'The Interpretive Wars over the Cold War, 1945–1960', in Gordon Martel (ed.), *American foreign relations reconsidered, 1890–1993*, London: Routledge.

Leffler, Melvyn P. (1999), 'The Cold War: What Do "We Now Know"?', *The American Historical Review*, Vol. 104, No. 2: 501–24.

Lepore, Jill (2013), 'The Force: How Much Military is Enough', *The New Yorker*, January 28: 70–6.

Leuchtenburg, William E. (1952), 'Progressivism and Imperialism: The Progressive Movement and American Foreign Policy, 1898–1916', *The Mississippi Valley Historical Review*, Vol. 39, No. 3: 483–504.

Leuchtenburg, William E. (1963), *Franklin D. Roosevelt and the New Deal, 1932–1940*, New York: Harper & Row.

Leuchtenburg, William E. (1964), 'The New Deal and the Analogue of War', in John Braeman, Robert H. Bremner and Everett Walters (eds), *Change and Continuity in Twentieth-Century America*, Athens, OH: Ohio State University Press.

Levy, Daniel (2006), 'Is It Good for the Jews?', *The American Prospect*, July/August.

Lichtenstein, Nelson (1989), 'Labor in the Truman Era: Origins of the "Private Welfare State"', in Michael J. Lacey (ed.), *The Truman Presidency*, Cambridge: Cambridge University Press.

Lieber, Keir A. and Daryl G. Press (2006), 'The End of MAD? The Nuclear Dimension of U.S. Primacy', *International Security*, Vol. 30, No. 4: 7–44.

Lieber, Keir A. and Daryl G. Press (2009), 'The Nukes we Need: Preserving the American Deterrent', *Foreign Affairs*, Vol. 88, No. 6: 32–51.

Lieberman, Robert C. (2009), 'The 'Israel Lobby' and American Politics', *Perspectives on Politics*, Vol. 7, No. 2: 235–57.

Lieven, Anatol (2004), *America Right or Wrong*, New York: Oxford University Press.

Limerick, Patricia (1987), *The Legacy of Conquest: Unbroken Past of the American West*, New York: Norton.

Lind, Michael (2012), *Land of Promise: An Economic History of the United States*, New York: Harper.

Lindsay, James M. (2002), 'Getting Uncle Sam's Ear: Will Ethnic Lobbies Cramp America's Foreign Policy Style', *Brookings Institution* [url: http://www.brookings.edu/articles/2002/winter_diplomacy_lindsay.aspx]

Lindsay, James M. (2003), 'Deference and Defiance: The Shifting Rhythms of Executive-Legislative Relations in Foreign Policy', *Presidential Studies Quarterly*, Vol. 33, No. 3: 530–46.

Lipset, Seymour Martin (1997), *American Exceptionalism: A Double-Edged Sword*, W. W. Norton & Company.

Little, Richard (2007), *The Balance of Power in International Relations; Metaphors, Myths and Models*, Cambridge: Cambridge University Press.

Lizza, Ryan (2011), 'The Consequentialist: How the Arab Spring Remade Obama's Foreign Policy', *The New Yorker*, May 2.

Luce, Edward (2012), *Time to Start Thinking: America and the Spectre of Decline*, London: Little, Brown.

Lukes, Steven (ed.) (1986), *Power*, New York: New York University Press.

Lukes, Steven (2005), *Power: A Radical View*, rev. 2nd edn, Basingstoke: Palgrave Macmillan.

Lynch, Mark (2007), 'Anti-Americanisms in the Arab World', in Peter J. Katzenstein, and Robert O. Keohane (eds), *Anti-Americanisms in World Politics*, Ithaca, NY: Cornell University Press.

Mabee, Bryan (2004), 'Discourses of Empire: The U.S. "Empire", Globalisation and International Relations', *Third World Quarterly*, Vol. 25, No. 8 (2004): 1359–78.

Mabee, Bryan (2012), 'Department of Homeland Security', in George Ritzer (ed.), *Blackwell Encyclopedia of Globalization*, Oxford: Blackwell.

May, Ernest R. (ed.) (1993) *American Cold War Strategy: Interpreting NSC 68*, New York: St Martin's Press.

McClintock, Michael (1992), *Instruments of Statecraft: U.S. Guerrilla Warfare, Counter-Insurgency, and Counter-Terrorism, 1940–1990*, New York: Pantheon Books.

McConnell, Grant (1966), *Private Power and American Democracy*, New York: Knopf.

McCormick, James (1998), 'Interest Groups and the Media in Post-Cold War U.S. Foreign Policy', in James M. Scott (ed.), *After the End: Making U.S. Foreign Policy in the Post-Cold War Environment*, Durham, NC: Duke University Press.

McDougall, Walter (1997), *Promised Land, Crusader State: The American Encounter with the World Since 1776*, New York: Houghton Mifflin.

MacIssac, David (1986), 'Voices from the Central Blue: The Air Power Theorists', in Peter Paret (ed.), *Makers of Modern Strategy*, Princeton, NJ: Princeton University Press.

McKay, David (2009), *American Politics and Society*, Oxford: Wiley-Blackwell.

McNeill, William H. (1982), *The Pursuit of Power: Technology, Armed Force and Society since AD 1000*, Chicago: University of Chicago Press.

McPherson, James M. (1990), *Battle Cry of Freedom: The Civil War Era*, London: Penguin.

Mack, Andrew (1975), 'Why Big Nations Lose Small Wars: The Politics of Asymmetric Conflict', *World Politics*, Vol. 27, No. 2: 175–200.

Madison, James, Alexander Hamilton and John Jay (1987 [1788]), *The Federalist Papers*, Harmondsworth: Penguin.

Mahnken, Thomas G. (2008), *Technology and the American Way of War Since 1945*, New York: Columbia University Press.

Mandelbaum, Michael (1981), *The Nuclear Revolution: International Politics Before and After Hiroshima*, Cambridge: Cambridge University Press.

Mandelbaum, Michael (1996), 'Foreign Policy as Social Work', *Foreign Affairs*, Vol. 75, No. 1: 16–32.

Mann, James (2012), *The Obamians: The Struggle Inside the White House to Redefine American Power*, London: Viking.

Mann, James (2004), *Rise of the Vulcans: The History of Bush's War Cabinet*, London: Penguin.

Mann, Michael (1986), *The Sources of Social Power, Vol. I: A History of Power from the Beginning to AD 1760*, Cambridge: Cambridge University Press.

Mann, Michael (1987), 'The Roots and Contradictions of Modern Militarism', *New Left Review* No. 162 (March–April): 35–50.

Mann, Michael (1993), *The Sources of Social Power, Vol. II: The Rise of Classes and Nation States, 1760–1914*, Cambridge: Cambridge University Press.

Mann, Michael (2001), 'Globalization and September 11', *New Left Review*, No. 12: 51–72.

Mann, Michael (2005), *Incoherent Empire*, London: Verso.

Mann, Michael (2011), *Power in the 21st Century*, Cambridge: Polity Press.

Mann, Michael (2012), *The Sources of Social Power, Vol. III: Global Empires and Revolution, 1890–1945*, Cambridge: Cambridge University Press.

Mann, Thomas E., and Norman J. Ornstein (2007), *The Broken Branch: How Congress is Failing America and How to Get It Back on Track*, New York: Oxford University Press.

Mann, Thomas E. and Norman J. Ornstein (2012), *It's Even Worse than it Looks: How the American Constitutional System Collided with the New Politics of Extremism*, New York: Basic Books.

Mannheim, Karl (1960), *Ideology and Utopia: An Introduction to the Sociology of Knowledge*, London: Routledge & Kegan Paul.

Maraniss, David (2008), 'Clinton, Thinking about Tomorrow', *Washington Post*, Thursday, August 28.

Markovits, Andrei S. (2007), *Uncouth Nation: Why Europe Dislikes America*, Princeton, NJ: Princeton University Press.

Markusen, Ann, Peter Hall, Scott Campbell and Sabina Detrick (1991), *The Rise of the Gunbelt: The Remapping of Industrial America*, New York: Oxford University Press.

Mastanduno, Michael (2009), 'System Maker and Privilege Taker: U.S. Power and the International Political Economy', *World Politics*, Vol. 61, No. 1: 121–54.

May, Ernest R. (1955), 'The Development of Political-Military Consultation in the United States', *Political Science Quarterly*, Vol. 70, No. 2: 161–80.

May, Ernest R. (1992), 'The U.S. Government, a Legacy of the Cold War', in Michael J. Hogan (ed.), *The End of the Cold War: Its Meanings and Implications*, Cambridge: Cambridge University Press.

Mayers, David (2007), *Dissenting Voices in America's Rise to Power*, Cambridge: Cambridge University Press.

Mayhew, David (1977), *Congress: The Electoral Connection*, New Haven, CT: Yale University Press.

Mead, Walter Russell (2007), 'Jerusalem Syndrome: Decoding the Israel Lobby', *Foreign Affairs*, Vol. 86, No. 6: 160–8.

Mead, Walter Russell (2002), *Special Providence: American Foreign Policy and How It Changed the World*, London: Routledge.

Mead, Walter Russell (2009), 'A Hegemon's Coming of Age: A Brief History of American Foreign Relations', *Foreign Affairs*, Vol. 88, No. 4: 138–43.

Mearsheimer, John J. (1990), 'Back to the Future: Instability in Europe After the Cold War', *International Security*, Vol. 15, No. 1 (1990): 5–56.

Mearsheimer, John J. (2001), *The Tragedy of Great Power Politics*, New York: W. W. Norton.

Mearsheimer, John J. (2010), 'The Gathering Storm: China's Challenge to US Power in Asia', *The Chinese Journal of International Politics*, Vol. 3: 381–96.

Mearsheimer, John J., and Stephen Walt (2006), 'The Israel Lobby', *London Review of Books*, Vol. 28, No. 6 (March 23). http://lrb.co.uk /v28/n06/mear01.html.

Mearsheimer, John J., and Stephen Walt (2007), *The Israel Lobby and U.S. Foreign Policy*, New York: Farrar, Straus & Giroux.

Merom, Gil (2003), *How Democracies Lose Small Wars: State, Society, and the Failures of France in Algeria, Israel in Lebanon, and the United States in Vietnam*, Cambridge: Cambridge University Press.

Miller, Greg (2011), 'Under Obama, An Emerging Global Apparatus for Drone Killing', *Washington Post*, 28 December.

Mills, C. Wright (1956), *The Power Elite*, Oxford: Oxford University Press.

Moore, Barrington (1966), *Social Origins of Democracy and Dictatorship: Lord and Peasant in the Making of the Modern World*, Boston, MA: Beacon.

Moran, Michael (2012), *The Reckoning: Debt, Democracy and the Future of American Power*, Basingstoke: Palgrave Macmillan.

Morgan, Ted (2004), *Reds: McCarthyism in Twentieth-Century America*, New York: Random House.

Morgenthau, Hans J. (1965), *Vietnam and the United States*, Washington, DC: Public Affairs Press.

Morris, Charles R. (2008), *The Trillion Dollar Meltdown*, New York: Public Affairs.

Morriss, Peter (1987), *Power: A Philosophical Analysis*, Manchester: Manchester University Press.

Morton, Adam David (2007), *Unravelling Gramsci: Hegemony and Passive Revolution in the Global Economy*, London: Pluto.

Murray, Williamson and Allan R. Millett (2001), *A War To Be Won: Fighting the Second World War*, Harvard, MA: Belknap Press.

Myrdal, Gunnar (1996) [1944], *An American Dilemma*, reprint edn, London: Transaction Publishers.

Nagl, John (2005), *Leaning to Eat Soup with a Knife: Counterinsurgency Lessons from Malaya and Vietnam*, Chicago: University of Chicago Press.

Nathan, Andrew and Andrew Scobell (2012), 'How China Sees America: The Sum of Beijing's Fears', *Foreign Affairs*, Vol. 91, No. 5: 32–47.

Nelson, Anna Kasten (1981), National Security I: Inventing a Process (1945–1960), in Hugh Heclo and Lester M. Salamon (eds), *The Illusion of Presidential Government*, Boulder, CO: Westview Press.

Nelson, Anna Kasten (2007), 'The Evolution of the National Security State: Ubiquitous and Endless,' in Andrew Bacevich (ed.), *The Long War*, New York: Columbia University Press.

Neustadt, Richard E. (1990), *Presidential Power and the Modern Presidents: The Politics of Leadership from Roosevelt to Reagan*, New York: Free Press.

Nexon, Daniel H. (2009), 'The Balance of Power in the Balance', *World Politics*, Vol. 61, No. 2: 330–59.

Niday, Jackson A., II (2008), 'The War against Terror as War against the Constitution', *Canadian Review of American Studies*, Vol. 38, No. 1: 101–17.

Nye, Joseph S. (2002), *The Paradox of American Power: Why the World's Only Superpower Can't Go It Alone*, Oxford: Oxford University Press.

Nye, Joseph S. (2003), 'U.S. Power and Strategy after Iraq', *Foreign Affairs*, Vol. 82, No. 4: 60–73.

Nye, Joseph S. (2011), *The Future of Power*, New York: Public Affairs.

Obama, Barack (2007), 'Renewing American Leadership', *Foreign Affairs*, Vol. 86, No. 4: 2–16.

Obama, Barack (2009a), 'A Just and Lasting Peace: Nobel Peace Prize Lecture', Oslo City Hall, 10 December.

Obama, Barack (2009b), 'Remarks by President Obama', Prague, Czech Republic, 5 April.

Obama, Barack (2009c), 'Remarks by the President in Address to the Nation on the Way Forward in Afghanistan and Pakistan', United States Military Academy at West Point, West Point, New York, 1 December.

Obama, Barack (2009d), 'Remarks by the President on a New Beginning', Cairo University, Cairo, Egypt, 4 June.

Obama, Barack (2009e), 'Remarks by the President on National Security', National Archives, 21 May.

Obama, Barack (2011), 'Remarks by the President on the Middle East and North Africa', State Department, Washington, DC, 19 May.

OpenSecrets (2012), Center for Responsive Politics, http://opensecrets.org

Ornstein, Norman J. and Thomas E. Mann (2006) 'When Congress Checks Out', *Foreign Affairs*, Vol. 85, No. 6: 67–82.

Overy, Richard (2006), *Why the Allies Won*, rev. edn, London: Pimlico.

Packer, George (2007), *The Assassins' Gate: America in Iraq*, London: Faber and Faber.

Paine, Thomas (1995 [1776]), 'Common Sense', in *Rights of Man, Common Sense and Other Political Writings*, ed. Mark Philp, Oxford: Oxford University Press.

Panitch, Leo and Sam Gindin (2003), 'Global Capitalism and the American Empire', in Leo Panitch and Colin Leys (eds), *The Social Register 2004*, London: Merlin.

Panitch, Leo and Sam Gindin (2012), *The Making of Global Capitalism: The Political Economy of American Empire*, London: Verso.

Pape, Robert (2005a), *Dying to Win: The Strategic Logic of Suicide Terrorism*, New York: Random House.

Pape, Robert (2005b), 'Soft Balancing against the United States', *International Security*, Vol. 30, No. 1: 7–45.

Parker, R. A. C. (1989), *Struggle for Survival: The History of the Second World War*, Oxford: Oxford University Press.

Patterson, James (2005), *Restless Giant: The United States from Watergate to Bush v. Gore*, Oxford: Oxford University Press.

Paul, David M and Rachel Anderson Paul (2008), *Ethnic Lobbies and US Foreign Policy*, Boulder, CO: Lynne Rienner.

Paul, T.V. (2005), 'Soft Balancing in the Age of U.S. Primacy', *International Security*, Vol. 30, No. 1: 46–71.

Perkins, Bradford (1993), *The Cambridge History of American Foreign Relations, Vol. 1: The Creation of a Republican Empire, 1776–1865*, Cambridge: Cambridge University Press.

Pew Global Attitudes Project (2010), *Obama More Popular Abroad Than At Home, Global Image of U.S. Continues to Benefit*, Washington, DC: Pew Research Center for the People the Press.

Pierre, Andrew J. (1982), *The Global Politics of Arms Sales*, Princeton, NJ: Princeton University Press.

Polanyi, Karl (1944), *The Great Transformation*, Boston, MA: Beacon Press.

Pollard, Robert A. (1989), 'The National Security State Reconsidered: Truman and Economic Containment, 1945–1950', in Michael J. Lacey (ed.), *The Truman Presidency*, Cambridge: Cambridge University Press.

Porter, Bruce D. (1994), *War and the Rise of the State: The Military Foundations of Modern Politics*, New York: Free Press.

Posen, Barry R. (2003), 'Command of the Commons: The Military Foundation of U.S. Hegemony', *International Security*, Vol. 28, No. 1: 5–46.

Powell, Jefferson (2002), *The President's Authority over Foreign Affairs: An Essay in Constitutional Interpretation*, Durham, NC: Carolina Academic Press.

Quiggin, John (2010), *Zombie Economics*, Princeton, NJ: Princeton University Press.

Rachman, Gideon (2010), *Zero-Sum World: Politics, Power and Prosperity After the Crash*, London: Atlantic Books.

Radu, Michael (2004), 'A Matter of Identity: The Anti-Americanisms of Latin American Intellectuals', in Paul Hollander (ed.), *Understanding Anti-Americanism*, Chicago: Ivan R. Dee.

Reichard, Gary W. (1986), 'The Domestic Politics of National Security', in Norman A. Graebner (ed.), *The National Security: Its Theory and Practice, 1945–1960*, Oxford University Press.

Reus-Smit, Christian (2004), *American Power and World Order*, Cambridge: Polity.

Rice, Condoleezza (2000), 'Promoting the National Interest', *Foreign Affairs*, Vol. 79, No. 1: 45–62.

Rice, Condoleezza (2008), 'Rethinking the National Interest', *Foreign Affairs*, Vol. 87, no. 4: 2–26.

Richardson, James L. (1997), 'Contending Liberalisms: Past and Present', *European Journal of International Relations*, Vol. 3, No. 1: 5–33.

Ricks, Thomas E. (2006), *Fiasco: The American Military Adventure in Iraq*, London: Penguin.

Ricks, Thomas E. (2010), *The Gamble: General Petraeus and the Untold Story of the American Surge in Iraq, 2006–2008*, Harmondsworth: Penguin.

Robinson, Piers (2008), 'Media and US Foreign Policy', in Michael Cox and Doug Stokes (eds), *US Foreign Policy*, Oxford: Oxford University Press.

Robinson, William I. (1996), *Promoting Polyarchy: Globalization, US Intervention and Hegemony*, Cambridge: Cambridge University Press.

Romney, Mitt (2010), *No Apology: The Case for American Greatness*, New York: St Martin's Press.

Roosevelt, Franklin D. (1938), *Public Papers and Addresses of Franklin D. Roosevelt, Volume 2: The Year of Crisis, 1933*, New York: Random House.

Roosevelt, Theodore (1904), 'Fourth Annual Message', 6 December. Online by Gerhard Peters and John T. Woolley, *The American Presidency Project*. http://www.presidency.ucsb.edu/ws/?pid=29545.

Rosati, Jerel and Stephen Twing (1998), 'The Presidency and U.S. Foreign Policy after the Cold War', in James M. Scott (ed.), *After the End: Making U.S. Foreign Policy in the Post-Cold War Environment*, Durham, NC: Duke University Press.

Rosenberg, David Allen (1983), 'The Origins of Overkill: Nuclear Weapons and American Strategy, 1945–1960', *International Security*, Vol. 7, No. 4: 3–71.

Rosenberg, Emily (1993a), 'U.S. Cultural History', in Ernest R. May (ed.), *American Cold War Strategy: Interpreting NSC 68*, New York: Bedford/St. Martin's.

Rosenberg, Emily S. (1993b), 'The Cold War and the Discourse of National Security', *Diplomatic History*, Vol. 17, No. 2: 277–84.

Rostow, Walt (1990), *The Stages of Economic Growth: A Non-Communist Manifesto*, 3rd edn, Cambridge: Cambridge University Press.

Rothkopf, David (2005), *Running The World: the Inside Story of the National Security Council and the Architects of American Power*, New York: Public Affairs.

Ruggie, John Gerard (1998), *Constructing the World Polity: Essays on International Institutionalisation*, London: Routledge.

Saull, Richard, (2007), *The Cold War and After*, London: Pluto.

Savage, Charlie (2007), *Takeover: The Return of the Imperial Presidency and the Subversion of American Democracy*, New York: Little, Brown.

Savage, Charlie and Mark Landler (2011), 'White House Defends Continuing U.S. Role in Libya Operation', *New York Times*, June 15.

Schlesinger, Arthur M. (2004), *The Imperial Presidency*, rev. edn, New York: Mariner Books.

Schroeder, Paul (1994), 'Historical Reality vs. Neo-realist Theory', *International Security*, Vol. 19, No. 1: 108–48.

Schwartz, Herman (2009), *Subprime Nation: American Power, Global Capital, and the Housing Bubble*, Ithaca, NY: Cornell University Press.

Schwartz, Herman (2010), 'Structured Finance for Financed Structures: American Economic Power Before and After the Global Financial Crisis', in Martijn Konings (ed.), *The Great Credit Crash*, London: Verso.

Schweller, Randall L. (1994), 'Bandwagoning for Profit', *International Security*, Vol. 19, No. 1: 72–107.

Schweller, Randall L. and Xiaoyu Pu (2011), 'After Unipolarity: China's Visions of International Order in an Era of U.S. Decline', *International Security*, Vol. 36, No. 1: 41–72.

Scott, James C. (1985), *Weapons of the Weak: Everyday Forms of Peasant Resistance*, New Haven, CT: Yale University Press.

Seavoy, Ronald E. (2006), *An Economic History of the United States: From 1607 to the Present*, London: Routledge.

Seelye, Katharine Q. (2004), 'Cheney's Five Draft Deferments During the Vietnam Era Emerge as a Campaign Issue', *New York Times*, May 1.

Shaw, Martin (1991), *Post-Military Society: Militarism, Demilitarization and War at the End of the Twentieth Century*, Cambridge: Polity.

Shaw, Martin (2005), *The New Western War of War*, Cambridge: Polity.

Sheehan, Neil, Hedrick Smith, E.W. Kenworthy and Fox Butterfield (1971), *The Pentagon Papers*, New York: Bantam Books.

Sherry, Michael S. (1995), *In the Shadow of War: America since the 1930s*, New Haven, CT: Yale University Press.

Sherry, Michael S. (2003), 'A Hidden-Hand Garrison State?', *Diplomatic History*, Vol. 27, No. 1: 163–66.

Singer, P.W. (2009), *Wired for War: The Robotics Revolution and Conflict in the 21st Century*, Harmondsworth: Penguin.

Singh, Robert (ed.) (2003), *Governing America: The Politics of a Divided Democracy*, Oxford: Oxford University Press.

Singh, Robert (2012), *Barack Obama's Post-American Foreign Policy: The Limits of Engagement*, London: Bloomsbury.

Skocpol, Theda (1992), *Protecting Soldiers and Mothers: The Political Origins of Social Policy in the United States*, Cambridge, MA: Belknap Press.

Skowronek, Stephen (1982), *Building a New American State: The Expansion of National Administrative Capacities, 1877–1920*, Cambridge: Cambridge University Press.

Smith, Tony (2000), *Foreign Attachments: The Power of Ethnic Groups in the Making of American Foreign Policy*, Cambridge, MA: Harvard University Press.

Smith, Tony (2007), *A Pact with the Devil: Washington's Bid for World Supremacy and the Betrayal of the American Promise*, London: Routledge.

Sobel, Richard (2001), *The Impact of Public Opinion on U.S. Foreign Policy since Vietnam: Constraining the Colossus*, Oxford: Oxford University Press.

Stein, Arthur A. (1984), 'The Hegemon's Dilemma: Great Britain, the United States, and the International Economic Order', *International Organization*, Vol. 38, No. 2: 355–86.

Stephanson, Anders (1995), *Manifest Destiny: American Expansion and the Empire of Right*, New York: Hill & Wang.

Strange, Susan (1987), 'The Persistent Myth of Lost Hegemony', *International Organization*, Vol. 41, No. 4: 551–74.

Strange, Susan (1988), *States and Markets*, London: Pinter.

Stuart, Douglas T. (2008), *Creating the National Security State*, Princeton, NJ: Princeton University Press.

Tilly, Charles (1985), 'War Making and State Making as Organized Crime', in Peter B. Evans, Dietrich Rueschemeyer and Theda Skocpol (eds), *Bringing the State Back In*, Cambridge: Cambridge University Press.

Tilly, Charles (1991), 'Domination, Resistance, Compliance ... Discourse', *Sociological Forum*, Vol. 6, No. 3: 593–602.

Tilly, Charles (1992), *Coercion, Capital and European States, AD 900–1990*, Oxford: Blackwell.

Tilly, Charles (2004), 'Terror, Terrorism, Terrorists', *Sociological Theory*, Vol. 22, No. 1: 5–13.

Tocqueville, Alexis de (2003), *Democracy in America*, trans. Gerald E. Bevan, London: Penguin.

Todd, Emmanuel (2006), *After the Empire: The Breakdown of the American Order*, New York: Columbia University Press.

Trachtenberg, Marc (1991), 'The Nuclearization of NATO and U.S.–West European Relations', in *History and Strategy*, Princeton, NJ: Princeton University Press.

Treverton, Gregory (1988), *Covert Action*, London: I.B. Tauris.

Trubowitz, Peter (1998), *Defining the National Interest: Conflict and Change in American Foreign Policy*, Chicago: University of Chicago Press.

Trubowitz, Peter (2012), 'Regional Shifts and US Foreign Policy', in Michael Cox and Doug Stokes (eds), *US Foreign Policy*, 2nd edn, Oxford: Oxford University Press.

Truman, Harry S. (1961), 'Special Message to the Congress Recommending the Establishment of a Department of National Defense, December 19th, 1945', *Public Papers of the Presidents, Harry S. Truman, 1945*, Washington, DC: GPO.

Truman, Harry S. (1963), 'Special Message to the Congress on Greece and Turkey: The Truman Doctrine. March 12, 1947', in *Public Papers of the Presidents, Harry S. Truman, 1947*, Washington, DC: GPO.

Tucker, Robert W. and David C. Hendrickson (2004), 'The Sources of American Legitimacy', *Foreign Affairs*, Vol. 83, No. 6: 18–32.

Turner, Frederick Jackson (1986), *The Frontier in American History*, Tucson: University of Arizona Press.

Turner, Graham (2008), *The Great Credit Crunch: Housing Bubbles, Globalisation and the Worldwide Economic Crisis*, London: Pluto.

United States Department of Defense (2010), *Nuclear Posture Review Report 2010*, Washington, DC: GPO, 1–30.

United States Department of Defense (2012a), *Fiscal Year 2013 Budget Request*, Washington, DC: GPO.

United States Department of Defense (2012b), *Sustaining Global Leadership: Priorities for 21st Century Defense*, Washington, DC: GPO.

United States Department of the Army (2007), *Counterinsurgency Field Manual (FM 3-24)*, Chicago: University of Chicago Press.

United States National Intelligence Council (2008), *Global Trends 2025: A Transformed World*, Washington, DC: GPO.

United States National Intelligence Council (2012), *Global Trends 2030: Alternative Worlds*, Washington, DC: GPO.

United States National Security Council (1948), 'U.S. Objectives with Respect to the USSR to Counter Soviet Threats to U.S. Security', *Foreign Relations of the United States, 1948, Vol. 1*, Washington, DC: GPO.

United States National Security Council (1950), 'NSC 68: United States Objectives and Programs for National Security', in Ernest R. May (ed.) (1993), *American Cold War Strategy: Interpreting NSC 68*, New York: Bedford/St. Martin's.

United States Senate (n.d.), 'Treaties', At: http://www.senate.gov/artand history/history/common/briefing/Treaties.htm.

Viotti, Paul R. (ed) (2005), *American Foreign Policy and National Security: A Documentary Record*, Upper Saddle River, NJ: Pearson Education.

Vogel, David (1989), *Fluctuating Fortunes: The Political Power of Business in America*, New York: Basic Books.

Wade, Robert (2003), 'The Invisible Hand of the American Empire', *Ethics and International Affairs*, Vol. 17, No. 2 (2003): 77–88.

Wade, Robert (2008a), 'Financial Regime Change', *New Left Review*, No. 53 (Sept–Oct): 5–21.

Wade, Robert (2008b), 'The First-World Debt Crisis of 2007–2010 in Global Perspective' *Challenge*, Vol. 51, No. 4: 23–54.

Wade, Robert (2011), 'Emerging World Order? From Multipolarity to Multilateralism in the G20, the World Bank, and the IMF', *Politics & Society*, Vol. 39, No. 3: 347–78.

Walker, William O. (2009), *National Security and Core Values in American History*, Cambridge: Cambridge University Press.

Walt, Stephen M. (2000), 'Two Cheers For Clinton's Foreign Policy', *Foreign Affairs*, Vol. 79, No 2: 63–80.

Walt, Stephen M. (2005), 'Taming American Power', *Foreign Affairs*, Vol. 84, No. 5: 105–20.

Waltz, Kenneth N. (1959), *Man, the State and War: A Theoretical Analysis*, New York: Columbia University Press.

Waltz, Kenneth N. (1979), *Theory of International Politics*, New York: McGraw-Hill.

Wapshott, Nicholas (2011), *Keynes Hayek: The Clash that Defined Modern Economics*, New York: Norton.

Weber, Max (2009a), 'Politics as a Vocation', in H.H. Gerth and C. Wright Mills (eds), *From Max Weber: Essays in Sociology*, new edn, London: Routledge.

Weber, Max (2009b), 'The Protestant Sects and the Spirit of Capitalism', in H.H. Gerth and C. Wright Mills (eds), *From Max Weber: Essays in Sociology*, New edn, London: Routledge.

Weber, Max (2009c) 'The Social Psychology of the World Religions', in H.H. Gerth and C. Wright Mills (eds), *From Max Weber: Essays in Sociology*, new edn, London: Routledge.

Weigley, Russell F. (1977), *The American Way of War*, Bloomington: Indiana University Press.

Weigley, Russell, (2001), 'The American Civil-Military Cultural Gap: A Historical Perspective, Colonial Times to the Present' in Peter D. Feaver and Richard H. Kohn (eds), *Soldiers and Civilians: The Civil-Military Gap and American National Security*, Cambridge, MA: MIT Press.

Weiner, Tim (2008), *Legacy of Ashes: The History of the CIA*, London: Penguin.

Weiss, Linda (1998), *The Myth of the Powerless State: Governing the Economy in a Global Era*, Cambridge: Polity.

Weiss, Thomas G. (2003), 'The Illusion of UN Security Council Reform', *The Washington Quarterly*, Vol. 26, No. 4: 147–61.

Weiss, Thomas G. (2011), 'Fundamental UN Reform: A Non-starter or Not?', *Global Policy*, Vol. 2, No. 2: 196–202.

Welch, David (1992), 'The Organizational Process and Bureaucratic Politics Paradigms: Retrospect and Prospect', *International Security*, Vol. 17 (Fall): 112–46.

Weldes, Jutta (1996), 'Constructing National Interests', *European Journal of International Relations*, Vol. 2, No. 3: 275–318.

Wendt, Alexander (1999), *Social Theory of International Politics*, Cambridge: Cambridge University Press.

Westad, Odd Arne (2005), *The Global Cold War*, Cambridge: Cambridge University Press.

Wheeler, Nicholas J. (2000), *Saving Strangers: Humanitarian Intervention in International Society*, Oxford: Oxford University Press.

White House (2002), *The National Security Strategy of the United States of America*, Washington, DC: GPO.

White House, Office of Management and Budget (2012a), *Fiscal Year 2013 Budget of the Government of the United States*, Washington, DC: GPO.

White House, Office of Management and Budget (2012b), *Historical Tables, Budget of the United States Government, Fiscal Year 2013*, Washington, DC: GPO.

Whitfield, Stephen J. (1996), *The Culture of the Cold War*, 2nd edn Baltimore: Johns Hopkins University Press.

Williams, Michael J. (2005), 'What is in the National Interest? The Neoconservative Challenge in IR Theory', *European Journal of International Relations*, Vol. 11, No. 3: 307–37.

Williams, William Appleman (1962), *The Tragedy of American Diplomacy*, New York: W.W. Norton.

Williamson, John (2004), 'A Short History of the Washington Consensus', *Institute for International Economics*, September.

Wilson, James Q. (1989), *Bureaucracy: What Government Agencies Do and Why They Do It*, New York: Basic Books.

Wohlforth, William C., Richard Little, Stuart J. Kaufman et al. (2007), 'Testing Balance-of-Power Theory in World History', *European Journal of International Relations*, Vol. 13, No. 2: 155–85.

Wood, Gordon S. (1991), *The Radicalism of the American Revolution*, New York: Vintage.

Woods, Ngaire (2010), 'Global Governance after the Financial Crisis: A New Multilateralism or the Last Gasp of the Great Powers?', *Global Policy*, Vol. 1, No. 1: 51–63.

World Bank (2013), *World Development Indicators*, http://data.world-bank.org/indicator.

Wright, Lawrence (2006), *The Looming Tower*, Harmondsworth: Penguin.

Yergin, Daniel (1977), *Shattered Peace: The Origins of the Cold War and the National Security State*, Boston, MA: Houghton Mifflin.

Young, Marilyn (1991), *The Vietnam Wars, 1945–1990*, New York: Harper Perennial.

Zakaria, Fareed (1998), *From Wealth to Power: The Unusual Origins of America's World Role*, Princeton, NJ: Princeton University Press.

Zakaria, Fareed (2009), *The Post-American World*, London: Allen Lane.

Zegart, Amy (1999), *Flawed by Design: The Evolution of the CIA, JCS, and NSC*, Stanford, CA: Stanford University Press.

Zolberg, Aristide R. (2006), *A Nation by Design: Immigration Policy in the Fashioning of America*, Cambridge, MA: Harvard University Press.

Index